NOT THAT RICH

To my grandpa, who taught me that even the craziest dreams are worth believing in.

CONTENTS

FALL		**11**
CHAPTER 1.	TRISHA, HUNTER, AND SIERRA	13
CHAPTER 2.	TRISHA AND RAY	25
CHAPTER 3.	HUNTER AND JACK	31
CHAPTER 4.	HUNTER	43
CHAPTER 5.	PAMELA	53
CHAPTER 6.	HUNTER AND PAUL	61
CHAPTER 7.	THE STRANGER	71
CHAPTER 8.	PAMELA AND TRISHA	77
CHAPTER 9.	HUNTER	85
CHAPTER 10.	MATT AND THE STRANGER	93
CHAPTER 11.	SIERRA AND HUNTER	101
CHAPTER 12.	PAUL	113
CHAPTER 13.	RAY, TRISHA, HUNTER, AND SIERRA	119
CHAPTER 14.	JACK, TRISHA, AND HUNTER	131
WINTER		**141**
CHAPTER 15.	TRISHA AND PAMELA	143
CHAPTER 16.	MATT	151

CHAPTER 17. HUNTER   159

CHAPTER 18. THE STRANGER   165

CHAPTER 19. SIERRA AND JACK   171

CHAPTER 20. PAMELA AND TRISHA   179

CHAPTER 21. RAY AND TRISHA   191

CHAPTER 22. MATT   199

CHAPTER 23. JACK   207

CHAPTER 24. PAUL AND FELIX   211

CHAPTER 25. TRISHA AND HUNTER   219

CHAPTER 26. TRISHA   233

SPRING   **241**

CHAPTER 27. PAMELA   243

CHAPTER 28. MATT   251

CHAPTER 29. JACK   257

CHAPTER 30. FELIX, PAUL, AND SIERRA   263

CHAPTER 31. HUNTER   273

CHAPTER 32. RAY AND TRISHA   279

CHAPTER 33. FELIX   289

CHAPTER 34. TRISHA AND PAMELA   297

CHAPTER 35. JACK, PAUL, AND FELIX   303

CHAPTER 36. SIERRA AND HUNTER   313

EPILOGUE   319

AUTHOR'S NOTE   323

CHARACTER LIST   333

ACKNOWLEDGMENTS   337

APPENDIX   341

"Don't confuse the small things that don't matter with the big ones that do."
—GRANDPA

FALL

CHAPTER 1

TRISHA, HUNTER, AND SIERRA

TRISHA

Hunter:	Yo.
Hunter:	You know those AP retakes?
Trisha:	Uh, duh.
Hunter:	Yeah so obv still pissed, but I thought Winchester let it go cuz of the new school year...
Trisha:	??
Hunter:	But they didn't.
Trisha:	What do you mean they didn't?
Hunter:	It's a police case now.
Trisha:	WTF why?
Hunter:	No clue. Angry parents wanting revenge I guess.
Trisha:	That's so extra!
Hunter:	Yep. It's Winchester after all.
Trisha:	True. BTW, why are you texting me? I'm literally across the quad from you.

Hunter: Can't you see I'm with Sierra ;)

Trisha: o_o

Trisha put down her phone and nudged her best friend Pamela, who was taking selfies on her phone.

"Trish!" Pamela exclaimed. "This better be good. Incredible lighting doesn't last forever. It took me four tries before I was happy with my winged eyeliner this morning!"

"Pam, the AP thing is a POLICE case now!"

Pamela arched one of her well-defined, perfectly threaded eyebrows. "What? Seriously? Doesn't the Pasadena police have anything better to do than to hunt down some random high schooler who screwed over the AP nerds?"

"It's Pasadena. What do you expect?" Trisha smirked and wondered for the hundredth time who had stolen the AP exams[1] last Spring and forced a quarter of the school to retake their exams over the summer, including her brother and her.

"No idea. My brother just texted me about it," Trisha responded with a shrug. She stretched out her slim, sun-kissed legs and leaned back to bask in the Californian sun. It was the first day of school at Winchester High, one of the most prestigious college preparatory high schools in the San Gabriel Valley, or SGV for short. Trisha glanced across the quad at her brother and the "it" girl of the sophomore class, Sierra Jones, nuzzling each other.

---

1   AP exams, otherwise known as Advanced Placement courses, offer college-level curricula and examinations to high school students. There are many nicknames for AP courses such as APUSH, which stands for AP US History. The more AP exams you take, the more of an overachiever you are.

I wonder what it must be like to be that tall, that beautiful, and that popular. Trisha looked down at her flat, shapeless body with dismay.

"Of course you got the information from Hunter." Pamela interrupted her thoughts, tossing her thick, waist-length hair behind her shoulder. "Hunter knows everything now that he has joined the Tree People. He probably got it from Stacy Williams."

Tree... people?

"Did you just nickname Hunter's new friend group Tree People? They're not tree huggers or elves, just popular."

"Trish, honey, isn't it obvious? There isn't any popular crowd just called 'the popular group.' They always have a clique name. Just think of the Plastics, the Pink Ladies, and the Pretty Little Liars. I think the Tree People perfectly suits them. They're always under that big oak tree anyway."

Trisha pursed her lips. She wasn't a fan of putting people into categories at school, partially because she already hated being labeled the sophomore class's overachieving perfectionist. However, she could also tell this was an argument she wasn't going to win. When Pamela made up her mind, it was made up.

"Pam, what's your schedule like today? Do you have a third block?" Trisha asked, changing the subject.

"Nope. How about you?" Pamela mumbled, preoccupied with her phone again, swiping through photo filters for her latest round of selfies.

"None too! I love this new block schedule." The start of the new school year also meant a new and improved class schedule. In an effort to help its students adapt to college life early on, Winchester adopted a three classes a day, eighty minutes each block schedule.

"Slow down, girl. It's only sophomore year. We've still got PSATs, SATs, SAT IIs, and APs—not to mention snatching boyfriends to break our hearts." Pamela winked at Trisha before returning her attention back to her phone.

Trisha's new smartphone dinged. She swiped it open and began giggling instantaneously. "Your vids are always so good." Trisha continued to laugh while staring at a brief video of Pamela surrounded by multi-colored glass and dancing zebras. Video Pamela, with her eyes the color of rich honey and light brown complexion, bashed her long, false mink eyelashes seductively.

"Of course. I finally reached one million followers this summer. I have to keep everyone on their toes," Pamela said matter-of-factly.

"I still don't understand where you find time for making all of this." Trisha shook her head in a mixture of disbelief and jealousy. Trisha rarely used social media. She told everyone it was because she barely had enough time to sleep, let alone scroll through pretty pictures and funny videos, but in reality, she simply never felt like she was interesting enough or pretty enough for that. Instead, she lived vicariously through Pamela.

"Want to grab boba after our second block finishes?" Trisha asked, tearing her eyes away from her phone. "I have a massive craving for Tiger Sugar or Half and Half."

"Babe, you know I never say no to boba, despite the fact that it may or may not be Halal. Plus, there's been this boba challenge floating around." Pamela began imitating holding a straw with her eyes closed and stabbing the air. "I'm sure my followers would love to see me try to stab a boba cup with my eyes closed."

"Great. It's a plan then," Trisha snickered, ignoring her best friend's usual antics. "I'm going to head to AP Calc now. I'm trying to grab the back seat."

"Trisha Wang in the back row?" Pamela raised her eyebrows in melodramatic astonishment. "What is this? New year, new me?"

Trisha rolled her eyes. Despite what the rest of her classmates thought, she didn't like to sit in the front row of class—unless it was crucial material that required neat and color-coded note-taking, of course. "You know how much I hate math. I need to get away from it as much as possible, including physically."

Pamela laughed. "Right, and that's exactly why you're in an advanced math class, huh?"

"I still need to uphold my Asian model minority stereotype, 'kay? Anyway, see you at one-thirty by my car." Trisha swung her backpack over her shoulder and began to walk away, understanding how ironic it was that she hated math but was still good at it. It was hard to be bad at something when your parents had you in private tutoring since elementary school.

"Mkay, see ya!" Pamela's focus glued back to her phone screen. She began swiping through online dating profiles of boys who looked questionably older than their advertised teenage years.

HUNTER

Across the quad, Hunter Wang watched as his sister walked toward the Zhou Center, a recently remodeled state-of-the-art building named after a very wealthy donor to the school. He looked down at the girl with platinum blonde hair and piercing blue eyes leaning against his right shoulder.

"Sierra, how many APs are you taking this semester?"

The girl propped herself up against the bench. "Three—AP Chem, AP Lang, and APUSH. Why?"

"Nothing, just curious." Hunter watched a brave squirrel skitter across the quad with a stolen potato chip in its mouth. "Ugh, I miss being a carefree sophomore—when you only had to worry about your grades and extracurriculars. You should enjoy it while it lasts."

Sierra glanced at Hunter; her mouth curled into a frown. "It's only the first day of school and you sound more stressed out than usual already."

Hunter rubbed his short, black hair nervously. "Yeah, sorry. I feel like my schedule is going to be insane this year. I signed up for five AP classes and all the college essay writing has been awful. Having to retake four AP exams last month didn't help either." Hunter let out a tired exhale. "My last chance to max out my SAT score is only a month and a half away. I'm going to be so MIA this semester."

Sierra put a perfectly manicured, reassuring hand on his arm. "Hunter, *chill*. It's going to be okay. Didn't you get a fifteen-forty last spring? That's an incredibly good score!"

"Sierra, you don't understand. I'm *Asian*. That means I need to get at least a fifteen-eighty on the SATs to be truly competitive for Stanford.[2] Did you know Asians have to get at least one hundred and forty points higher on the SAT to be considered on equal footing with a white applicant?" Hunter grimaced as if his own words had just stabbed him. "I need

---

2   As of 2020, the SAT is based on two sections—evidence-based reading and writing (EBRW) and math for a total of 1,600 possible points on the SAT. The ETS, or Evil Testing Service as students call it, changes it up every so often for "improvements" *cough.*

to be in the top twenty-five percent scoring zone to mean anything to HYSP."[3]

Sierra furrowed her eyebrows. "I get that you're Asian, Hunter, but you shouldn't always use that as—"

"How are my two favorite love birds doing?" A boy with warm, brown eyes wrapped his lanky arms around the couple from behind. He looked between the two of them and took a step back. "Sorry, am I interrupting anything?"

"Nah, you're fine, Matt." Hunter waved his hand dismissively. "How was Korea? It was weird not seeing you for an entire month."

"Ugh, it was incredibly boring. What's the point of owning an apartment in Itaewon, *the* nightlife district in Seoul, when you're not allowed to go out after nine p.m.?" Matt dramatically threw his hands up in the air. "On top of that, my grandma wanted to see me *all* the time. I don't even understand what she's saying half the time!"

"Aww, Matt. Your grandma just wants to spend more time with her precious grandbaby," Sierra teased.

"Yeah, I get that, and I feel bad for not knowing Korean... but what am I supposed to do? I'm a quarter Chinese and half German. Am I supposed to learn Chinese and German too?"

"Yes," Hunter deadpanned while giving Matt a deep, sarcastic stare.

Matt shot Hunter a glare. "You're one to talk, Hunter. You can barely speak Mandarin and you're *full* Chinese."

"Fair enough," Hunter grinned and gave Matt a fake punch on the shoulder. "You're right. Despite Chinese school

---

3   Acronym to represent some of the most competitive, prestigious, and private (oh, and of course, expensive) colleges—Harvard, Yale, Stanford, and Princeton.

every Saturday, I can barely write my name in Mandarin. Any other highlights?"

"Nope, unless you count being forced to watch K-dramas with my mom," Matt shrugged. "You know, *SKY Castle* was actually pretty good."

"I *love* that show! Stacy introduced me to it last year," Sierra flashed a mischievous smile. "All the upper-class moms quite literally killing each other to help their kids get into top colleges made me have crazy Winchester vibes."

"*Yes*, I got the chills," Matt squealed.

"Okay, I've officially lost you both," Hunter said, breaking up the conversation. "Anyway, I'm going to drop by the dining hall for coffee before AP World. Anyone want to come—"

"Me!" Matt interjected before Hunter could even finish his question. "Coach Bron was brutal this morning. I get that he wants us to get to CIF Waterpolo regionals[4] this year, but man, you would think he would know that muscle is built over time and *not* in two hours at five-thirty a.m. on a Monday."

"Tell me about it," Hunter agreed, swinging his black leather backpack behind him. He turned to Sierra. "See you for lunch?"

"Yep, I'll be here," she leaned in toward Hunter and gave him a peck on the cheek. Her comforting strawberry scent lingered as she pulled away from Hunter. "By the way, I think the dining hall is attempting to make sushi again."

---

4   CIF, or the California Interscholastic Federation, is the governing body for high school sports in California.

"Gross. Why do they always attempt ethnic food with all the wrong recipes? I'm all for sushi, but not Winchester dining hall sushi." Matt buried his head into his hands.

Sierra chuckled, "They're just trying to adapt to all the different ethnic tastes on campus! Anyway, see you both later."

"See ya," Hunter waved goodbye. He tilted his head in a silent "let's go" to Matt, and the two of them began to walk toward a tall wooden building surrounded by palm trees.

SIERRA

Sierra looked at Hunter walking away and sighed. She felt like the college admissions process brought out the worst in people. For Hunter, the stress manifested by making him this high-strung ball of anxiety. For her older brother Paul, he used bullying everyone around him, including their little brother Felix, as a form of stress-release.

Am I going to be like this in two years when I'm a senior too?

Out of the corner of her eye, Sierra saw her best friend Stacy Williams emerge from the school parking lot.

Did she leave to get an oat milk latte again?

Sierra wasn't sure. Stacy was still a dot out in the distance. Winchester's 120-acre campus was open and vast, which gave students and faculty full views of everyone from afar, but that also meant it was a workout to get anywhere on campus.

A few minutes later, Stacy barely got within earshot of Sierra before launching into a gossip tirade. "Guess what? I heard from Steven, who heard from Tracy, who heard from Omar, who heard from Ji Woo, who heard from Ren that there are *two* new junior boys in town." Stacy, with her hourglass figure and densely braided hair, stopped abruptly in front of Sierra.

She continued, "One is this epically hot, quiet guy named Ray Martinez... rumor is he is a genius on top of being delicious, and the second guy is this dude named Jack Zhou. He came to school today driving a Lexus LFA. I just saw it in the parking lot. I googled it, and the car is, like, at least three hundred and seventy-five *thousand* dollars! Could you believe it? Not to mention he was dressed head to toe in Armani."

Sierra burst into laughter. Stacy looked like she was about to turn faint from excitement. "Haha, okay, Gossip Girl. Got anything else?"

"Sierra, you know I always have more," Stacy said with a wink before taking an exaggerated breath.

"Jack strolled up to Dean Rand's office this morning, and no one knows what happened inside, but next thing everyone knew, Dean Rand came out with a hand on Jack's back, smiling from ear to ear. Besides at your brother, have you ever seen Dean Rand genuinely *smile* at someone?"

Stacy stared intensely at Sierra. She had barely shaken her head no when Stacy spoke again.

"After he shook Jack's hand profusely, Jack marched away from the office, almost forgetting that he had left his Hermés backpack behind." Stacy crouched down next to Sierra, who was sitting on the grass as she whispered in her ear, "The best rumor of all—Steven's dad, who is on the board of trustees, says it was Jack's family who donated the fifty million dollars over the summer."

Sierra raised her eyebrows. She wasn't too fazed by Jack's clearly extensive luxury collection. She was in a simple Alexander McQueen mini dress herself at the moment. Everyone always came to the first day of school dressed head-to-toe in luxury goods and driving (or, for the freshmen, chauffeured in) a shiny brand-name car. It felt like some nonsensical show to see whose family could buy out the other's. But this $50 million donation was something new. Yes, Winchester had plenty of donations every year, but none as big as the $50 million anonymously gifted over the summer. She wondered if Hunter had met or heard about Jack yet, given how fast the Asian moms of Winchester spread news amongst each other.

"So, how good is this gossip?" Stacy dropped her oversized Louis Vuitton tote down next to Sierra with a clatter, sending a myriad of blushes, mascara, and eye shadow rolling out of it.

"Stacy, I think it's going to be quite a year," Sierra responded with an amused smile.

CHAPTER 2

TRISHA AND RAY

TRISHA

Another year at Winchester, Trisha groaned internally as she walked into her AP Calculus AB class. She tunnel-visioned on the empty desk at the back corner of the room, opposite to the smartboard and stack of new tablets Winchester passed out to students every year.

As the first person to enter the room, she quickly made her way to the desk and dropped her fake Burberry backpack from a random street market in Hong Kong down on the ground. Trisha never cared for luxury goods, but she didn't like to stand out for not fitting into the lavish aura of Winchester's bubble either.

She pulled out her sketch book and began doodling—her primary method of escapism in all aspects of life.

"Hey Trisha! How was your summer?" A bubbly girl with coral lipstick and violet-colored contact lenses flopped into the seat in front of Trisha mid-doodle.

Trisha smiled brightly. "It was great, Ren. How was yours?"

"It was alright. My parents forced me to go to a PSAT boot-camp while they flew off with my baby brother to our Napa villa," Ren rolled her eyes. "I could have studied there too."

Ren's attention quickly drifted away as the classroom began to fill with the buzz of more excited classmates swelling with stories of summer adventures. By the time the clock hit 9 a.m., a whopping eight people sat in the classroom.

The door opened and closed with a loud thud, instantly bringing down the classroom's volume level to a zero. A middle-aged man with a clean-shaven face and muscular build strolled in. "Welcome to AP Calculus AB class! My name is Mr. Johnson, and I'll be your teacher for the year. I'm so excited to get to know you all."

Trisha stifled a chuckle. While Mr. Johnson was excited to get to know everyone, everyone already knew about him. Like many teachers at Winchester, the students had already discussed, psychoanalyzed, and theorized about him. Mr. Johnson doubled as the school's triathlon and cross-country coach and enrolled himself in one of the most intensive long-distance triathlons every year called the Ironman. Rumor had it that he ate so healthily, peanut butter was dessert for him. Needless to say, there were already many conversation threads across multiple social media channels that happened prior to this class.[5]

"Now, who has their textbooks already?" Mr. Johnson continued. Trisha stopped sketching a picture of her family's American Eskimo, Cuddles, and raised her hand along with the other half of the class. The other half just laid back in their

---

5   This week's teacher topic—"Who would win in a faculty Olympics tournament?" Mrs. Stevens from basketball, Mr. Lansing from volleyball, Mr. Lim from baseball, or Mr. Johnson from cross-country? Most people had their bets on Mr. Johnson.

seats staring at Mr. Johnson like they dared him to make them use textbooks. *Of course they wouldn't have textbooks. They'll just photocopy each other's, plus answers, anyway.*

Winchester was well known for having a strict honor code governed by an Honor Council made up of the student body.[6] If any student was caught cheating, stealing, dealing drugs, or even having sex in the school's chapel (which happened every year), they were shipped off to the Honor Council. Depending on someone's reputation and likability on campus, the council members' punishment recommendations were entirely subjective and did not prevent the highly resourceful Winchester students from cheating either.

Trisha wasn't even surprised when the school revealed last year that someone had stolen AP tests to study prior to the actual exam. *We're already wired to believe we can get away with everything—because we do.*

Trisha's internal mulling was interrupted abruptly by the front door flying wide open. A sweaty, panting guy stumbled into the room.

Mr. Johnson, with a look of surprise, collected himself and cleared his throat. "Hello. Welcome to AP Calculus AB. Can I help you?"

"Yeah," the boy said, straightening himself out.

Trisha suddenly found it a struggle to breathe. With striking green eyes, thick eyebrows, and unbearably smooth, tan skin… this guy was *hot*.

---

6   The Honor Council investigates violations of the Honor Code, a code created by Winchester's founder over a century ago to align the school's students to a strict promise of integrity. The Honor Council recommends penalties for offenders to the head of school and are selected under the impression that council members serve as honorable role models to the rest of the student body.

"Sorry for being late, Mr. Johnson. This campus is *huge*. How can you not get lost around here? The dining hall is literally the size of my school's old gym," the boy said in an impossibly deep voice. "Anyway, I'm Ray Martinez. New junior transfer."

He finished off his introduction with a dazzling smile that exuded laid-back confidence. Trisha felt her pulse pick up. She ripped her eyes away from the front of the classroom and desperately searched for something else to focus on.

She settled on her drawing of her dog. *Get it together, Trisha. When did hot, unattainable guys ever pay attention to you?*

"Welcome, Ray. Welcome to Winchester. It's great to have you with us, and yes, I completely understand how easy it is to get lost here," Mr. Johnson greeted in a knowing voice. "I'm sure you'll get used to it in no time. Now, please take a seat, I'm about to pass out the syllabus for the year."

"Awesome. Thanks." Ray walked over passed the front row, then the second row, and then, much to Trisha's mixture of joy and dismay, right to the empty seat beside her. He slipped his long, lean body onto the chair and dropped his faded, threadbare backpack onto the ground before looking up—and catching Trisha staring directly at him.

Oh, my.

RAY

Well, that was awkward, Ray thought to himself as he took a double-sided page syllabus from the stack being passed around. He was not only the new kid at school, but he had also shown up late for the first class.

I'm such a newbie cliché.

Ray tried to shrug off the embarrassment. It wasn't his fault this insane school seemed to stretch the same size of his entire neighborhood in Azusa. *Speaking of Azusa...* Ray felt a sudden twinge of sadness. He knew the first day at Winchester would be hard as a new junior transfer, but he didn't realize *how* hard it would be without seeing the familiar faces of his friends.

He didn't have a choice though. He had to do it for Tommy. *Tommy...*

Ray tightened his jaw, willing away the memories of coming home to find his mom slumped on the ground sobbing hysterically against the phone, just like when his father passed away from cancer when he was ten.

He closed his eyes and took a deep breath, reinforcing the wall of numbness he built for himself following his brother's death last year. As he felt his pain subside, he tried to refocus his mind on the alternate universe that was Winchester.

This school is so... loaded....

Looking around, Ray saw a lot of white and Asian kids, which was still more diverse than his old high school that was over 90 percent Hispanic.[7] However, it felt even more homogenous than his old high school thanks to the very clear displays of fancy looking backpacks, jewelry, watches, and shoes on full display—not to mention the crazy nice cars outside.

Ray felt like a fish out of water.

Hold up... is that a white board or a screen? And why does the teacher have such a big Mac on his desk? Teachers at his old school never got the luxury of high-quality tech. In fact,

---

7   In the San Gabriel Valley, the area is more like a "salad bowl" as opposed to a "melting pot," where ethnic neighborhoods that are predominantly made up by one ethnicity exist next to one another.

they even had to withhold white board markers from students because there wasn't enough in the school budget to purchase them for everyone.

Ray looked down at the syllabus and flipped through the schedule. Even that was weird. There were school camping trips and expensive sounding out-of-state outings littered across the syllabus. *I hope they're not expecting me to pay for this.* Winchester had given him a full-ride to come here, but they didn't mention anything about additional money for figuring out how to afford to fit in.

"Mr. Johnson, there's a typo on this syllabus. One of the dates says it's Monday but that date is a Tuesday."

Ray arched an eyebrow and looked over at the girl sitting next to him with her hand straight up into the air. He smirked. He had caught her staring at him earlier, probably judging the new weirdo in the class. Her cheeks had instantly blushed a crimson red when he made eye contact with her. As if she was a rabbit caught in a trap, she immediately used her shiny, black hair to shield her face. He almost laughed out loud by her frightened reaction.

And he felt like he was about to laugh out loud again.

Seriously? Who calls out a typo on a syllabus, or even checks it that thoroughly?

"Ah, good catch Trisha. Thank you. That should be a Tuesday," Mr. Johnson replied.

Ray continued to stare at Trisha as she nodded her head and took out some colorful marker to cross out the date on the syllabus.

Ugh. Overachiever alert.

Still, Overachiever Trisha was kind of cute.

CHAPTER 3

HUNTER AND JACK

—

HUNTER

I'm about to puke.

Ever since he could remember, Hunter would get motion sickness from even the slightest amount of lurching. Unfortunately, being in LA, that meant having to sit through hours of traffic with waves of nausea on a regular basis. The only time Hunter really tolerated driving was when he was the driver.

Yet, here I am, in the passenger seat, suspended from driving and getting kidnapped by Mom to go to some fancy mommy get-together in Beverly Hills.

Usually, when Hunter was dragged to these types of events, he'd get Matt to go too. Their moms were best friends, after all. Matt, however, bailed at the last minute today in order to game. "Way to have my back," Hunter silently muttered.

Now, Hunter was on his own.

A car horn blasted in his ear as he clutched the armrest in horror while his mom swerved dramatically in the car lane. His mom perpetuated the "Asian women are poor drivers" stereotype. She wasn't just a poor driver, but an incredibly reckless one. Twice in the last half hour she almost hit someone or got rear-ended herself by abruptly stopping. She was too busy calling people on her phone to pay attention.

"Mom, I don't understand why I have to go to this get-together," Hunter whined as soon as his mom hung up her phone. "Your friends only talk to me for all of five minutes anyway and it's very disturbing when they squeeze my biceps like I'm some stuffed animal. They don't understand the concept of personal space."

"Hunter, stop complaining, especially after you scratched this car," his mom huffed.

Hunter rolled his eyes. How long was his mom going to hold his teeny tiny car accident over him? It wasn't his fault that the tiniest scratch on his mom's new Mercedes-AMG GT cost five grand in repairs. Hunter hadn't even hit anything significant, just the brick wall outside of Matt's house. In his mom's eyes, it was still unforgivable.

As punishment, Hunter was under her every wish and command, at least more than he usually was already. Today, he'd been commanded to play the son that every mother wishes to have and wants their daughter to marry for his mom's friends.

"Zi Wei, my new client, will be joining us as well with her son, Jack," his mom continued. "He just transferred to Winchester and is only a year below you. I'm sure you can be a good *ge ge*[8] to him and take care of him at school. You'll become really good friends and then you'll thank me for this meeting."

---

8   Mandarin word for "brother." Brother and sister terms in Chinese culture are used loosely to address friends, regardless of a biological relationship, who are older or younger. It makes everyone seem more intimate than they actually are.

Hunter couldn't believe what he was hearing. "Jack Zhou? We're meeting *Jack Zhou*?"

"Oh good, you know him already."

"Mom, he's insane. He came to school dressed head to toe in designer. And not just normal Winchester designer clothes, like high fashion as if he belonged on a NYC fashion week runway. On the first day of AP Calc BC he was texting openly on his phone. When it got confiscated, he just whipped out *another* one. Jack even dared Dr. Stevens[9] to confiscate the second one too—he said he could just buy five more."

"Calculus BC as a junior? Smart boy."

"Mom, that's not the point! We'll never be friends. We're from different planets."

"Hunter, it's only going to be for two hours. His family could be one of my biggest clients yet. Zi Wei and her son are renting a house for twenty thousand dollars a month. Imagine what their budget is like for purchasing one. My commission would be your entire college tuition."

Hunter paused and took in his mom's last statement. His parents always thought about finances in relation to tuition dollars. Attending college was a necessity for his family, and Hunter's parents made sure paying for private education and applying for student loans would never be barriers for Trisha's and his success.

He still remembered one night back in elementary school when he had had another bout of insomnia due to test nerves. He slipped downstairs to eavesdrop on the late night "adult" conversation. A persistent topic was how to afford the best

---

9   Dr. Stevens, the teacher for advanced level Calculus and Statistics, also holds a PhD in math. He used to teach for Cal State Pomona as a professor, but Winchester snagged him after offering to pay for his child's Winchester tuition.

education for Trisha and him while trying to make ends meet on only his dad's salary.

At the time, his mom had only just reentered the workforce after being a stay-at-home mom, and she could barely sell any houses considering it was during the '08 financial crisis. He will never forget how his mom declared she'd rather eat only rice for every meal than not give her children every single educational opportunity. When Hunter finally fell asleep that night, he vowed to become the top of every class and not let his mom down.

He felt a wave of guilt and shame wash over him.

"Uh, hey Mom, uh, thanks for... thanks for covering expenses for me," Hunter stammered.

His mother glanced over at him with bewildered eyes. "What? What are you thanking me for? Did you get in trouble at school?"

Hunter scratched the back of his head awkwardly. "Nothing. It's just, I feel like Trisha and I don't tell Dad and you thank you sometimes."

His mom shifted uncomfortably in her seat. "It's fine. I'm your mom. Thank me by getting into Stanford and being on your best behavior with Jack."

Hunter couldn't tell if he should be offended that his mom dismissed his gratitude or laugh because he always forgot how bad his parents were at dealing with expressing emotions, including with one another.

"Don't worry Mom. I gotchu," Hunter replied. "What should I call Jack's mom by the way? Auntie Zhou?"

His mom tsked. "No, no. You call her Auntie Xu because Xu is her maiden name... Jack's father and she never got married, so she never took his last name. Her full name is Xu Zi Wei."

"Interesting..." Hunter tilted his chin in confusion. "Why did they never marry?" In Hunter's memory, having a kid out of wedlock was blasphemous in China.

"It's a long story, but basically, Jack's dad has a wife already," his mom quickly explained. "Auntie Xu is the *xiao san*. Don't *ever* speak of this in front of them though."

"Ohhhh," Hunter's mind began to connect the dots hearing the term *xiao san,* or "little third," used to describe mistresses in China. "Got it. Auntie Xu it is. I'll just bro out with Jack."

"What do you mean 'bro out?'" his mom snapped. She narrowed her eyes as if Hunter had just cursed.

"No, Mom, it's not a bad thing. Like, bro as in brother. It's slang." *Ugh. She'll never get it.* Hunter couldn't wait to joke about this with Trisha later.

"Oh! How sweet you already see him as a brother," his mother beamed as another car honked at them.

Hunter facepalmed.

JACK

"Is it really necessary for me to be here?" Jack moaned in Mandarin as he hit the back of his head against the car seat with a frustrated thud. "Can't I just drop you off and pick you up later?" He just pulled up to a valet parking booth with his mom in tow. Thanks to the fact that the visa for his mom's Chinese chauffeur was delayed, Jack was forced to drive his mom around for the past few weeks as a replacement driver.

It's just her excuse to make me spend more time with her. Jack hated the overbearing presence of his mom.

She leaned toward the Bentley car mirror to check the bags underneath her eyes. "Yes, it is. You need to make friends with the ABCs so you can have friends at your new school…. Do you think my bags look really dark?" his mom responded back in Mandarin, the only language she knew despite her frequent trips to the US these days.

Jack clenched his jaw. His mom had some irrational notion that by surrounding him with more American Born Chinese, or ABC for short, he'd learn how to assimilate into Western culture better. It felt like she made it her singular mission in life to compare him against everyone at all costs.

"No, Mom. Also, if there really are eye bags it's your fault for staying up so late." Jack flung the car door wide open as an eager valet attendant came over to take the keys.

"It's not my fault! You know with the time difference between LA and Shanghai I have to be up late in order to talk to your dad," his mom pouted like she was a five-year-old child.

"You mean schmoozing up to him while he's staying with his real family," Jack snorted.

His mom's eyes lit up like fire. "Say that one more time."

"Dad. Is. With. His. Real. Family," Jack said with exaggerated slowness.

His mom slammed the car mirror closed and turned around to give her son an icy glare. Jack shrugged back at her in response. His mom knew his words were true. His dad was Wang Zhou, a billionaire from Shanghai who struck his fortune in the garment industry and eventually grew his empire to include media and entertainment, technology, and commercial real estate along Shanghai's Bund. He wasn't just known for being a shrewd businessman, however. Jack's dad was also infamous as a womanizer.

While on a business trip to Shenzhen, a major city in China's Guangdong province, Jack's thirty-eight-year-old dad met nineteen-year-old Xu Zi Wei at a Beijing Dance Academy performance of *Mazurka*.

"She was like a bird," Jack's dad once described to him. "She was delicate yet determined in her dancing. She glimmered on stage. I *needed* to speak with her afterward. When she told me about how hard she worked to get from a small rural town in the Sichuan province into the best dance academy China has to offer by age ten, my heart became hers. My one week in Shenzhen with her was like a dream."

But then reality hit.

Once the one week was up, Jack's dad returned to his wife and four-year-old son in Shanghai, believing his week-long affair with Zi Wei would fade into the universe—just like the string of affairs before her. What he didn't realize? Zi Wei was pregnant.

Today, Jack is known as the "happy accident" to his father, the "shameful family secret" to his older half-brother, and the "best and worst decision" of his mother's life. After discovering her pregnancy, Jack's mom almost aborted him, until she found out the baby was a boy. Thanks to China's thousands-year-old preference for males over females, as a son, even an illegitimate one, Jack's life was saved. With China's one child policy[10] tacked on top of that, Jack became an instant treasure in his mother's belly.

---

10 The one child policy was a birth planning program from 1980-2015 where the People's Republic of China restricted families to only one child. The policy created an entire cultural shift, sparking the creation of terms like *xiao huangdi*, or "Little Emperor." Needless to say, Jack grew up like a little emperor.

Jack's dad reluctantly accepted the new baby's existence. Despite his extramarital affairs, Wang Zhou had an ironically stable relationship with his wife who chose to turn a blind eye to his adultery for the sake of their then four-year-old son, Sam. The appearance of a new child to challenge Sam for succession rights almost led to a divorce, but his dad agreed to give Sam more stakes in his businesses than Jack in order to appease Sam's mom.

Jack's mom fought desperately to change that. She wanted the majority of Wang Zhou's companies to go entirely to him.

"Do you know what I've sacrificed for you, ungrateful child?" Jack's mom demanded while she reached for her Birkin bag.

"Yeah, yeah," Jack said, still uninterested. "Your star career. You wanted to become a ballerina or movie star. You've only repeated this thousands of times already."

"Not just that. I had to be locked away for thirteen years in Shenzhen like some unwanted nobody, thanks to you," his mom seethed, referring to how Jack's dad put them up in a luxury apartment in Shenzhen in order to have them live separately from his main family.

"Hah," Jack scoffed. "Was it really so bad? You thought living in a four million dollar, four-bedroom apartment with maids, private chefs, and even a personal masseuse was bad?"

"That was never mine and you know it. That was all for *you*." His mom snatched out a pair of sunglasses from her purse and sniffed. "He gave you not a silver, not a golden, but a platinum spoon in your mouth. All of your baby clothes were tailor-made out of the finest silk in the summer and softest cashmere in the winter, regardless of the fact that you'd grow out of them within only a few months. Your favorite teddy bear was a two million dollar Louis Vuitton teddy bear, for goodness sakes, with eyes made of sapphires and diamonds."

Jack drummed his fingers against the car seat. *It's not like I ever asked for any of these things.*

"Yeah, yeah, I get it. Yay me," Jack replied blandly.

His mom stuck her pair of Dior sunglasses on and opened the car door, much to the relief of the valet attendant who was clearly perplexed by the argument unfolding in front of him. "You need to learn some respect, especially after you got kicked out of school last year."

Jack gritted his teeth. *Not this again.* Was he ever going to live this down? Prior to transferring to Winchester, Jack had been a student at Phillips Exeter Academy, a boarding school on the East coast with alumni that included billionaire tech founders, US presidents, and leaders scattered across industries.

Getting into Phillips Exeter was like getting a golden ticket into the Ivy League, every Chinese parent's dream. For his Exeter acceptance present, Jack's dad gave him a $5.2 million Patek Philippe watch and presented his mother with a diamond encrusted, ten carat Sri Lankan sapphire bracelet for all of her child-rearing efforts. With a tuition of $55,000 per year, Exeter was filled with the true global elite. There were the Russian chemical billionaire's twins, the Saudi Arabian royalty, and the *chaebol*[11] kids from Korea. Everyone had money, and that was one of the school's biggest assets—many parents believed being wealthy also meant being well-connected, so why not start getting their kids connected at a young age?

---

11   *Chaebol* refers to large, dynastic family-controlled firms known for wealth and political power in Korea.

Unfortunately, Jack's life at Exeter was cut short halfway through thanks to Khalid Khan, a Saudi Arabian classmate who had distant ties to the Saudi Arabian royal family and direct ties to the oil behemoth, Saudi Aramco. Khalid was not only always head to head with Jack on grades, but also openly trying to trample on Jack's wealth in front of his friends. If Jack bragged about how his mom shipped him a $2,600 box of Chocopologie Chocolate Truffles, Khalid would buy them for the whole dorm. If Jack showed off the newest edition gaming laptop, Khalid would recreate his room to have three gaming computers the following week.

"*Ma*, you know getting kicked out wasn't my fault," Jack lamented. He swung himself out of the car and slammed the door.

"Really?" his mom demanded, getting out of the car as well. "You mean you didn't stab someone with scissors?"

"It barely even drew blood!" Jack glowered. During sophomore year, Khalid Khan had taken one-upping Jack a step too far when he strolled into Jack's room during study hours and told him he had just bought the same exact Patek Philippe watch that Jack's dad had gifted him, and Jack had snapped. He picked up a pair of scissors that had been sitting on his desk and slashed Khalid's hand.

Chaos immediately broke loose following the incident. Khalid's parents threatened to slap a lawsuit on the school for failing to protect their child and another lawsuit on Jack for hurting their child. There was no way Exeter would allow their pristine reputation to be destroyed. So, they expelled Jack instead.

"That's still no excuse," his mom insisted, now briskly walking toward the Lady M Cake Boutique in the distance as Jack trailed behind her. "Maybe I've spoiled you too much.

I still remember having to pay off the neighbor after you nearly blinded his son with sand when you were ten. You know money can't solve all of your problems. You need connections too, and you basically handed them all away by getting kicked out of Exeter!"

Jack's mom abruptly stopped walking. "You know, your dad used to be nicer to me when you were at Exeter," she whispered. "Sam didn't get into Exeter, so when you got in, he was ecstatic. I thought you'd be able to compete with Sam for succession rights. You were worthy for once."

Ah, the classic Mom guilt trip. Jack swore he could see a vein in his mom's neck throbbing. Jack's dad was fairly absent his entire childhood life. Instead of spending time with his parents, Jack's days were filled with English, Chinese, French, math, chess, badminton, piano, violin, and art lessons. By the age of seven, Jack had become a badminton champion and consistently scored the highest grades in his class. It still wasn't enough to please his dad, at least not until he got into Exeter. In a tight-knit, high society circle, his son's, even an illegitimate son's, acceptance into *the* elite boarding school gave his dad instant bragging rights.

And then that smug Khalid got me expelled. Jack clenched his hands into fists.

Now, Jack was at Winchester—a private school his parents managed to place him in after donating $50 million to their scholarship fund. It was less prestigious, less well-known, and certainly poorer than Exeter, but it was better than being back in Shenzhen trying to study for China's notoriously difficult college entrance exam, the *gaokao*.

At least I can go back to being one of the richest kids again.

Jack stared at his mom from behind. With a new school that was a private day school rather than boarding school, his mom now joined him in the US, at least for as long as her visa would allow. He wished his mom's tourist visa was one month long rather than six months. Even in their $52 million sprawling five-acre mansion in Arcadia equipped with a tennis court, waterfall, eight-car garage, separate guest house, fifteen bedrooms and nineteen bathrooms, Jack still couldn't get away from his mom's constant nagging.

His mom started walking again, waving to a small, pale women with cropped black hair and an overly happy expression along with a tall, tan guy poorly dressed in shorts, a t-shirt, and flip flops that had stepped out of Lady M out in the distance. "Are you coming or not?" Jack's mom snapped, bringing Jack out of his thoughts.

"Yes. Whatever."

CHAPTER 4

HUNTER

——

"Yes, I'll be there tomorrow for the oxygen facial," Hunter's mom confirmed into her phone in Mandarin before hanging up.

Hunter surveyed the plaza around him. Despite the numerous mainstream stores like Lululemon and Pottery Barn littering the shopping plaza, he couldn't help but notice the new Korean skincare store and Chinese hot pot chain that had just opened up right next to them. He wasn't surprised. In the SGV, you were better off knowing a language that wasn't English to navigate the place. Restaurants, cafes, and even some tutors in the area only spoke ethnic languages. Hunter hated it because every Mandarin encounter embarrassed him. While Hunter grew up speaking Mandarin at home, he still spoke it with an Americanized, "ABC," accent.

"Zi Wei! Oh, it's so good to see you again!" Hunter's mom exclaimed suddenly, looking over at two figures walking toward them.

Hunter's eyes widened as he got a better look at Auntie Xu and Jack close up. As expected, Anutie Xu's mustard yellow silk dress with bright red flowers, paired with bedazzled Louboutin heels, was so flamboyant Hunter had an urge to shield his eyes. Jack, on the other hand, had the casual billionaire look down. His slide sandals, cashmere-looking sweats, and relaxed white cotton tee with a long overcoat in the 80-degree weather made Hunter wonder if Jack had somehow missed the memo about LA's heat. The two's fashion choices mixed together looked so odd Hunter almost burst out laughing.

"You as well. You look so skinny!" Auntie Xu greeted in hurried Mandarin. "What have you been doing to have such slim legs? You'll have to tell me your secret."

Hunter's mom laughed, clearly flattered, "*Me* skinny? Don't be ridiculous. Look at these hips. You're the one who still looks twenty, with that tiny dancer body of yours." Hunter felt like his ears were already bleeding, and it had only been thirty seconds.

Welp. Here goes nothing. "Nice to meet you, Auntie Xu," Hunter said with a polite smile.

He immediately turned to Jack. "And it's Jack, right? I think I saw you walking around at school last week." Hunter extended his hand.

"Yep." Jack reached over and half-heartedly shook Hunter's hand before turning away to look at... the clouds, maybe? Hunter suspected this afternoon was going to drag way longer than he had anticipated.

Hunter's mom piped in, "I can see our boys becoming such good friends already. Hunter is such a good *ge ge* to my daughter Trisha and I'm sure he'll be the same to Jack at school. Hunter isn't Chinese enough, so I'm sure he'll learn a lot from Jack."

"Jack has been so excited to meet Hunter," Auntie Xu replied, clearly putting words in her son's mouth. "Where is Trisha today? She's one year younger than Jack, right?"

"Yes!" his mom beamed. "Trisha wanted to come so badly today, but she unfortunately had dragon boat practice."

Psh. Yeah right. Trisha was *relieved* when she realized there was a time conflict with the Beverly Hills get-together. Always the people-pleaser, this morning she had done a false groan along with an, "Oh mom, I'm *so* sorry I can't go with Hunter and you," before flashing a "sucks to suck" smile at Hunter on her way up the stairs.

"Such talented children! I didn't think dragon boat racing would even be available in the US. Jack, you'll have to learn from *ge ge* and *mei mei*, okay?" Aunti Zi Wei said while clasping her hands together like Hunter and Trisha's "goodness" would somehow rub off on her aloof son.

"Yep," Jack responded, now nudging a pebble with his foot.

There was a few seconds of awkward silence before his mom perked up again. "Let's go into Lady M! The girls have been waiting to meet you and they're all so excited. Have you tried Lady M before? It's exquisite."

His mom coaxed Auntie Xu and Jack into the beaming white storefront with royal blue highlights and towers of cakes behind glass windows. Hunter trailed behind the group. While he appreciated the minimalist aesthetic that seemed to now indicate wealth and good interior taste, he never understood why a thin slice of a signature Lady M mille crepe cake was $9.

"Oh yes. They have a storefront in Shenzhen I used to frequent a lot," Auntie Xu responded. "I like this one much more though. Way less crowded. Chinese stores are like *ren shan ren hai*."[12]

_____

12 Chinese idiom that translates directly into "People Mountain People Sea" and refers to having a lot of people in one place. It's honestly a useful

The two mother and son pairs walked toward two women chatting enthusiastically at a small table in the corner. "Caroline, Susan, we're back! This is the mother and son I told you both about—Zi Wei and Jack. Zi Wei, these are my friends Susan Miller and Caroline Tan. Susan is the mother of Hunter's best friend, Matt Miller, and Caroline's daughter, Laura Tan, just started at Winchester as a freshman this year."

"It's a pleasure to meet you, Zi Wei! And look at your son Jack. So tall and strong." Auntie Tan placed her hand on Jack's bicep and gave a squeeze. Hunter winced for Jack. *There goes Auntie Tan again.*

Auntie Tan had a long list of victims who at one point had their arms, cheeks, or one poor girl's belly fat pinched by her. Ninety percent of her conversations involved topics such as weight and superficial beauty, which also explained her breast implants and monthly botox injections.

How does someone like Auntie Tan end up with a daughter as sweet as Laura?

Hunter still remembered a house party in which he had accidentally walked into Auntie Tan's daughter, Laura, throwing up in the bathroom. She said it was food poisoning, but he knew that only thirty minutes prior Auntie Tan had publicly scolded Laura for going from a whopping ninety-five to one-hundred pounds over the summer while visiting her grandparents in China. Hunter had muttered a quick "feel better" before closing the door.

"Poor Laura." Hunter took a seat before quickly realizing he had said that out loud.

---

proverb if you think about what Times Square in NYC looks like during the holidays.

"What was that, Hunter?" Auntie Tan asked sharply, turning toward him. He felt like a deer in headlights. While he was constantly annoyed by Auntie Tan, he also knew to never piss her off. Her dense superficiality also came equipped with a fiery temper.[13] Hunter was in so much trouble.

"Oh, Hunter just said poor Laura for not being able to be here, right, Hunter?" Auntie Miller said as she swooped in to help him out. Hunter let out a silent sigh of relief. Auntie Miller spoke up less during Mandarin conversations amongst the Aunties, being half Cantonese and half Korean. However, she was always ready to step in when she felt that conversations were getting too heated, or, in Hunter's case, when kids misspoke.

"Yes, uh, exactly. I feel so bad because I know how much Laura likes Lady M," Hunter quickly chimed in.

"Hunter, that's sweet of you to think of Laura. You two should really hang out more," Auntie Tan said with a twinkle in her eye. "But it's good Laura isn't here. I can't have her eating anymore and ruining her figure. I've been trying everything with her, but she's still putting on weight. How will she ever find a rich Chinese husband if she becomes a balloon?"

Hunter clenched his jaw. Laura was like a little sister to him and he didn't like anyone, including her mom, ridiculing her.

---

13 It was this same fiery temper that got Caroline Tan through her bitter divorce when she found out her husband had been detained in China for tax evasion and laundering, along with having an entire second family with kids that she never knew about. Her intense need to stick a middle finger to him led her to build a toy manufacturing empire that overtook her ex-husband's own. Almost every kid between the ages of three to ten in the US has now touched a Chinese made toy imported in by Caroline Tan.

Auntie Miller, with her sixth sense, stepped in again to change the topic. "Has the school made any progress on finding who stole the AP exams last year yet? Matt was so upset that he had to retake it this summer."

"What happened with the stolen AP exams?" Auntie Xu asked inquisitively, now seated across from Hunter. Jack looked up as well, stopping whatever game he had been playing on his phone.

"It was this scandal we had at Winchester last year," his mom explained. "Someone broke into Winchester the week of the exams and then stole a couple of booklets from the storage room to study ahead of time. The school didn't realize anything was missing until *after* all the kids had taken their exams. After months of back and forth, everyone had to retake them over the summer."

"It was ridiculous," Auntie Tan fumed. "My daughter was lucky enough to have not even entered Winchester yet, but there is no way I'm letting this cheater off the hook. I am not paying nearly forty grand for my daughter to have to retake exams."

More like not wanting to pay nearly forty grand so Laura's chances at an Ivy League might be jeopardized over cheating scandals.

"Ladies, here are your cakes," a server said in a peppy voice, with a large platter holding multiple cake slices in one arm. Rather than choose their own slices, Hunter's mom placed an order for each of the four mille crepe cake flavors and the strawberry shortcake.

After the moms were done taking cake photos, Hunter hungrily dug into a bite. The thin layers of matcha melted into his mouth. *Okay, maybe this is worth nine dollars,* Hunter thought with satisfaction. At least he didn't have to feel guilty about spending the money, especially since his mom could afford it now. Ever since mainland Chinese wealth had begun pouring into the SGV in droves, his mom's real estate commissions had shot up. It felt like overnight, the family bank account had inflated with cash.

And that was also when his parents began arguing 24/7.

Hunter looked over at Jack. *I wonder where his dad is at.* He decided to attempt small talk with this perplexing dude. "What was the first week at Winchester like for you?" Hunter asked.

Jack took his gaze away from the window and his humorless eyes fell onto Hunter's welcoming expression.

"It was boring. Everyone is too poor."

"Oh, uh," Hunter was taken aback. He couldn't tell if Jack was being sarcastic or not. *Do Chinese people even get sarcasm?* His mom definitely didn't.

"*Jack,*" Auntie Xu hissed.

The table immediately fell silent.

"Haha, just joking Mom," Jack deadpanned.

Maybe Chinese people understand sarcasm after all?

"Jack is just teasing," Auntie Xu laughed in an overly high-pitched voice. "He's always been this way with his strange sense of humor. He knows what being poor is actually like. Right, Jack? Remember how you volunteered in rural China that one summer and taught all the village children how to play chess? We have a video of him doing it too." Auntie Xu whipped out her phone and began searching for the video.

Hunter was not convinced. Head-to-toe Gucci Jack? It's more likely Jack was sent out to rural China for a single day, put up in the best available unit in the village, and then filmed with the children before being sent promptly back to his mansion. It had unfortunately become a common scheme amongst parents in order to get their kids to look like humanitarian leaders on college applications.

Hunter knew that to outsiders, this elaborate ploy sounded insane, but after hearing about how a family friend at Wharton had paid someone to take the SAT for her in Taiwan, and *multiple* Winchester students supposedly paid someone to write their college essays, Hunter no longer knew the lines between reality and outrageousness when it came to college admissions spend.

Hunter looked over at the progress of the cakes. The plates now sat not empty, but exactly half-empty on the table.

"I am *so* full. Caroline, why are you barely eating anything? Try more!" his mom demanded, distracting Auntie Xu long enough for her to, thankfully, stop looking for that video of Jack.

"Don't be silly, Phoebe. You barely ate anything," Auntie Tan shot back. "I swear I ate more than everyone combined!"

Hunter buried his face in his hands and looked up to find Jack doing the exact same thing beside him. Chinese moms for some reason had this unbearable obsession with their bodies yet also pushed food onto one another constantly. It made zero sense.

"Have you heard about Tina's twins?" his mom said, changing the topic.

"You mean Fiona and Chris?" Auntie Tan's eyes glimmered with strange curiosity.

"Yes! Those two. Tina is so blessed. Remember how they both got into Harvard and Stanford last year? Apparently, *both* of them want to be doctors." His mom sighed wistfully. "She's so lucky."

Auntie Tan scoffed. "Can you imagine them as *doctors*?"

Hunter could not help but want to eye roll for the tenth time that day. The moms all had such a love and hate relationship with the Lu family. Fiona and Chris were the children that all the Asian moms wanted, and therefore were intensely jealous of Auntie Lu for.

"I bet those college acceptances aren't even real," Auntie Tan continued. "With the amount of money Tina has from her princeling[14] parents along with the tech money her husband has, I bet she paid off the colleges just like that ring of parents in the college admissions bribery scandal."

Yup. Of course Auntie Tan would bring up the Chris and Fiona's princeling grandparents and their seemingly limitless access to wealth.

"I'm really confused by this college admissions scandal that everyone is talking about. How much were the bribes?" Auntie Xu asked with a perplexed expression.

Auntie Miller spoke up, "I think it varied, but one of the parents gave 1.2 million dollars in bribes to have their daughter listed as a fake star recruit for the Yale soccer team."

"*Only* 1.2 million dollars?" Auntie Xu exclaimed. "No wonder they got caught! They were either too poor or too stingy. The asking amount should have been for fifty million dollars at least. Let me tell you ladies..." Auntie Xu trailed off and a flash of panic passed through her eyes.

"Um..." Auntie Xu stammered. "Not that I know a lot about bribery amounts, but a friend of a friend once donated one hundred million dollars to an Ivy League for constructing a new building and it was an instant guaranteed acceptance

---

14 "Princelings" refer to descendants of senior Chinese Communist Party officials with incredible influence and wealth. Kind of ironic, don't you think?

for her son. No sneaking around involved at all. The school just wrote it into their endowment fund."

Interesting.... Hunter thought to himself. He knew there was a lot of resume padding done to make your application stand out in the college admissions process, but spending that kind of money for it.... he shook his head.

Is a fancy college name really worth that much?

Hunter looked over at Jack. *I wonder what he's thinking.* Auntie Xu's awful attempt at dodging the fact that she engaged in bribery made him wonder if Jack ever felt guilty about the whole ordeal, or if he felt like the whole thing was something totally normal.

CHAPTER 5

PAMELA

———

Pamela just wanted to escape. In a land of the free, home of the brave, she felt anything but. Her parents didn't care about her (only about her grades), and she felt like she had to be a constant role model to her annoying little siblings. Besides Trisha, everyone around her was insufferable. But even Trisha didn't completely get her. Pamela needed more, and she found that outlet through doing everything her parents hated—being around boys her parents would never approve of, smoking, partying, drinking, and growing her ever expanding collection of drugs.

Today wasn't any different. Pamela walked down her home's marble staircase, avoiding a toy at the bottom of it that her youngest brother Nirav had left behind. She inhaled the lingering scent of freshly made beef nihari and grabbed her car keys from the kitchen counter. With the beginning of the school year and her recently obtained driver's license, Pamela felt that fleeing her stifling life had never felt so close.

"*Abba, Ammi,* I'm heading out to study with Trisha!" she yelled, lying casually. She was, in fact, heading out to see her mildly attractive drug dealer, Calvin Reddy.

"Wait a moment," her mom said, appearing from the kitchen. "Take Anika with you. She's bored and can use some of your *didi*[15] advice. I need to head into the office today."

"*Ammi*," Pamela groaned. "It's a Sunday! Why are you going into the office?" All her parents ever did was work.

What's the point of children when you're never around to take care of them?

"Don't talk back, Pamela, and do as I say," her mother snapped. "There has been a hack in the database systems and your dad is on a work trip, so I need to go fix it."

Pamela's parents had immigrated to the US from Pakistan under the H1B visa as highly skilled technology workers. It wasn't long before they made their way up the corporate ladder, became C-suite executives, and then started their own tech consulting firm. Somewhere along the way, and Pamela had no idea how, her mom also had Pamela and her siblings, Anika, Rohan, and Nirav.

"What about Rohan and Nirav?" She sometimes felt like her parents only had so many kids because they knew Pamela would be able to provide free childcare. Even with all of their upper middle-class wealth, her parents never hired a nanny to help around the house.

"I'm going to drop them off at Uncle Kiani's," her mom said.

"Then why can't Anika go to Uncle Kiani's as well?" Pamela felt the icy metal of her keys dig into the palm of her hand. She didn't want her copy-cat little sister tailing her.

"I promise that I'll be good," Anika chimed in a sing-song voice from upstairs, clearly eavesdropping on the conversation.

"No, absolutely not," Pamela replied firmly.

---

15   Urdu for "older sister."

"But I really want to spend time with you," Anika whined, now running downstairs, "The girls at school have been so mean to me recently. You're the only one who knows how to deal with it."

Pamela's eyes narrowed, "What?"

"One of the girls keeps on saying I'm too dark to play Juliet in the upcoming school play."

Pamela's chest tightened. *Racism never stops.* When Pamela was in elementary school, she had her *hijab* torn off her head for no reason one day by Joffrey Lee, a boy who had always called Pamela names like "terrorist." While Pamela was already used to his bullying tactics, tearing off her *hijab* was a new level of abuse. When her parents reported it to the school when Pamela arrived home in tears, they were bluntly told that nothing could be done. Joffrey's parents were large donors to the school and, therefore, untouchable.

Pamela stopped wearing her *hijab* after that day, and her parents, perhaps out of hopelessness and guilt, never mentioned it to her again.

Pamela felt a shot of sadness bury inside of her stomach. *Hmm, I guess it is only for a few hours.*

"Fine. Whatever," Pamela relented to her mom's demands. "Anika, go get in the car."

"Yay!" Anika exclaimed, already bounding down the stairs and racing to the garage.

"I'll be right there," Pamela waved at her sister nonchalantly. "I just need to tell Trisha."

While having Anika around definitely threw a curveball into her trip to purchase drugs from Calvin, she already had a backup plan. She slipped into the laundry room and closed the door behind her.

Pamela pressed a button and speed dialed Calvin. It rang for several seconds before a groggy voice picked it up.

"Pamelaaa, wassup?"

"Hey, I'm on my way over right now. I'd like the usual stash. Put it in some sort of textbook, though. My baby sister is going to be in the car."

"Wow, corrupting your baby sister now too, huh? Is she hot like you?" Calvin responded in an amused voice.

"Shut up, Reddy. Just do as I say," Pamela snapped and promptly hung up the phone. Her lips curled upwards.

Reddy was efficient and gave her fair prices on his selection. He was not only the most unlikely drug dealer as a junior chemical engineering major at Caltech, he also didn't care that Pamela was only sixteen. In fact, probably because of her age (and looks, of course), he gave her discounts all the time on a long list of uppers.

Pamela walked into the garage and got into her mom's old Tesla, now Pamela's new car. Anika was already sitting in the backseat waiting.

"Anika, I'm going to need to swing by Caltech really quickly before going to the boba shop to meet Trisha," Pamela stated smoothly. "There's this textbook that I need to get from a friend."

"Who do you know at Caltech? Is it a boy? What's his name? Do Mom and Dad know?" Anika fired off a list of questions like she was reading a shopping list.

"Shut up, Anika," Pamela scowled. *She's always so annoying.* "No, Mom and Dad don't know, but don't you dare tell them either. I'll tell Dad you're the one who knocked over that cup of water on his laptop."

Anika immediately fell silent at the threat. *That should do the trick.* Pamela pulled out of the garage and began to speed toward the freeway.

"Why did you sleep all day yesterday?" Anika began again, still clawing for any information about her older sister.

Pamela exhaled impatiently. Her siblings always noticed things she didn't want them to notice. It was exhausting. Yesterday, after taking some Adderall to help her pull an all-nighter to write an essay, she crashed at 6 a.m. in the morning. With her parents so busy with work, they hadn't even noticed that Pamela didn't actually wake up until 3 p.m. Clearly, it didn't go unnoticed by everyone, though.

"I was up. I was just taking a nap in the middle of the day. You must be confused," Pamela replied dismissively. It wasn't her fault Pamela had an overwhelmingly large workload from courses, extracurriculars, and building her online influencer presence. Using Addy was the only way she could juggle everything and get through every long night and exam.

It certainly is much easier than breaking into the school for AP exams.

Pamela wished she was as brave as the AP exam thief. Instead, she was just an empty, pitiful shell. Addy at least let her feel like she was invincible. Well, for a little while, until the crashes came with killer migraines, insomnia, and muscle tremors that made her want to scream in despair. But she had a sort of Stockholm syndrome for the drug—even after it tore her apart, she'd always go crawling right back to it.

"Hmm," Anika mumbled, not quite convinced. "I checked your follower count the other day, by the way. Do you know your fans are calling you the Pakistani ABG[16] now?"

Pamela smiled. Her dedicated followers were always hyping her up, and Anika was in that follower group. Anika was an annoying little sibling, but she knew when not to tattle. Her parents had zero clue that Pamela spent large amounts of time posting makeup videos and style tips to over a million people's social media feeds on a daily basis.

"Pakistani ABG," Pamela thought out loud, "that's a new one."

"Yeah," Anika sighed whimsically. "I wish I could be more like you."

Pamela scoffed. "Anika, you're an eighth grader with straight A-pluses in every class except for PE. You're the favorite in the family. What are you talking about?" Pamela flipped on the car's right clicker and exited the freeway.

"Don't remind me about grades," Anika groaned. "I would have an A-plus in PE if I didn't have to fast for Ramadan."

Pamela rolled her eyes as she turned onto California Boulevard. "Stop being an overachiever like Trisha, would you?"

She pulled into a parking lot near Milikan Pond beside a bearded guy with messy black hair, deep-set chocolate brown eyes, and a long stubble beard that sometimes made Pamela wonder what it would feel like to run her hand across it.

"Reddy!" Pamela shouted though her car window. *Just the man to bring me into the darkness.*

---

16   ABG, or "Asian baby girl," is a stereotype born out of the SGV which refers to, according to Anika's recent search of Urban Dictionary, "A special type of Asian girl who enjoys going to clubs partying and drinking with friends. Loves to get boba and shop. Usually an Instagram model or influencer."

Reddy walked over to the car window, flashing a wolfish grin. "Hey, Pamela," he said. He looked into the back seat and saw Anika. "Hello, baby Pamela."

Pamela tried to stop her fluttering heartbeat as she shot an icy glare at Reddy's chiseled face. He got the message and smiled even wider. "Here's the textbook. Don't study too hard." He stifled a laugh as he handed a molecular biology textbook over to Pamela. "You need your beauty sleep, you know," he finished with a wink.

"I'll Venmo you later for the textbook." Pamela tried to make her voice sound as smooth and casual as possible. Calvin's girlfriend was notorious for being an evil, possessive skank, and Pamela knew she'd be in real trouble if she even caught a whiff of him flirting with her. Before Calvin could respond, Pamela mumbled a "see ya later" and sped off.

Pamela rubbed the dented cover of the textbook with longing. She yearned for the moment when she can take one of the little white pills again. They aided her into fading more and more into the shadows of a different world day by day. She couldn't wait to do the one thing her parents cared about most—get into college—and then vanish into a different universe altogether.

"I can't believe you're studying molecular biology!" Anika cooed in the backseat.

CHAPTER 6

HUNTER AND PAUL

HUNTER

College admissions: the years—yes, years—long event in the SGV. Beginning from when they're born, SGV babies had their lives laid out in minute detail. The goal? To get into one of the nation's leading colleges to prove that the family reached the American Dream. In Hunter's family, a brand-name college really just meant Harvard, Yale, Princeton, MIT, or Stanford. Anything beyond that was deemed either not good enough, too small, too isolated, or not well known enough amongst his parents' friends to brag about.

It wasn't just Hunter's family that thought this way. The irrational philosophy ran deep within the Winchester community—it was extremely rare to find a family where the parents allowed their kids to choose whichever school was the "right fit" for them. In the parents' minds, rankings and prestige were everything.

As a result, Hunter had no choice but to hop on the bandwagon and slave away toward that elusive college acceptance letter. After years of pulling all-nighters for essays and exams, studying for the SAT, and carefully selecting extracurriculars to show that he was a well-rounded athlete, school leader, and community member, Hunter was finally a senior at Winchester.

It was finally the year of college applications.

Winchester's dedicated college admissions office gave the senior class the most attention—starting out with monthly Winchester "College Success" assemblies as soon as school began.

"Everyone, please grab a seat," a striking, voluptuous woman in a business suit and ruby red high heels announced. "We will begin shortly."

"Does Mrs. Browser ever *not* wear heels?" Matt asked as the two of them took a seat next to each other in Fowler Auditorium, a massive 800-person capacity building named after an old faculty member who had taught at Winchester for fifty years before retiring.

Hunter smirked. "I'm sure she wears fluffy bunny slippers at home." He slumped deeper into the chair. He hated these anxiety-inducing meetings. People who actually needed it ditched the meetings anyway.[17]

"By the way," Matt whispered, making sure no one within earshot could hear them. "What's your college list again?"

"Hmm, it's here," Hunter replied, whipping out his phone and showing Matt a list of college names on the screen. During Hunter's last one-on-one meeting with Mrs. Browser, he worked with her to get his college application list broken out into three categories—the Reaches (Harvard, Yale, Stanford), his Targets (USC, Johns Hopkins, UC Berkeley, and

---

17 Although, rumor had it that Mrs. Browser, Winchester's college counselor, always hunted the ditchers down one way or another. She needed to maintain Winchester's 100 percent college acceptance rate.

NYU), and three safety schools that he didn't even want to think about landing in.

"Where's MIT?" Matt asked, staring at Hunter's impressive list.

Hunter pursed his lips. "MIT didn't make the list. Mrs. Browser point blank said I wouldn't be accepted and shouldn't apply."

"I get the feeling," Matt looked down sadly. "Mrs. Browser told me I wasn't good enough to have Brown or Dartmouth on my college list."

The entire formation of a Winchester student's ten school college list (nothing more and nothing less) happened under the watchful reviewing eye of Mrs. Browser, who had connections with all the top colleges after working on multiple college admissions committees throughout her twenty-year long career. According to Sierra's best friend Stacy, whose dad was a Winchester faculty member, Mrs. Browser made more than any other faculty member after getting poached from Harvard Westlake, a competing private school in the area.

"I'm sorry, man, that's so irritating," Hunter grimaced. "I don't like how Winchester tries to limit which colleges we can apply to. They always try to sell it as not wanting to waste our efforts on colleges where we don't have any chance with, but everyone knows there's some invisible quota where only a couple of us can be accepted into each of the top colleges every year."

Matt nodded. "Agreed, but honestly, I can't complain. She's letting me apply to BU and NYU at least, and I honestly don't care where I go as long as it's in a big city on the East Coast. I'm tired of Cali." Matt leaned in toward Hunter. "I heard she outright rejected Katie Hurst for applying to any of her dream schools, and she left the room crying," he said in a hushed voice.

"Oof. She's our best basketball player, though. Maybe she can go through the sports recruiting route," Hunter said sympathetically.

"Yeah, definitely. Also, with or without MIT, your list is crazy good," Matt commented with a twinge of jealousy in his voice.

Hunter shrugged. He knew with his GPA, extracurriculars, standardized testing scores, and Winchester's reputation within the college admissions world, he wouldn't end up in any school below the top fifty rankings. It was getting into his dream school, Stanford, that seemed impossible.

The way Hunter saw senior year, it could be broken out into four chunks:

- **Part 1**—Take the SAT in October to get a near-perfect score (especially since Asians were expected to score higher) before early admissions and early action deadlines, and gather letters of recommendations from his favorite teachers.

- **Part 2**—Write the most solid personal statement possible that showed his "inner self" and submit it to his top choice school, Stanford, for early action.

- **Part 3**—Submit the remaining applications for regular decision, even if he did get into Stanford. After all, the beauty of early action was that he didn't have to commit to any one school, so why not try his chances at the other Ivies as well?

- **Part 4**—Senioritis[18] time. Party like there's no care in the world but only let grades slip so much where a college doesn't end up noticing and rescinding its offer.

Since it was only the beginning of his senior year, Hunter was solidly in part one. Therefore, he was spending day and night studying for the SAT in October as his last chance before applying to Stanford. Problem was, Hunter was exhausted, and it was only the first month of school. While he did try to get a head start on his Common App[19] personal statement over the summer with one of the many private college counseling coaches in the area,[20] Stanford's eleven supplemental prompts had made him stop dead in his tracks. Now, Hunter was regretting it because, on top of studying for the final SAT and writing the college essay, he was also juggling four AP classes, co-captaining this water polo season, being a solid VP for his class—oh, and of course, a good boyfriend to Sierra. He was running on five hours of sleep per night along with insomnia from all the stress.

Hunter sometimes wondered if death was better than what he was living through. The one thing that really kept him going was the idea of how proud his parents would be when he finally got his college acceptance letter. All he wanted was a droplet of recognition from them.

And so, Hunter continued grinding without pause.

---

18 "Senioritis" refers to when second semester seniors slack off after college applications are over knowing that their future grades will no longer matter for their college applications.

19 Common App, or Common Application, is an undergraduate college admission application that can be used in one go to apply to more than 800 colleges, mostly in the U.S.. It makes life a lot easier!

20 Hunter's mom felt like having only Mrs. Browser as a college counselor didn't give her son enough one-on-one attention for perfecting his college application

He felt a large shadow come near him and turned to his side. He stiffened. He stared into the spitting image of Sierra's blue eyes, except instead of love and kindness, Paul Jones's eyes had a permanent evil glint in them.

"'Sup, Paul."

PAUL

Whoever invented college admissions should be thrown into Guantanamo.

It was a disgusting process that really only favored the ultra-rich and those emotionless nerds at school. In fact, he stared at one now.

"What's up, Hunter," Paul tossed back. His lips curled in disgust.

Paul hated how Hunter talked to him with such familiarity. Hunter used to be the dorky kid that he could shove around and cheat off of freshmen year, but after one summer away and a growth spurt, Hunter suddenly thought it was *okay* to be on the same level as Paul and stop handing homework answers over to him. Not only that, he had to *share* the water polo captain position with Hunter this year. He didn't understand what Coach Bron, or anyone for that matter, saw in him.

Now, the loser is dating Sierra, Paul thought with disdain. He couldn't stand the thought of Hunter's geeky hands all over his baby sister.

And the unbelievable nerve they had to hide their relationship from me. It made Paul look like an idiot when he found out from his friends that his gorgeous sister was dating the biggest loser of his class. He blamed the dawn of the tech bros up north in Silicon Valley. Suddenly, everyone thought being a dork was cool.

"Hi, Hunter," Paul waved with a gigantic smile, keenly aware that Mrs. Browser was only steps away from them. "How was your summer?"

Hunter stared at Paul suspiciously before he saw who was standing near them. "It was okay, lots of studying," Hunter muttered.

"I wouldn't expect anything less," Paul said through gritted teeth.

"Students, please take your seats!" Mrs. Browser boomed from behind. Paul reluctantly took the only empty seat remaining next to Hunter.

He sulked in his seat as he looked at everyone around him. *I wonder who else has USC on their college list?* As he began to prepare for the college admissions process, Paul realized how stacked the odds were against him. Sure, Paul had good genes (six-foot and two inches, blonde-hair, blue eyes, and eight percent body fat last time he checked at Equinox), grades,[21] and pedigree, but money and standardized test scores still eluded him. He desperately wished his parents would have enough money[22] to just donate a building to USC and get an automatic acceptance like someone did for a never-to-be-mentioned Ivy League last year.

On the testing front, Paul swore the test was rigged. He had to slave away while people like Hunter could just twiddle their thumbs and an A would pop out. Paul even heard that some testing institutions in China and Korea had instructors

---

21 Paul knew which teachers and classes were the easiest to get an A in, so he always chose his courses for upcoming semesters based upon this to maintain his 3.8 GPA. If he got a teacher for a course that was notoriously difficult, Paul would just walk into Dean Rand's office, talk about golf, and then get switched easily into the other section with the easier teacher.

22 The Jones family only had a net worth of $16.5 million—not nearly enough to Paul.

either taking the exams for students or leaking the answers to students prior to the exam.

Meanwhile, even with one-on-one tutoring at $150 per hour, Paul still scored in USC's lower twenty-fifth percentile for SATs last spring. This time around for the October SAT, though, Paul had found a brilliant way to game the system by getting diagnosed with ADHD. Thanks to a family friend doctor connection, Paul now got four and a half hours on the SAT rather than three and a half for his "learning disability," despite the fact that Paul didn't actually have ADHD. The extra hour would help Paul take more time to figure out the right answer. His mom thought he was a genius for discovering this loophole.

"Students," Mrs. Browser said, now standing at the top of the auditorium stage. "Welcome to the year of college admissions!"

The entire ninety-eight-person senior class turned toward Mrs. Browser anxiously.

"First of all, I'd like to commend everyone for your years of hard work leading up to this year. This will be one of your hardest, but happiest, years as you get into colleges that will define the next four years of your life." Mrs. Browser paused, staring into the crowd like a fortune-teller. "At an institution like Winchester, with a one-hundred percent college acceptance rate, *everyone* will be attending a college, I guarantee it. That being said, you will only get into somewhere if you listen to and follow everything that I say. Don't apply to colleges that are not on your college list, and don't do anything that will jeopardize your college acceptances, especially after admittance."

Paul smirked. *I can't wait for second semester senior year.* Paul already imagined himself partying and making out with some of the new, hot freshmen girls he spotted the first day of school.

"As you all know, someone tampered with the AP exams that were given out last spring," Mrs. Browser continued. "While this is an ongoing investigation, we know that the majority of students who took the stolen AP exams last spring were juniors, which means there's a high likelihood one of you sitting in the auditorium today was the thief who decided to crawl in through the vents and play mission impossible."

Mrs. Browser stopped speaking. The auditorium began to stir uncomfortably with whispers amongst the students.

After a moment, Mrs. Browser suddenly clapped her hands together, silencing the murmuring immediately. "I'm only going to say this once—colleges will not accept cheating and abating, let alone thievery. If you know anything about the stolen AP tests last year, I expect you to report this information to Dean Rand immediately. I will not be wasting my valuable time on undeserving students during the college admissions cycle."

Paul stared at his nail beds, unbelievably bored. *When were they ever going to stop talking about the dumb AP tests?*

CHAPTER 7

THE STRANGER

The Stranger never understood the world of the SGV. He didn't understand the insane struggle for success and recognition, nor did he understand why a person's self-worth was decided by a piece of paper from some fancy college that only rich people could afford. He didn't understand any of it.

Ever since he could remember, he had always felt like an outsider—within his family, within his community, within the region. Yet, he went along with conforming and becoming the "perfect" kid anyway.

The Stranger flipped open his laptop and let his fingers flow at his usual 112 words per minute speed across the keyboard. In a few minutes he was on the Dark Net,[23] pinging other users about his latest successful hack into a large financial institution for their customer data. He always vetted his data before selling it—only those with a bank account amount of $1 million and over would have their data sold to other users.

They could afford a few hacked accounts.

---

23   A small part of the deep web that is often used for nefarious purposes.

At the age of one, the Stranger was enrolled into Montesorri, a school founded on the principle of "holistically" developing children, or in other words, kid geniuses. It worked, but not in the way his parents had hoped. He developed an avid interest in technology from an early age, and the wealth of knowledge on the web allowed him to see what was actually going on in the world compared to the superficial bubble his parents created for him.

"Meowwww." A fat, orange tabby cat hopped onto the Stranger's desk, attempting to sit on the keyboard.

"Buttercup!" he scolded. "Not now. You can't just jump onto my laptop whenever you want." The Stranger plucked up Buttercup and plopped him on the ground.

He ignored Buttercup's glare and continued typing furiously, taking various bids for his dataset containing 100,000 customer names and personal information. He scratched his neck and winced. His neck had an itchy, painful sunburnt glow from getting dragged off earlier in the day to some outdoor philanthropy event.

By day, he was enrolled in all the best tutoring that money could buy. In monetary terms, that meant $29,870 for music and art classes, $104,000 for a Chinese tutor, and $56,600 for golf lessons per year. This did not even include the private school tuition, admissions counselors, college preparatory courses, college tuition, and study abroad programs he had, or would need, to spend money on in the future. All in all, through some quick mental math, the Stranger concluded that his parents would spend approximately $1.7 million on educating him by the time he graduated from college.

He was spoiled. He was privileged. And he hated it.

By night, the Stranger prowled the internet for new techniques to hack into accounts and amass an income that even towered his dad's. The internet was the best education he had ever gotten.

"If only they knew their money is all pointless," the Stranger muttered out loud. Buttercup jumped onto the desk for a second time at the sound of his voice. This time, he acquiesced his position and allowed his cat to sit on his forearms while he typed awkwardly on his keyboard.

The Stranger's parents focused solely on expanding their wealth and power. Consequently, in order to exude a perfect image, his parents controlled everything about his life with firehose douses of intensive parenting and having their kids compete with all the other children in the area.

The Stranger pressed enter on his keyboard and heard a ding on his phone almost simultaneously. The edge of his lips curved upward. *Pay day.* Five hundred and fifty thousand dollars just deposited into his offshore bank account under a false name.

In a way, his parent's quest for perfect, high-achieving children forced him to become one of the most brilliant and youngest masterminds on the Dark Net. He had an IQ of 161, photographic memory, and the ability to speak four languages. He also suffered from OCD, exacerbated by his suffocating parents, and experienced extreme introversion because he couldn't figure out how to talk to normal kids his age.

Buttercup began to knead the Stranger's arm. "Do you really have to do that?" He picked up Buttercup and held him like a baby. Buttercup wasn't too happy with it. In one twist, he jumped down onto the floor, nicking his arm on the way down.

"Buttercup!" he shouted in exasperation. The scratch hadn't drawn any blood, but it laid perfectly on top of one of the Stranger's scars. *Hmm. Haven't thought about this one in a while.*

The scar was of the many injuries the Stranger sustained from a family member growing up.

I think this one was from when I was promised to be taught how to bike, but was pushed down a steep hill instead.

In the Stranger's eyes, his family member was the epitome of everything that was wrong with the system based on power, wealth, and looks. The family member was a sociopath in the making. Yet, others seemed to turn a blind eye to the manipulative and abusive behavior and say, "It wasn't intentional." It infuriated him. But what could he do? Even his teachers and friends at school didn't believe this outwardly "perfect," "empathetic," and "gracious" person could be so callous and evil behind closed doors.

Ironically, it wasn't even the physical punches that hurt him the most—those he could recover from. It was the emotional blows that tore down every shred of self-confidence he had. As they got older, his family member began to physically abuse him less and less, especially once the Stranger grew bigger and learned how to fight back. However, the emotional abuse never stopped.

The Stranger heaved a giant sigh and walked toward his bathroom. He walked past Buttercup, who didn't look guilty in the slightest.

He rolled his eyes. "What am I going to do with you?" The cat meowed and scurried past him.

Once the Stranger began middle school, he became fast friends with an online gaming buddy named Suzie024. They seemed to share all the same interests in music and, despite being so young in age, a deep desire to change the world. Suzie024 was terrible at gaming but it made the Stranger like her even more. He felt like he could help and protect someone, something that he often lacked the opportunity to do for himself.

While all of their discussions happened over instant message, Suzie024 soon became his go-to person for all his rants about school, the SGV, and most importantly, his family. After months of chatting over instant message, the Stranger decided it was time to try video calling sometime. Since Suzie024 was all the way in Philadelphia, it was impossible to meet up in-person. That night at 6 p.m., the Stranger logged online and messaged Suzie024 that he was ready. He waited in excitement as the video call screen loaded, but instead of the sweet girl he had been confiding in for months, he was greeted with a white wall.

"Looking for me?" the Stranger heard behind him, making him yelp.

He turned around to find his family member smiling menacingly. "What's with that open-mouthed expression? Aren't you happier to see me in real life than over a video camera?"

The Stranger wanted to die on the spot. He knew there was a risk that Suzie024 wasn't who she said she was, especially since they had met online. He even considered hacking into Suzie024's laptop at some point to verify her identity, but his conscience won out. As their friendship grew stronger, the Stranger's emotions made him sloppy. He wanted so desperately for his friendship to be real that he let his guard down. Betrayal and devastation were only the surface of what the Stranger felt. He told Suzie024 *everything* about himself—how he felt about his parents, how lonely he felt, and how he felt like an absolute outsider. Perhaps what was the most mortifying, the Stranger had confessed to Suzie024 that he had developed a crush on her.

After weeks of taunting from his family member and finding pages of their chat printed out and pasted across his bedroom, the Stranger felt like he hit a dark, hopeless wall. He simply didn't see the point of living anymore.

One day, after secretly hoarding a mixture of drugs from his family's medicine cabinet, the Stranger got into his bathtub fully clothed and swallowed a handful of pills. Halfway through, he began to hear incessant yowling from Buttercup.

He shuddered at the memory of that day in the bathroom. After hearing Buttercup, something inside of him told him this wasn't the right way out. He promptly changed his mind and forced himself to throw up everything he had consumed.

The Stranger looked over at Buttercup, now laying on his side on his bed. The Stranger couldn't help but find dark humor in his memories. *Twelve-year-old is saved by hungry cat. That should be a headline somewhere.*

CHAPTER 8

PAMELA AND TRISHA

PAMELA

"What are you looking at, Trish?" Pamela asked from her sprawled out, belly-down position on the Wang's chaise sectional. Like most school days, Pamela came over to the Wang house after her last class.[24] It was one of the only places where she could safely run her growing social media community. While both Trisha and her parents were never home due to their busy work life, Pamela had little siblings who liked to invade her privacy and tattle on her to her parents, unlike Trisha. Besides her little sister Anika, no one else in her family knew about Pamela's influencer status.

Trisha giggled hysterically. "A cat video."

"Let me see that," Pamela demanded. Trisha walked over to Pamela from her side of the sectional and handed her

---

24 While Trisha and Pamela started out as enemies in kindergarten after arguing over a princess tiara sticker, their rivalry quickly blossomed into the friendship of a lifetime. Sure, on the outside Trisha was the perfectionist, straight-edged overachiever while Pamela was the cool, hot, rule-breaker that every boy wanted to date. But on the inside, they both shared a strong sense of loyalty, independence, and hunger to leave the San Gabriel Valley bubble.

the phone. The video showed a cat jumping three feet into the air in horror at the sight of a cucumber.

Pamela burst out laughing too. "Dumb content is getting better and better every day." She handed the phone back to Trisha and lifted her lethargic body up from the couch.

"I'm going to grab something to eat." Pamela made a beeline for the Wang's disgustingly well-stocked kitchen that she enjoyed putting a dent in. Pamela had no qualms treating the Wang home as her own.

"Hungry again?" Trisha's voice echoed from the living room. "You just had three mooncakes!"

"I haven't had anything to eat since yesterday, okay!" Pamela challenged. She walked over to the stainless-steel fridge and flung open its high-tech vacuum seal door. She rummaged around, pushing aside two cartons of eighteen-pack eggs, a gigantic carton of soymilk, ginger, tomatoes, a large cantaloupe, and a family-size bag of apples.

"Trish, did you go to Costco again?" Pamela asked, her voice reproachful. "I can't believe that after *finally* learning how to drive all you really do is go to Costco!"

"Maybe," Trisha shouted in an embarrassed voice from the other room. "I couldn't help it. It's out of habit! I used to go weekly with Uncle Mike and my grandparents when they were still around."

Pamela shook her head. "You don't have that many people in the house anymore," Pamela admonished, grabbing a Chinese swiss roll cake from behind the soymilk. "Although, I'll gladly pretend to be extended family if it means I can always access the fridge."

"You already have unlimited access!" Trisha jested. Pamela tore off the cake's plastic wrapping and took a gigantic bite out of the light and fluffy vanilla sponge cake layered in whipped, creamy goodness. She strode back into the living room, ignoring the cream that was getting all over her hands.

"How is your uncle doing, anyway?" Pamela asked, collapsing back onto the chaise. "Didn't he fall in love with an air stewardess?"

"Yep. He's pretty good. Lives in San Diego with her now."[25]

"And your grandparents?" Pamela took another large bite out of the cake.

"They're also good. Happy in their luxury retirement community in Beijing."[26] Trisha walked over to Pamela and stuck her face next to Pamela's hand and ate the last bite of the cake.

"Hey," Pamela protested, "that was mine!"

"Uh huh, right. Like that was totally not from my fridge," Trisha said sarcastically.

Pamela made a dramatic eye-roll. "I feel like your house has gone from 'I seriously can't find any available bathroom' to super silent in the past two years."

"Agreed." Trisha's shoulders slumped. "To be honest, I used to hate feeling like I could never get any privacy in the house, but now the house just feels depressing. At least when

---

25 Uncle Mike tells everyone that he had ensnared the attention of a gorgeous air stewardess on a twelve-hour plane ride with his charm. The real story is not as romantic as it sounds. Uncle Mike was throwing up in the tiny bathroom the whole time from air sickness and his now wife helped him clean up afterward. He managed to ruin her shoes in the process and took the opportunity to exchange numbers to replace the shoes as an excuse.

26 The grandparents' decision to move back to Beijing after Trisha and Hunter became self-sufficient teenagers was a highly controversial one. It led to a months-long debate since, traditionally, parents lived with their adult kids in multi-generational households until they passed away. However, Trisha's grandparents, usually incredibly traditional, insisted that the decision was final.

my grandparents were around, they forced everyone to have family meals."

Pamela could hear the intense sadness in Trisha's voice. She quickly tried to pivot the conversation toward something happier.

"Family meals are *the worst*," Pamela exclaimed. "I'm always lectured about how deficient I am, how I need to find a husband ASAP, and how I'm an awful example for my little siblings. It's a good thing you don't have to have them!"

Trisha nodded, but the sadness in her eyes persisted. Pamela attempted to pivot to a new strategy.

"Have you talked to your parents about this? Maybe you all need a family vacation or something."

"Hah," Trisha scoffed, "I wish. My parents barely speak now, unless it's about coordinating logistics over Hunter and me. They're basically divorced, just not on paper."

Well, this convo clearly isn't going well. Pamela shifted around nervously. She usually was good at cheering Trisha up, but when it came to family issues, Pamela felt like a deer in headlights. *I can barely handle my own family. And tossing drugs at Trisha isn't a solution either.*

Just then, the entrance to the garage opened to reveal Hunter and Matt, both lugging their water polo duffels and backpacks.

TRISHA

"'Sup," Hunter said as soon as he saw Trisha and Pamela looking over at them.

"Hey, girls," Matt waved.

Trisha waved back at them, trying to shake off the dark rabbit hole of emotions she had fallen into.

"What are you up to?" Hunter asked, dropping his duffle bag into the family's shoe closet and slipping into fuzzy velvet house slippers.

"Nothing, just hanging around," Trisha mumbled. *Just wondering why our family is falling apart, the usual.*

Matt dropped his duffle bag on top of Hunter's and yawned loudly. "I'm ready to take a nap, Hunter."

"Same, that workout was brutal," Hunter nodded in agreement while stretching out his arms. He looked at Trisha. "Trish, did I see you flirting with that new junior boy Ray in the library today?"

Trisha's blood rushed to her cheeks. *This is why having a sibling in the same school sucks.*

When she didn't respond right away, Hunter lifted his eyebrows questioningly. "Trish, have you been hiding someone from me?"

Trisha heard Pamela stifle a laugh beside her.

Her face was now as red as a tomato. "I haven't been hiding anything, okay! Ray and I just have been hanging out a lot lately. I need him as a study buddy. He's, like, crazy smart, like so smart he can probably recite a textbook word for word."

"Trish, why does your romantic life even sound nerdy?"

"Oh my gosh, stop!" Trisha said, wanting nothing but to duck underneath her living room furniture at the moment.

"Okay, okay," Hunter raised his hands up in defeat. "Introduce me to him sometime when you're *studying.* I'll quiz him on Trisha knowledge."

"Whatever, I'll think about it," Trisha said, desperately wanting to change the topic. "Just don't tell Mom and Dad about it... you know how they get about the idea of us dating someone not... Asian..."

"Of course. I'm not dumb. They only started to accept Sierra after they realized she looked like a model." Hunter cringed. "All they can think about now is beautiful babies."

Suddenly, a gasp from the corner of the living room drew everyone's attention to Pamela gaping at her phone.

"Pamela, what's wrong?" Trisha asked, concern in her voice.

"Someone is going through all my photos on my social media and calling me a 'slutty whore,'" Pamela raged. "What is wrong with this chick?"

Hunter, Trisha, and Matt quickly huddled around Pamela's phone.

"Do you know this person?" Matt asked.

"I'm trying to figure out her real name. So far, I know she's this other influencer from Polytech High, but I don't recognize her." Everyone around her stirred uncomfortably as she swiped and dug into the girl's social media account. "Shit!" she shrieked, causing everyone around her to jump.

"That's why!" Pamela roared. "She's Reddy's girlfriend! Ugh, I swear, I'm going to make Reddy pay for this."

Trisha was deeply confused. Wasn't Calvin Reddy Pamela's drug dealer? Why was his girlfriend attacking Pamela online then?

"Pam..." Trisha began hesitantly, "what does this have to do with Reddy?"

Pamela flipped toward Trisha, her eyes dancing like fire. "I may or may not have slept with him this past weekend."

"What?" Now it was Trisha's turn to shout. "With *Calvin Reddy*?"

"Uhhhh," Hunter cast an uncomfortable glance at Matt. "Should we leave?"

"No. Stay. Listen to me talk about how I slept with my drug dealer," Pamela deadpanned, now systematically deleting comments from her profile.

"Yeah, we're gonna go." The boys didn't wait a second longer before dodging upstairs and away from the drama they clearly did not want to be part of.

Trisha wasn't sure if she should be furious, worried, or both.

"Isn't this illegal? Isn't this statutory *rape* to sleep with him?" Trisha demanded.

"Yeah, I guess," Pamela said. "But honestly, the sleeping together part wasn't such a big deal. We were drunk after a rave, and things just happened. It was consensual... although def regretting it now."

Pamela finished deleting all the messages and pressed the button to block Calvin's girlfriend from her social media profile. "This was supposed to be a one-night stand that was never going to be mentioned again. I can't believe Reddy was idiotic enough to tell his girlfriend, or maybe ex now."

Pamela threw her phone, and then herself, face first onto the couch. "What a mess," she groaned into the sofa. She jolted up suddenly and flashed a mischievous smile at Trisha. "Want some warm Grey Goose? I still have half a bottle in my trunk."

"From when?"

"From when I stole it from Reddy's place the morning after." Pamela winked.

"Pamela!" Trisha made a strangling motion with her hands.

CHAPTER 9

HUNTER

———

Hunter collapsed onto his bed and let out a gigantic sigh of relief. After the SATs, SAT IIs, countless AP exams, extracurriculars, volunteering work, maintaining a 4.0, writing the college personal statement, crafting the college supplemental statements (who came up with ten word limits?), and paying the exorbitant college application fee... he finally submitted his Stanford early action application.

One application down. Nine more to go.

Despite still having many applications to fill out, Hunter could now recycle his essays and use the Common App to apply to regular decision colleges simultaneously.

Maybe Sierra and I can spend more time together now that college apps aren't 99 percent of my life...

Hunter's throat tightened. They were only a month and a half into the new school year, but it had been an incredibly rocky start.

Bzz. Hunter checked his vibrating phone.

Sierra: Congrats on finishing the app.
Sierra: Are you ready to talk now?

Hunter scowled at the text message. He immediately typed out:

Way to be passive aggressive. Nice use of a hard period.

Hunter was about to hit send when he paused and quickly deleted the text. *I'll just be adding fuel to the fire.*

He buried his head into his pillow.

"Uh... you okay?" Trisha's voice entered the room.

Hunter lifted up his head and glared at his sister standing at the doorway.

"How many times have we talked about knocking?" he protested.

"Sorry, I just thought I'd drop by and tell you congrats on finally submitting your app." Trisha walked over to Hunter's bed and sprawled halfway onto it, leaving her feet dangling off the ground. "Shouldn't you be happy? You've been the *best* boyfriend in the world to Sierra lately, after all."

"Haha. Very funny," Hunter tossed up his hands. "I've apologized! You know that!"

"Was it a genuine one, though?" Trisha said, eyeing him accusingly. "If I remember correctly, you called her when she was already in Santa Monica and told her sorry for not being able to make it. Did you apologize to her again after?"

"Uhhhh," Hunter winced at Trisha's judging gaze.

Last weekend, after promising Sierra he'd take her surfing, he ended up bailing to make some last-minute adjustments to his Stanford essay. Unfortunately, he stood Sierra up *after* she already showed up to Santa Monica beach.

"Okay, so yes, maybe I didn't make a perfect apology yet," Hunter replied. "But you know how busy I have been!"

"Seriously? That's your excuse? If I were Sierra, I'd never talk to you again," Trisha huffed. "I think this is the fourth time you've flaked on her in, like, three months?"

"Actually... fifth time..."

"My point exactly!" Trisha got up from the bed and crossed her arms. "You need to be a better boyfriend. I'm not going to walk around school being known as the baby sister of another douchebag senior."

"Trish. Chill," Hunter exclaimed. "I'm nowhere near as bad as Paul."

"Don't tell me to *chill*. I hate it when girls are stepped on, and it's even worse when it's by my own brother!"

"Fine, fine," Hunter acquiesced, knowing he was going to lose this argument. "You're right. I'll do better. Just please get off my back. You aren't even dating anyone. Who made you the relationship expert?"

Trisha gave Hunter a death glare.

Hunter gulped. "Just kidding.... Anyway, I need to head to water polo practice now. Coach Bron added an extra swim practice this afternoon."

"Whatever. Just get your life together, will you?" Trisha stomped out of the room.

Hunter watched his little sister leave the room with a blank stare.

I swear, we were born out of order.

***

Two hours of swimming later, Hunter was exhausted. After the team lost the match against Polytech last week, Coach Bron decided to take out his frustration by drilling the team hardcore and instating "optional" 5 a.m. practices. Hunter couldn't tell which of his muscles *weren't* sore.

Matt stumbled over to Hunter's locker and dropped straight down on the floor as the other drenched players casually walked around him, clearly used to Matt's antics. "That was brutal. I could gorge on ten In-N-Out burgers right now."

Hunter chuckled as he rubbed his dripping wet hair. "I believe it. Would you actually make some gains after that?"

Matt rolled himself up with dirt particles clinging to his back. "Excuse me, bodybuilder fanatic. Not every guy can be blessed with both height and mass. Plus, unlike you, I have abs." Matt gestured toward his stomach.

Hunter rolled his eyes. "Skinny packs don't count, dude."

Matt faked offense. "You're just jealous." He flung open his locker door and pulled out an oversized t-shirt before throwing it on.

Hunter mirrored Matt. They never took showers in the locker rooms. Winchester had an entire fund for an organic herb garden, yet they couldn't afford to give their swimmers mold-free showerheads.

Suddenly, the front door swung open, hitting the concrete wall behind it with a slam. Hunter snapped his head to the direction of the sound and cursed under his breath. *My favorite person in the world.*

"Get out!" Paul yelled at no one in particular.

The locker room erupted into chaos as lockers banged closed and boys shuffled out, including Matt.

Hunter placidly threw on his shirt and turned toward Paul. "Seriously? Just because we're seniors doesn't give us the right to throw temper tantrums like toddlers."

Paul took a step toward Hunter, baring his teeth. "Today is not the day to be pissing me off."

Hunter grabbed his backpack and swung it over his shoulder. "Whatever," he said and began to walk toward the door.

"Hey, Hunter," Paul called out.

"What?" Hunter turned around and briefly saw a fist before it connected with his face. He crashed straight onto the floor.

"What in the world?" Hunter sputtered, completely caught off guard.

"That's for pissing off Sierra," Paul sneered, towering over him.

"Are you out of your mind?" Hunter's cheek began to throb painfully.

"Don't you know Kung Fu? I thought you could take a punch better than that."

"What decade are you in, you racist asshole?" Hunter growled. He launched himself up and tackled Paul to the ground. The impact of their bodies hitting the concrete floor knocked the air out of Hunter for a second before a dull burst of pain shot up his knee, but the need to get back at Paul overrode his entire sensory system.

Paul struggled to throw Hunter off of him as Hunter raised his fist, ready to punch off the condescending smirk on Paul's face. He swung his fist down, and then his fist froze inches above Paul's face.

If I beat up Paul, what would Sierra think? Hunter couldn't risk upsetting Sierra even more.

His moment of hesitation left a clear opening for Paul and within seconds, Hunter was flipped onto his back and punched in the stomach.

"Are all Asian men so weak?" Paul scoffed.

Hunter groaned as he clutched his ribcage and watched Paul haul himself back up and walk toward the door.

"I don't know what Sierra sees in you. I used to think she was attempting to be 'woke' by dating an Asian guy, but now I can see she's just delusional. If you knew any better, you'd stay away from her. She should be dating a real American," Paul snarled in a low and threatening voice.

Hunter dragged himself off the ground and watched Paul open the door and come face-to-face with Matt.

Matt squeaked in fright. Paul burst out in a cold and sardonic laugh. He shoved Matt out of his way before marching away toward the school parking lot.

As soon as Paul stepped a safe distance away from him, Matt rushed into the locker room.

"Dude, are you okay? What happened?" Matt cried, his voice laced with worry. "Why did you not just leave? I thought you were right behind me."

Hunter pulled himself up. "Just Paul being an asshole, as usual. He barely gave me a bruise."

Matt shuddered. "Yeah, but standing up to bullies only works when they're actually rational human beings. Paul is not rational. He's a psychopath."

Hunter grimaced, clutching his side. "Well, it was worth a shot nonetheless."

"Did you hit him too?" Matt asked, picking up Hunter's backpack for him.

"I almost did, but then I stopped." Hunter sighed sharply. "For Sierra's sake, I didn't want it to go too far. The last thing she needs is her boyfriend and brother beating each other up. And, let's be real here... it would take two of me to take down Paul."

Matt smiled meekly. "Well, if it makes you feel any better, it would have taken three of me. Did he say why he was so pissed off? I heard a lot of yelling."

"Nah, he just told me to stay away from Sierra as per usual, and that was it," Hunter shrugged like it was nothing.

Except it wasn't. Hunter didn't want to admit it, but Paul's words had stung him.

His entire life he managed to avoid any direct racial slurs or remarks made against him. The community he grew up in had always been predominantly Asian, and while there were still jokes and stereotypes about race, Hunter never experienced anything as racially charged as what Paul just said to him.

Does my existence really bother Paul that much? Is this what others actually think behind closed doors, and Paul just happened to say it out loud? Hunter felt self-disgust rise up in his throat.

His dad had always told him to "man up" and ignore others, but Paul's words clearly got to him.

"Are you sure you're okay, Hunter? You're looking a bit pale."

"Yeah, I'm fine... I think I lost my appetite, though." Hunter gave Matt a small, reassuring smile. "I think I'm going to just go home for the day. Sorry, man. I know you're starving."

Matt seemed uneasy about dropping the topic but went along with it. "Okay... just let me know if you need to see a nurse or something. I'll head to the dining hall for a snack instead."

Hunter put an arm over Matt and ignored the stinging pain on his side. "Sounds good. AYCE[27] KBBQ tomorrow? Let's get that *galbi* grilling and pretend the marinated meat is Paul."

"Yes, please!"

---

27 Slang for "all you can eat." Pronounced like "ACE."

CHAPTER 10

MATT AND THE STRANGER

———

MATT

Matt was *starving*. Water polo practice always left him ready to eat an elephant. Luckily, there was the 5,000-square-foot Thompson Dining Hall, open from 9 a.m. to 5 p.m. every day, equipped with a salad bar, soup station, and a variety of entreé and dessert choices. Best part, Matt didn't have to pay for it. Well, sort of—his parents paid for it, since it was all neatly baked into his $38,000 annual tuition fee.

Matt made a beeline for the peanut butter and jelly sandwich station. He dug through various loaves of bread neatly stacked against the corner of the table and settled on a plain bagel. While waiting for his bagel to toast, he snatched two granola bars piled inside a woven basket and began inhaling them. He stared at the other baskets filled with oranges, apples, and bananas, thought about grabbing a fruit as well, then decided against it. *Too healthy.* The smell of baked bread began to fill his nostrils and he heard the toaster oven ding.

Like a hyena, he snatched up a slice and began to slather on crunchy peanut butter from a large bowl.

I hope Mom is making bibimbap tonight. Matt was the skinniest guy in his class, but probably the one who ate and thought about food the most. It also helped that both his parents were phenomenal cooks who could whip up a variety of cuisines. Unlike many of his other friends growing up, Matt was a multicultural melting pot. He loved to brag to Hunter about being the only "quarter Korean, quarter Chinese, and half White boy who looked Filipino" in all of the San Gabriel Valley.[28]

Matt was tearing at his peanut butter sandwich when he heard footsteps behind him. He looked up to see the new kid, Jack, walking over to the 24/7 snack station. Matt wanted to laugh out loud. From afar, Jack looked like a ghost. Jack was dressed head to toe in white: he wore an oversized white limited-edition Supreme hoodie, white sweatpants, and white sneakers that were labeled with a ginormous Gucci logo. Jack stopped right next to Matt and picked up a granola bar with his index and thumb finger as if it was a dirty rag.

Hmm, should I introduce myself? It's probably difficult being the new kid. Almost everyone at Winchester had gone through the same pipeline private school system together since pre-school, which basically made it one gigantic clique for outsiders to break into. He turned toward Jack.

---

28 Matt's mom is half Chinese and half Korean, while his dad is German. His parents had met at a Catholic youth study group at Indiana University—his mom was an arts history major, and his dad was a film major. Both of them moved to LA with barely anything in their pockets, but his dad quickly moved up the ranks in Hollywood. Matt's dad is currently one of the most sought-after producers in Hollywood, while somehow also making plenty of time to plan church events for the local community.

"Hey, Jack. I don't think we've officially met yet. I'm Matt Miller."

Jack turned around with a confused and slightly annoyed expression. "Oh. Hey."

"Not a fan of the snacks here, huh?" Matt commented, watching Jack stare scornfully at the peanut butter station.

"I don't understand why this station is so messy. I'm used to three-hundred-and-fifty-dollar peanut butter and jelly sandwiches."

"Three hundred and fifty dollars?" Matt exclaimed. "No way! How?"

Jack shrugged. "Gold leaf, all-natural peanut butter, imported French jam, and New Zealand Manuka honey... just the usual."

Matt's mouth fell open. "Wow, well, okay," he cleared his throat, "um, anyway..."

Matt stretched out his hand and continued his introduction. "I'd like to welco—ahh!" Before he could complete his sentence, he hit the butter knife that had been teetering on the jelly bowl with his outstretched hand, sending it flying straight onto Jack's snow-white hoodie. It clattered loudly to the ground, leaving an oozing trail of grape jelly behind.

"Oh, shoot!" Matt shouted. "I am *so* sorry, dude. Let me help you clean that up."

Matt quickly grabbed napkins from a dispenser to wipe off the trail of jelly making its way toward Jack's pants.

Jack's expression quickly changed from surprise to disgust. "What are you doing? Get away, you gay," Jack shouted—his Chinese accent thickening as he said the word "gay."

Matt jumped back as if he had been electrocuted by Jack's words. "Hey, I'm just trying to apologize. No need to call me names."

"But you *are* gay," Jack responded in a matter-of-fact voice. Matt, for once, was speechless. An uncomfortable silence descended between the two as Jack took off his Supreme hoodie to reveal another white shirt. Jack chucked his hoodie onto a dining hall chair and turned to walk away.

Jack's abandonment of his hoodie broke Matt from his silence. "Hey, dude, you can't just leave your hoodie here. The dining hall is not laundry service."

"I don't want it anymore. Keep it. Throw it away. Whatever," Jack muttered, disappearing from view through one of the dining hall's many exits.

Matt picked up the plush hoodie and stared at it dumbly. He felt like Jack had just dumped an avalanche into his psyche.

"Well, that guy sure is awkward." An irritated voice floated from the far-left corner of the dining hall's fireplace lounge.

Matt turned around to find Pamela peeking her head out from one of the couches. She sat up and yawned loudly.

"Ugh. That noise woke me up from my nap. I've barely slept in days, and the only time I get some actual shut-eye, a guy dressed like he's ready for an Asian funeral[29] covered in grape jelly ruins it." Pamela walked over to Matt and picked up the leftover white hoodie. "Can I keep this? It's probably worth, like, one thousand dollars. I can easily sell this online."

"Uhm. Yeah, sure," Matt stammered.

Pamela smiled. "Thanks." She began to pick at the grape jelly stain and then asked, "So, was what he said true?"

"Was *what* he said true?" Matt said, his face starting to steam.

"You know exactly what I'm asking. Not to stereotype, but you're *obsessed* with learning all the K-pop girl group dances.

---

29 White rather than black is often worn in mourning in Asia.

You're, uh, also not very discreet when you draw BTS's faces with hearts around them during AP Chem, and... I've seen how you look at Hunter."

Matt's eyes darkened. "Pamela, you don't know what you're saying. Don't make shit like that up. Even if what you're saying is true, you know no one would ever accept me."

"Matt, we're in *California*. We're in the most liberal and most LGBTQ-friendly state." Pamela gave him a look that made him feel like he had just said the dumbest thing ever.

"Yes, but I'm also a *Miller*. Son of extremely *Catholic* parents and a father who just became a deacon on top of that. They even met at church! This would ruin my life."

Pamela fixed her eyes onto Matt's. "I'm only going to say this once and never bring this up again unless you do so first. Regardless of who you are, anyone who truly loves you would just want you to be happy, including me. And if you don't consider me a family member by now or a friend, you're crazy."

Pamela leaned in and wrapped her arms around Matt in a massive hug. "You deserve all the love in the world, including love for yourself."

Pamela turned around and walked out of the dining hall with the white hoodie draped over her shoulder.

THE STRANGER

LAST YEAR SPRING

After almost taking his own life, the Stranger was done sitting around on the sidelines. He wanted revenge.

I'm going to make every person who has ever wronged me suffer.

The Stranger logged onto his computer and checked his Sub7 program, which he used for hacking into different laptops.

He smiled. *Bingo. Port 27374 is running today.* He quickly typed into his butterfly keyboard and, in a few keystrokes, took control of his family member's laptop. He fist-pumped into the air.

And the arrogant bastard has no idea.

Buttercup came over and sat next to him, staring at his screen as he systematically opened and closed files. It was just what he had expected—the laptop contained a jumble of sports website data, porn, poorly labeled documents, messages, and more porn.

The Stranger quickly copied and pasted a list of usernames and passwords from a document conveniently titled "passwords" on the hacked laptop and then opened up a chat application to read through the messages:

J: Yo, studied for the APs yet?

SwollMF: Nope. I'm so screwed.

A plan quickly began forming in the Stranger's head. *I can work with this.*

He logged onto the Dark Net again and quickly posted to one of the forums—"SEEKING PROFESSIONAL THIEF."

The Stranger got out of his chair and began to pace. Buttercup continued staring at him as he walked in circles around his room.

He heard a *ding* come from his laptop. The Stranger quickly walked back to his gaming chair and sat down.

FA0216:	What are you looking to steal?
Stranger:	Exams from a high school with private security.
FA0216:	Are you playing me? Can't you just hack into a computer for tests or something?
Stranger:	I am not. I need the school to figure out the tests are stolen.
FA0216:	Uh... how much $$$?
Stranger:	20K. 10K now, 10K after... if the job is done right.
FA0216:	Prove to me that your money is real and then we can talk.

The Stranger immediately went into his offshore account, took a screenshot of the balance, and sent it over.

FA0216:	Those are a lot of zeros ☺ deal.
FA0216:	My name is Olivia.

For the next hour, the Stranger corresponded with Olivia over an encrypted call, exchanging details with her about the heist. The Stranger began to laugh hysterically as soon as he got off the call. He couldn't remember the last time he actually looked forward to something.

He picked up Buttercup and swung him around while the cat meowed, confused. He stopped swinging suddenly and picked up one of Buttercup's paws with his thumb and index finger.

"Jeez, Buttercup. Why are your nails so long?" The Stranger started looking around the room for Buttercup's nail-cutter.

CHAPTER 11

SIERRA AND HUNTER

SIERRA

"Hey, make me a smoothie too."

Sierra turned her head to see Paul in the kitchen, his Range Rover keys in hand. "Oh, hey." Sierra was not in the mood to talk to Paul. She had texted Hunter earlier to talk about their issues, but he still hadn't responded yet.

"How was water polo practice?" Sierra asked while going back to the freezer to take out more frozen pineapple.

"The usual. Coach Bron being loud." He smirked. "I saw Hunter. Whipped him into shape too."

"What is that supposed to mean?" Sierra tilted her head in puzzlement. She dropped blobs of frozen pineapple into the blender and pressed the start button.

"It means I beat the living daylights out of him!" Paul shouted over the blender.

Sierra jabbed the off button. "You did what?" she demanded.

"His face was annoying, so I decided to kick him around a bit. Why are you so worked up? Didn't he not show up to your date the other day?"

"Paul! You can't just go around beating people up, *especially* when the person is my boyfriend."

"Why are you yelling at me? I got back at him for you." Paul walked over to the blender and pressed the on button again. The whirring noise sent Sierra's heading spinning more than it already was.

She stared in disbelief as her older brother stopped the blender, added some protein powder into the cup, and then started the machine again.

Why is he being like this? He only gets into these moods when something happens. Sierra quickly searched her head for any important events lately.

Paul stopped the blender, removed the cup, and began to slurp straight from it.

A thought dawned on Sierra. "Paul, did you get your SAT scores today?" she asked carefully.

"Maybe," Paul replied nonchalantly. He put down the blender cup. "It was a shitty score, in case you're wondering. Also, have you seen my Rolex?"

"Stop trying to change the subject, Paul. Why do you keep on doing this?" Sierra exclaimed in exasperation. Ever since they were young, Paul always had anger issues. He had never raised a finger toward her, but he had no qualms with beating up all the other kids for no reason if he was in a bad mood. Her parents always turned a blind eye to his behavioral problems, probably because their dad wasn't any better.

"It was only a little kick. He's still your perfect goody-two-shoes boyfriend—just maybe a little bit black and blue now," Paul laughed menacingly.

"I can't deal with this conversation anymore." Sierra stalked toward the stairs.

Once in her bedroom that was the size of a studio, she slumped onto her king-sized bed. Her heart pumped so hard she could hear it.

What do I do now? Sierra couldn't decide if she should call Hunter. He had been a pretty lousy boyfriend recently, but not so lousy where he deserved to be beat up by Paul.

She whipped out her phone and looked at her text messages. There were always messages waiting for her. Sierra acknowledged that her blonde-haired, blued-eyed Jones look, coupled with her volleyball athleticism, propelled her instantly into Winchester's popular crowd. Ironically, despite how much she stood out on campus, Sierra felt like the most invisible person in the world. No one truly understood her. Even her closest friends felt like they were only her friends because they would look beautiful together.

Sierra opened her chat with Stacy. Unlike everyone else, Stacy was Sierra's one true friend. They had known each other since kindergarten, before looks, wealth, and status determined school cliques.

Stacy: Girl I have SO much to fill you in on.
Stacy: CHARLES DREAMY EYED PETERS.
Stacy: ASKED ME TO WINTER FORMAL.
Stacy: !!!!
Stacy: !!!!!!!!!!

Sierra laughed out loud. Stacy always brought a smile to her face. She texted back "happy for you." She hadn't even navigated to a different screen yet before Stacy responded:

Stacy: What's wrong?

Stacy's sixth sense when a friend was in trouble, as usual, was right.

Sierra:	Paul beat up Hunter.
Stacy:	?? Why??
Sierra:	He was in one of his "moods" again. He didn't do so well on the SATs.
Stacy:	Only in the SGV will someone go cray because they did poorly on an exam.
Sierra:	Yeah...
Sierra:	Ima text you back later. Just want to nap RN.
Stacy:	:(okay... feel better.

Sierra put down her phone and slumped down onto her bed. All she wanted was a warm, comforting embrace from Hunter right now, but it felt so far away. She closed her eyes.

LAST YEAR FALL

The first day back at school after Thanksgiving break, Sierra meandered through the musky scented library rows that circulated around the sprawling Winchester library. She had just finished *Anna Karenina* by Leo Tolstoy, an 864-page book finished in three days. There was a sense of urgency and suffocation that Sierra felt she could relate to in the book. She hoped she could find something similar again amongst the shelves.

Maybe some Edgar Allen Poe.

Sierra walked over to the literature shelf, and after peering around, she found *The Complete Tales and Poems by Edgar Allen Poe* on the top shelf. She reached for the book and was startled when another hand bumped into hers. The book fluttered to the ground with a thud. She looked up to see Hunter Wang dressed in ripped jeans mirroring her surprised expression.

Isn't that the star goalie on Paul's water polo team?

"Oh, sorry, I didn't see you there." Sierra snatched her hand back, trying not to notice how sculpted Hunter's biceps looked in his tight-fitting t-shirt.

"Nah, you can have it. I was just curious, that's all," Hunter chuckled while combing his dark brown hair with his hands, as Sierra later learned, a tell-tale sign of nerves.

Sierra looked at him skeptically and mumbled a "thanks." She reached down to pick up the book.

"Did one of the English teachers assign Poe's stories as required reading?" Hunter asked.

"Hmm?" Sierra said, standing back up with the old, tattered book in hand. "What do you mean?"

Hunter paused for a moment before quickly muttering, "Sorry, my bad. I thought you were getting the book for a class or something."

"Can't I just like Edgar Allen Poe?" Sierra shot him an irritated glare. *Another guy who thinks I'm just some pretty girl.* She began to walk away.

"His prose is pretty haunting, isn't it?"

Sierra stopped and turned around, studying Hunter curiously. She was still annoyed, but besides some conversations with Stacy about Jane Austen, she rarely had a chance to talk about literature with others—it wasn't seen as "cool."

"He does..." Sierra said without thinking. "The biggest irony about Poe is that he is remembered today for being a mad genius, yet, while he was still alive, he had zero control over his own life."

"I wonder if that's what the world will think of us," Hunter followed up. "We're all brilliant in our own way for getting into this school, but we don't have any control over our own lives."

Sierra studied Hunter. It felt like he had just said out loud what was buried deep inside of her. As a Jones, she had to be *perfect*. Not just in terms of status, but also looks and demeanor. *Smile. Be everything at once. Hang with the popular crowd. Repeat.* Every day felt like a performance meant for everyone but herself.

Hunter stared back at her, his ears growing red. "Sorry, um... that got a little dark, huh?" He dug his shoe into the library carpet and began to swing it back and forth.

Is he nervous?

Sierra smiled. There was something different about Hunter. She couldn't place her finger on it, but he seemed—genuine.

"I think comparing us to Poe is a bit of a stretch," Sierra replied. "He was a drunken, raging man who married his cousin."

Hunter chuckled. "You're more than meets the eye. It's Sierra, right? Paul's sister?"

"Mhmm, and you're Hunter? I've seen you at Paul's water polo games."

"Oh, yeah. I'm on the team with him," Hunter said, brushing a hand through his bangs again and shifting his eyes away from hers.

Sierra suspected that Hunter didn't have the best impression of Paul, but she let it slide. "Why did you think I was reading this book for class?"

"Because it's rare to find someone who appreciates literature who isn't my AP Lit teacher these days," Hunter answered. His eyes twinkled. "Clearly it's my lucky day, since you're not my AP Lit teacher."

"Maybe it's mine as well," Sierra replied with a shy smile.

Sierra Jones, what are you doing right now? Are you flirting?

"Want to exchange books sometime?" Hunter suggested. "I have a gut feeling you're into some solid book titles."

There was a part of Sierra that wanted to shout *yes*. Instead, she cleared her throat and calmly responded, "Hmm, I've never done this before, but I like the idea. What if we end up choosing a book to exchange that the other person has already read?"

"Then we re-read it. If anything, that just reaffirms that we have similar book interests."

Sierra took a few seconds to ponder this proposal. It felt a little bit strange to exchange books with someone she just randomly bumped into at the library, but she did like the idea of getting closer to Hunter. She made her decision.

"How often would we exchange books?"

"How quickly can you read?" Hunter challenged.

"One hundred pages per day at least. Depends on how good the book is. I can do five hundred for a solid one."

Hunter whistled. "That's impressive. Okay, one book a week then. This time next week, same time and same place, I'll have a book for you."

And with that, Hunter turned and walked away, leaving Sierra confused by the abrupt departure but already excited for next week. And so, Hunter and Sierra's friendship, and eventual relationship, began. Since their first encounter, they exchanged dozens of books ranging from classics such as *The Count of Monte Cristo* by Alexandre Dumas to modern-day novels like *The Handmaid's Tale* by Margaret Atwood. Sierra had fallen particularly hard for a Japanese author named Haruki Murakami, an author who she had never heard of before prior to meeting Hunter. His works always left her diving deep into her subconscious realm, which would make Hunter laugh because he knew no one could escape Murakami's surreal grip.

HUNTER

PRESENT DAY

Hunter stewed in his Infiniti SUV outside of the Joneses' house. After the fight with Paul, he couldn't tell if he was more angry, sad, or just straight up confused. He hated how Paul had stripped him of his masculinity and made him feel targeted simply for his race. Now, he worried Sierra secretly felt the same way as her brother.

If you knew any better, you'd stay away from her. Paul's words echoed in Hunter's head. He saw Sierra walk out of her house and march toward his car.

"Hey, I saw your car from my bedroom window ten minutes ago, but didn't see you come out," Sierra stared inquisitively at Hunter. He felt her eyes linger on the fresh bruise on his cheek. She opened the door and got into the car.

"Paul told me you guys fought..." Sierra began softly. "I'm so sorry."

"We didn't *fight*, Sierra. Your racist brother just came at me for no reason and then *hit* me unprovoked," Hunter burst out. His suppressed rage suddenly bubbled up to the surface. "The only reason why I didn't hit back was because of *you*."

"Woah, there," Sierra put her hands up in front of her. "Look, I get that you're upset, Hunter. I'm upset too. I have a highly dysfunctional family—you know that. And Paul has always been the cherry on top for all of our dysfunction."

"Well, maybe you're dysfunctional too. Why *are* you dating an Asian guy when there is an army of dudes lining up to date you? Am I just some pity pick?" Hunter retorted back.

Sierra's face darkened. "Well, maybe I *should* date a guy who doesn't let my crazy brother's words get in his head and let them define him. Maybe I *should* date a guy who doesn't take me for granted all the time. Maybe I *should* date a guy who cares more about his girlfriend than spell checking his college essay for the tenth time!"

"Maybe I should just date an Asian girl who understands my struggles then."

Sierra's bottom lip trembled. *Oh, no.* Hunter braced himself as tears began to escape from her eyes.

"I can't believe you, Hunter. If this is what you think then we should just end it right now. I thought you'd be back to normal again after you submitted the Stanford app, but instead, you're *still* being an *asshole* and taking all your issues out on me."

Sierra's tearful plea dissipated Hunter's anger. He hated when she cried, mostly because he never knew how to handle them and was taught to always hold them back.

The car fell silent, minus Sierra's sniffles.

Sierra reached for the door handle when Hunter quickly muttered, "I'm sorry. I shouldn't have taken the fight with Paul out on you. I don't know what has gotten into me lately."

Sierra shook her head in disappointment. "What has gotten into you lately is that you have been pouring all of your negative emotions onto me. You don't treat anyone else this way. I get that this summer sucked, but that doesn't mean you can treat me like an emotional punching bag. I sometimes wonder if the closer we become, the more you feel like it's okay to treat me as a junkyard for your emotions."

Hunter fell back into silence, stunned. *Is that really what is happening?* He always shared his thoughts and emotions with Sierra. He just imagined that was what a relationship was like. He tried to think back to the last time he shared something that wasn't a rant about college or Paul.

He came up with nothing.

Hunter felt a wave of remorse slam down onto him. *Wow, I've been a real prick.*

He gingerly picked up Sierra's hand. She seemed like she was about to pull the hand away when he said. "I know I don't deserve you right now but give me another chance, Sierra. *I love you.* Think about our happy times together. We can go back there."

Hunter looked into her eyes imploringly and waited in the thick silence.

"I still love you... but..." Sierra finally said, "...but this is the *last* time. I'm so tired of fighting. You really have to start trying harder. You used to take me out to picnics underneath the stars and whisk me off to Griffin Observatory. Now all I get are nights reviewing your college essays for grammar errors."

Hunter couldn't help but let out a deep breath. *I can't lose Sierra. I just can't.*

"What are you doing now?" Hunter asked, squeezing her hand.

Sierra looked at him skeptically. "Trying to figure out how to forgive you."

"Fair enough..." Hunter said. "How about we drive to Little Tokyo right now? I'll get you the best matcha soft serve. My treat."

"If you think soft serve is going to make up for your past few weeks of behavior, you're so wrong, Hunter," Sierra glared. "It better be a lifetime's worth of soft serve."

Hunter broke into a wide smile. "If I can have you in my life for a lifetime, then it's absolutely a deal." He leaned in and kissed her on the cheek.

Sierra smiled, ever so slightly. It was incredibly small, but it gave Hunter hope that he could reclaim himself in her eyes.

CHAPTER 12

PAUL

—

Paul flicked the large California bear bobble head sitting on Dean Rand's desk. It wobbled so far back Paul though he had beheaded it, but then it snapped back with the bear's grinning face. Paul scowled. He was about to jump into the pool for water polo practice when Coach Bron barked at him to report to the dean's office. The visibly disgruntled water polo coach hated when his players skipped practice, and Paul knew there would be laps waiting for him when he got back.

This is so annoying. He had been in a particularly foul mood ever since he got his lousy SAT scores last week. Nothing put Paul in good spirits these days, except for maybe when he beat up Hunter.

Why am I here?

Paul knew from the rumor mill that Dean Rand had begun to work with the Pasadena police department to have "conversations" with any student who had to retake AP exams over the summer.[30]

---

30 According to rumors, the police department assumed only a student who was meant to take the exam would go so far as to break into a school and steal AP exam booklets. Stealing it for monetary value made no sense—it probably cost less than $4 per booklet.

Is that why I'm in this room? The police think that I stole the exams? Paul scoffed. *What nonsense.*

Paul was about to get up from his chair and pace the room when Dean Rand walked through the door with a serious looking woman sporting a tight bun in police uniform. *Guess it is an AP exam convo.* Paul stood up, ignored his loudly pumping heart, and put on his "golden boy" impression—a flashing smile, direct eye contact, and a voice that dripped with confidence.

"Hi, Dean Rand. What's up?" Paul asked in an easy-going manner.

"Hi, Paul. Thanks for coming in today. Please sit," Dean Rand directed. He pulled up a chair and turned to the woman in uniform. "After you, Sergeant Gomez."

"Thanks, Joseph," Sergeant Gomez responded before taking a seat.

"Paul, as you know, Winchester continues to pursue the thief that forced quite a large chunk of Winchester to retake their AP exams," Dean Rand began. "We called you in here today just to ask a few questions. You're not in trouble, but we're interviewing everyone that took an AP exam last year, which as you know is quite a few students." He waved a hand toward the officer. "Sergeant Gomez here is going to take some notes during this conversation."

Paul's eye twitched. He didn't like the way the lady stared at him with those predatory eyes. He suddenly felt an urge to smack her in the face.

"Yes, of course, and nice to meet you, Sergeant Gomez," Paul grinned, expertly crinkling his eyes to make it look more genuine. "How can I help you?"

Dean Rand cleared his throat. "Let's start off with the obvious—where were you the night the AP exams were stolen?"

"I was at home. My parents can confirm it." Technically, this was a lie, since Paul was out smoking and drinking with his friends. But he knew that his parents would cover for him, especially since, as long as it wasn't affecting his grades, they always turned a blind eye to drugs and alcohol.

Sergeant Gomez began scribbling in a little notebook. "And how did you feel about your scores?" Dean Rand continued.

Paul gave a crooked smile. "Really good. I studied super hard for them." Paul had received a five, the highest score, on all three of his AP exams. Sort of. Those were the scores he had until ETS voided his scores weeks later for the retake exam.

"That's great," Dean Rand commented, "And what about the retakes?"

Paul froze. The retakes? Because of how the tests were taken out of the cycle, the students hadn't received their retake scores yet. Why was Dean Rand asking about those?

Paul settled on a neutral response. "Er. They were alright. Sucked to have them over the summer. Why?"

"So, we received your retake AP exam scores already, Paul. It hasn't been released to the students yet due to obvious reasons. We wanted to talk to you today because you had scored all fives on your calculus, biology, and world history exams, yet for the retakes, you got two twos and a one. Is there a reason for dropping from full scores to low ones?"

Eff my life. Paul knew that he wasn't getting as many things correct on the AP exams during the retake compared to the first time around, but he didn't realize it would be by that much. "Ummm... well..." Paul was at a loss for words. He heard Sergeant Gomez stop scribbling and felt her narrowed gaze fall on him.

"I began seeing this girl," Paul blurted out. "And, uhh... she was super distracting, you know? High school stuff... I couldn't study and forgot everything before the retakes."

One of Dean Rand's thick eyebrows arched in surprise. "Well, that's not good to hear. You know college applications are right around the corner. Now is not the time for distractions." Dean Rand chuckled and shook his head. "Boys will be boys I guess."

Paul urged his face to turn red. "Yes, Dean Rand. Totally get it. All my fault, but I'll do better." Paul hesitated, and then asked in a naive voice, "Did I do something wrong? You know I would never do something so awful, right?"

Dean Rand glanced over at Sergeant Gomez, who had never taken her intense gaze off of Paul. "No, Paul, you're okay. We're just asking questions, that's all."

An awkward silence descended upon the room.

"If there's nothing else, Dean Rand, can I head back to water polo practice now? You know how Coach Bron gets around CIF time..."

"Oh, yes, yes. Of course. Thanks for coming in, Paul," Dean Rand said hurriedly. "And tell your dad I say hi. I'm still dumbfounded by his ace hit during our last golfing session. I look forward to playing against him in a few weeks at the Thanksgiving tournament."

"Will do, Dean Rand!" Paul got up and strolled casually to the door when he was stopped by Dean Rand's voice.

"By the way, Paul, I'd just like you to know that if the culprit steps forward now and confesses to the deed, the consequences will be lighter than having Sergeant Gomez and I identifying whoever broke into Winchester last Spring. Feel free to share this with your friends and classmates as well."

Paul turned his head back with a confident smile before saying, "Yes, sir," and walking out the door.

Paul left the building and headed straight for the school parking lot. There was no way he was going to go through some brutal swim hours right now. He wanted to go puke instead. *Why am I feeling like this? I didn't do anything wrong.*

CHAPTER 13

RAY, TRISHA, HUNTER, AND SIERRA

———

RAY

Ray learned early on that Winchester loved group projects, even when it came to math. Today, Mr. Johnson decided a calculus group project was long overdue following one of his 5 a.m. triathlon training sessions.

"Listen up kiddos—it's time for our favorite: group project time!" Mr. Johnson announced in an imitation sportscaster voice, his hair still drying from his post morning workout. "Your first group project of the year will require everyone to head to the grocery store."

"To the grocery store?" a big burly guy in the second row named Omar said in surprise. "I haven't stepped in one in ages. My family just has keto meals delivered to my house by a private chef."

"Well, Omar, maybe it's time for you to revisit the real world and give the grocery store a visit again," Mr. Johnson responded, unbothered by Omar's aghast expression.

Ray held back a facepalm. *Are people really that far removed from reality here? Or am I the one too far removed from Winchester's reality?* First of all, who does *group* math projects? His school just had problems one through whatever number at the back of a textbook chapter, and that was it. Mr. Johnson was definitely trying too hard to embrace the school's motto of *fine carent doctrina*, or "limitless learning" in Latin.

Second of all, what in the world is "keto?" Ray subtly shook his head and made a mental note to Google that later. Ray already knew by now that he was like a tiny guppy in a pool of very rich and loaded whales at Winchester. His old school had 1,300 students enrolled. Winchester had a third of that, with 400 students max per year. While he was used to class sizes of twenty-five to thirty-five students, Winchester had eleven students per class on average in order to give the young and privileged as much attention as possible. The only similarity between the two schools was that they were both old, except Winchester's age allowed it to develop honored traditions, relics, a generous alumni base, and a legacy of excellence. His old high school, meanwhile, needed to repair its plumbing system, replace its lockers, and oh, right, get some air conditioning for LA's increasingly rising temperatures.

"...and Ray, you're in a group together," Mr. Johnson's mention of his name broke Ray out of his thoughts.

"Sorry, who am I partnered with, Mr. Johnson?" Ray said in a fluster.

"Me." Ray turned around to locate the light voice that came from the corner of the room. His eyes landed on Trisha Wang.

TRISHA

Trisha stared at a box of barley rice tea. She loved H-Mart,[31] and she always felt very fortunate that the San Gabriel Valley never had a shortage of Asian food and groceries.

"Should we go with lie-chee or this Chinese character tea bottle first to measure for the surface area?" a voice said from behind, startling Trisha.

She flipped around and came face to face with Ray standing on the other side of their shared cart holding a can of preserved lychee fruit and a bottle.

"Ray, it's lychee, as in *lee*-chee. Not *lie,* unless you're trying to speak Cantonese. Also, the bottle you're holding is Japanese green tea. It just looks like Mandarin because it's the Japanese *kanji* characters." Trisha inherited her mother's impatience, and Ray was definitely testing it. "Let's measure the green tea first."

Ray handed the bottle to her and Trisha began to snap photos of it with her smartphone before switching to a phone app to measure the height and radius of the can. Satisfied, Trisha handed it back to Ray. "We can measure the surface area and volume later."

"Yep. Makes sense. I'm going to put this bottle back while you measure the *lychee* can."

Ray walked off, leaving Trisha squatting on the tiled floor taking pictures of the can. An elderly Korean lady walked past her and threw a judgmental glare.

Trisha knew how ridiculous it looked, but Mr. Johnson's assignment led to Trisha dragging Ray off to H-Mart for the very first time in his life. Trisha felt the corners of her mouth curve upward as she thought back to Ray's astonished face

---

31   H-Mart is a popular Korean-run supermarket chain.

when he found that the supermarket also had its own food court that sold buns, dumplings, Korean fried chicken, bento boxes, and tofu soup.

Trisha had to admit, she was secretly happy that she was assigned to be Ray's partner. There was something about his dangerously beautiful dimpled smile, thick caterpillar-like eyebrows, and forest green eyes that made Trisha's heart do backflips whenever she was around him. Ray returned, now with a box of Pocky sticks.

"Um, Trisha... what is this?" Ray asked, holding up the box.

"Well, as you can tell from the big letters, it's called Pocky. And as you can tell from the letters below, they're chocolate cream-covered biscuit sticks," Trisha answered, sarcasm dripping throughout her words.

"Ha. Ha. Very funny. I know how to read, Trisha. I meant what *is* it? I just saw a little kid throw the tantrum of the century because his mom refused to buy this."

Trisha laughed. "I'm not surprised. They're like an iconic Asian snack. We can try that along with everything else you wanted at the food court. I really need to take you to 99 Ranch as well; it's the Chinese supermarket everyone calls *da hua* around here."

Ray threw the Pocky into the cart. "I can't believe I've never stepped foot into one of these until now. I've always driven by H Marts in the area, but I've always been too weirded out to enter." He looked around at the colorful snacks lining the aisles and Korean aunties giving away food samples. "No offense, but Asians are like a mob around here."

Trisha gave him an offended look. "Uh, a lot of cities in the SGV are over fifty percent Asian now. It's impossible to avoid our Asian 'mob.'"

"Oh, no, no, I didn't mean it in a bad way," Ray said, putting up his hands, "I just meant that I would stick out like a sore thumb."

Trisha brushed her fingers through her long, thick ponytail. "To be fair, you kind of do. And also, it is pretty difficult to navigate a lot of the Asian businesses around here if you don't speak one of the languages." She began to push their cart toward the food court. "I swear, in San Marino, sometimes you're better off knowing Mandarin than English."

"In Azusa, you're better off knowing Spanish than English."

The two looked at each other for a second and burst out laughing.

"I really wonder how our cities became like this." Trisha waved her hand at everything around her.

Ray shrugged. "Our families immigrated here from China and Mexico. It makes sense for them to move to cities with the least amount of language and cultural barriers. For my parents, it was my neighborhood in Azusa. For yours, clearly San Marino."

"Yeah, but don't you feel like you're trapped in a bubble sometimes? Like, we all live in the same area and go to the same school, yet we never really learn about the other cultures around us."

"I guess... I never really thought about it that way before," Ray said, now lost in his thoughts. "I mean, if you want, I'll show you more of my hangout spots in Azusa if you show me around San Marino."

"It's a deal." Trisha grinned from ear to ear. "Lesson one— Korean barbeque."

Ray's stomach gurgled loudly. "Right on time."

HUNTER

I wonder what Trisha is up to right now, Hunter thought to himself. *Maybe I should bring back some egg tarts for her.*

Whenever Hunter had a sweet tooth attack, which happened very often nowadays with all the college admissions stress, he found himself dragging Sierra to his favorite bakery in the world, 85°C Bakery Café.[32] There was something about how over twenty different flavored breads ranging from savory to sweet, soft to crunchy, and small to large of freshly baked goodness would flood his nostrils upon entering the store that would instantly lift Hunter's mood.

It wasn't helping him forget about all his troubles today, though. He rubbed his hands back and forth in his hair nervously.

"What's wrong?" Sierra asked while reaching for a plastic tray and a pair of tongs at the entrance of the bakery.

"Nothing. Just the usual. I'm so done with this whole college application business," Hunter frowned. "I thought I'd feel like it would be smooth sailing after the Stanford application was submitted, but I still have all these doubts about whether or not I can get into any college."

"You're completely overqualified for a lot of colleges... why would you say that?" Sierra began to enter a single file line that had formed around the bakery bread casings.

"I guess..." Hunter hesitated. *Because my parents never told me that I was good enough? Because whatever I do, I've always failed in some way? Because my parents sacrificed everything to give me the best possibilities, and I'm reminded of that each and every day?*

---

32 A Taiwanese international bakery and cafe chain that had launched its US presence starting in the SGV. Locals like to call it 85C.

"I don't know..." Hunter finally said.

"Well, I think you're great. And I also think colleges would be dumb not to accept you," Sierra remarked, leaning in to pluck out a chocolate bun from one of the bread casings.

"I hope that's what they think of me," Hunter smiled, reaching into a refrigerated section for a coffee milk butter bread. "Thanks for the vote of confidence and for coming with me to 85C too, especially after Matt bailed. He's been so weird lately." Hunter frowned. Matt had been so skittish around him lately. *What is up with him?*

"Of course," Sierra beamed, "I know this always cheers you up, and it's not like I came here kicking and screaming either. I love this place too. "

"Thanks, babe." *How did I ever score someone as amazing as her?* "Nothing makes me happier than the big fat taro buns here to distract me from the world." Hunter lifted up one of the plastic doors holding half-foot buns with a smooth, marbled surface with swirls of white and lavender.

"I can't believe it took me fifteen years to figure out this place existed." Sierra bent down to reach into a lower compartment with a sign that said "fresh baked" and picked up a large brioche wrapped with purple paper. "Who knew that a brioche could be so fluffy and moist?"

"It's because it's a Japanese-style brioche. They're are all about the fluff. I'll take you to try Japanese fluffy pancakes sometime." Hunter licked his lips. "They're about two to three inches thick and come in all these flavors, like melon."

"That would be nice," Sierra beamed. "You've really been bringing your A-game to our dates lately."

"Well, it's the least I can do," Hunter noted, casting his gaze downward, "...especially after I was an absolute jerk to you."

Sierra grimaced. "Let's not talk about that anymore... I don't want to get mad all over again."

"Works for me," Hunter quickly acknowledged. He still felt like a dark cloud would come over him when he thought about the collision of events that happened to him last month—submitting his Stanford application, getting into a fight with Paul, and subsequently almost getting dumped by Sierra.

Hunter and Sierra made the entire loop around the bakery breads and collected an assortment of bread on their platter—there were multiple egg tarts, cheese dogs, berry flavored bread, and a Hawaiian-inspired chicken bun—on top of the brioche, taro, and coffee breads.

"Can I get an iced boba milk tea and an iced sea salt coffee as well?" Hunter asked the cashier.

"Yes. That will be twenty-four dollars and eighty cents, please. Do you have a stamp card with us?" The perky cashier girl asked.

"Yes, I do." Hunter pulled out a stamp card and credit card from his phone wallet and handed it over. "Here you go."

"Thank you very much!" The cashier replied and rang up the order while a second worker neatly folded the bread into individual plastic pouches and placed them in a large red and white box. The cashier completed the order and quickly handed the receipt back to Hunter before calling out "Next in line!" and signaling to Hunter and Sierra to walk away.

"Hunter?"

He turned his head toward the door and saw a petite, curvy girl with Prada sunglasses pulled to the top of her wavy, black hair in a fitted, silk dress.

"Laura!" Hunter exclaimed, waving his hand. Laura beamed and waved back to him.

Gah, it's so good to see her.

Laura Tan, the daughter of Auntie Tan and a freshman at Winchester, always brightened up Hunter's day with her bubbly personality.

He quickly swept Laura into a massive hug and let her go. She looked at Sierra standing next to him and waved at her too.

"Hi, Sierra!" Laura greeted sweetly. She immediately pointed to Sierra's drink. "You know my mom says drinking iced drinks aren't good for girls. It's awful for our bodies."

Sierra smiled tightly. "Hi, Laura."

SIERRA

Out of the numerous trips Hunter and Sierra had taken to 85C together, Sierra thought this trip by far was the worst.

Hunter and Laura sat across from her, laughing and smiling at each other while catching up on the latest Asian mom gossip. Sierra chewed on the straw of her iced coffee. She was usually not the jealous type, but the fact that Hunter was stressed out only moments ago and then shifted so quickly into a happy mood with the sight of *another* girl made Sierra want to run off to her parents' doomsday bunker in New Zealand.

Maybe it's because she's Chinese and therefore understands Hunter's struggles way better than you, a tiny voice in Sierra's head whispered. She felt herself begin to spiral into her insecurities. *Ugh. Stop it, Sierra.* She quickly took a long hard sip of her drink and tried to shake herself out of her sulking state.

"...and then the *feng shui* master told my mom I had to live in the master bedroom in order to bring better luck to my grades... so now I'm in the master bedroom of the house!" Laura declared.

"That's wild," Hunter responded enthusiastically.

"That must be so nice, Laura," Sierra said, attempting to add to the conversation. "I'd love to be in a master bedroom."

"It's actually not as great as it sounds. It's massive and has a nice view of all of Pasadena. You can even see downtown LA in the distance. But I'm also interrupted by my mom all the time because she still has everything in her master closet. I swear it's just an excuse to check in on me," Laura grumbled. "The good news is she likes to spend time in our Newport home on the weekends, so at least there's some down time then."

"Gotcha." Sierra had forgotten that Laura's mom hosted the Winchester Parents' Gala every year in her three pool, eight-bedroom, bowling alley and movie-theater equipped Newport Beach waterfront home. It always sent her mom into a jealous frenzy.

A scream erupted from Laura's phone, causing Hunter and Sierra to jump in their seats.

"Ah, sorry, that's my mom's new message tone. It screams whenever she sends me a text now," Laura laughed, embarrassed.

Laura swiped open her phone and looked at the text message. "Speaking of my mom, she's wondering where I am. I'm going to head back home now. Please don't tell her you saw me here. She hates the idea of me being around carbs."

"Yeah, duh," Hunter said knowingly. "See you later, Laura."

Laura waved goodbye at both of them and left.

"Well, that was nice," Hunter said, still smiling.

"Mhmm," Sierra uttered half-heartedly.

Hunter tilted his head in confusion. "What's wrong? Why are you pouting?"

"I'm not pouting. I just don't like the way you interact with one another like I'm not even around. It makes me feel like I'm the third wheel instead of the girlfriend."

Hunter rolled his eyes. "Sierra, you're being ridiculous. Have some sympathy. I've known Laura since I was in pre-school, and her mom is by far the most narcissistic and manic person I've ever met. Laura has to fend all of that by herself without any siblings and her dad out of the picture. She's all alone."

"Except she's not. She has you," Sierra pointed out. "How many dates between us has she ruined because she had some issue come up with her mom? How come you're the one she contacts every time and not Trisha? Let's face it. She likes you, Hunter, and I don't like how much she depends on you for all her emotional needs."

"You're being cruel and jealous," Hunter responded angrily. "I don't like this side of you."

"Well, don't bring it out of me then," Sierra snapped back.

Hunter looked like he was about to shout something back at her before taking a deep breath instead and saying quietly, "Let's not fight, okay? We finally just got to a good place. Look, it's my fault. I'm sorry. Less Laura time. More Sierra time." He reached for Sierra's hand and gave it a tiny squeeze.

Sierra felt the fire in her dissipate a little. She just wanted to feel like a priority again. *Why is that so hard to ask?* "You're right..." she bit her lip. "Okay, let's just drop it."

But a good chunk of her didn't want to drop it. Like many issues in her life, Sierra just buried it inside and locked it away for another day to think about, if ever. It was easier to drown out her problems with silence than confront what it might actually point to.

What is this actually pointing to, though? Sierra felt a shiver run down her spine. *Is this the beginning of the end?*

CHAPTER 14

JACK, TRISHA, AND HUNTER

JACK

When will Mom realize they only invited us here because of our money?

Jack finally got an entire week off from his dreadful school for Thanksgiving break and was looking forward to going back to Shanghai to see his dad.

But it was no longer happening. His dad made some lame excuse about wanting Jack to adapt to American life more by staying for its national holidays.

He sniffed. *I know it's just because Sam is back home from Princeton, and he doesn't want me there.*

He slumped his shoulders and looked around. It was a full Asian swarm tonight. His mom, the Wangs, those random aunties from Lady M last time, and he were standing in a revolving tower steakhouse in Downtown LA.

His mom "oohed" and "ahhed" at the full view of the LA skyline while furiously trying to take photos with the other Asian moms. They never seemed to tire of taking photos. A little white boy more engrossed with his iPad than his food sat next to his parents one table over. The parents glared at them in obvious annoyance.

"*Bao bei er zi*,"[33] Jack's mom called to him in Mandarin, "come help the *ayis*[34] and me take photos."

Jack pretended to not hear his mom as he checked his ex-girlfriend's Weibo, a Chinese social media platform with more than 500 million users. His ex had just posted herself in a tight-fitting dress outside one of Shanghai's hottest rooftop bars. Trisha spoke up next to him, "Auntie Xu," she said, "I can help you."

"Oh, you're such a *guai* and sweet girl, unlike my useless son," Jack his mom responded while Trisha got out of the seat next to him.

Jack looked up, hating how his mom's go-to description of him was "useless." "*Ma,* everyone keeps looking at us. You could have at least booked the entire restaurant," Jack sulked. He turned his attention back to his ex's photos, wishing he was back in Shanghai taking vodka shots for $50 apiece.

"Jack, you're in *America* now," Jack's mom said, attempting to say "America" in her deep Chinese accent.

He almost groaned out loud. *I hate it when she tries to say English words. It's so embarrassing.*

"Since you're here," his mom continued, "you should learn the American ways. You can't just book an entire restaurant and kick out all the diners like we'd do in China. Money won't buy them off here, especially when they look down on us for being Chinese."

---

33   Mandarin for "my sweet son."
34   Mandarin for "Aunties."

Jack grumbled, "We're not some poor immigrants that need to *kowtow* to the West and adapt to their culture. They should adapt to *us*. We don't need to feel any less than the West. We are *the* dominant world power."

All the aunties, along with Hunter and Trisha, looked uneasily between Jack and his mom. His mom, clearly embarrassed by Jack's outburst, demanded, "Who taught you this?"

"Dad, of course," Jack jeered.

His mom's pupils widened. *Hah. Let's see how she tries to scold me now. She never says anything when Dad is involved.*

Just then, Auntie Miller, the mother of that weird *hun xue,*[35] interjected herself into the conversation. "Zi Wei, no need to be upset. I like how opinionated your son is. He's not wrong. I remember how pressured I felt to blend in when I immigrated here in the eighties. Anyone who looked Asian was looked down upon."

Jack tilted back into his chair triumphantly. *See, Mom?*

His family could buy out any western brand. He wasn't like those other Chinese people who immigrated to the US with nothing and had to take inferior jobs in order for their family to survive. He was the new generation of Chinese. He had class, he had style, and he certainly was not fresh off the boat. He was fresh off a private jet.

Yet, here he was, surrounded by Asian families who were either single, unclassy divorcées, or so poor they only made $500,000 to $1 million per year. It was ridiculous. Did his mom have no pride?

He got up in a huff, surprising Hunter sitting on the other side of him.

---

35   Mandarin for "mixed blood." Refers to people of mixed ethnicities.

"Jack, where are you going?" his mom demanded as he stormed away. Jack knew he didn't have to respond. She was all about *mian zi*[36] in front of outsiders. She wasn't going to make a big deal about his poor behavior until they were alone.

As if on cue, his mom said, "Oh, it must have been the spicy food we had earlier today. His stomach must be upset."

The ladies gave one another skeptical looks and went back to posing for photos.

TRISHA

Well, that was awkward.

Trisha was relieved Jack had stormed off. The group certainly did not need any more drama.

Her mom started off the night by yelling at Hunter and Trisha after, apparently, they failed to make dinner reservations. As a result, the whole dinner party had to wait for forty-five minutes for a table while their mom scolded them loudly. *Mian zi*, in her mom's head, meant making sure the entire party knew how sorry she was and making it up to them by punishing the "culprits."

It's not our fault you didn't tell us and we can't read your mind. Trisha couldn't stand how her mom expected perfection but never verbalized what perfection was.

Tonight, especially, it was like all the Asian moms had become the most extra versions of themselves. The topics of conversation already went from sizing up knowledge of luxury purses[37] to demolishing all the achievements of their children in order for someone to say sweet things about them.

---

36 A Chinese concept of "saving face" where reputation and outside impressions are paramount to keeping social status.

37 Auntie Xu won that one since she not only knew about all the luxury purse collections but also owned the entire Birkin bag collection.

"Trisha is so talented at drawing. You'll have to have her sketch a picture for my upcoming birthday party," Auntie Tan flashed fakest smile to her mom. "I wish my Laura was that talented." She looked at her daughter with disappointing eyes then turned her gaze back to Trisha's mom. "She only knows how to play piano, unfortunately. She's too dumb to do anything else."

"Caroline, don't be ridiculous," her mom immediately replied. "Your daughter is a champion piano player. She played at Carnegie Hall in middle school. Trisha and Hunter are the stupid ones."

"Trisha," her mom said, now turning to her, "you're going to draw a portrait of Auntie Tan for her birthday, okay?"

Trisha smiled tightly. "Yes, of course." She turned her head over to Hunter and shot him a glance that the siblings had perfected for one another over the years. It was one that was mixed with annoyance, understanding, and "this again."

"Oh dear, isn't that Kelsey Jones? I think it is!" Auntie Tan whispered emphatically.

Sure enough, Mrs. Jones, with her platinum blonde hair in a high ponytail, strolled into the restaurant in her Prada heels with a tall, grey-haired man who looked like a less attractive and crueler version of George Clooney. His wrinkles gave the impression that he frowned more than smiled.

That must be Mr. Jones. Trisha shuddered. *He's literally everything I imagined him to be. I can't wait to tell Ray about him.* Her eyes filled with longing. Ray and her never left each other's side these days. She couldn't help but think maybe they were heading toward something more.

"Yes, that's definitely Kelsey and John Jones," Trisha's mom responded with disdain. Her harsh tone for the Jones parents shook Trisha out of her hopeful thoughts.

"Who are Kelsey and John Jones?" Auntie Xu asked with an inquisitive expression.

"She's another mom from Winchester. She has three kids—Paul, who is a senior, Sierra, who is a sophomore, and I think her youngest son, Felix, is in eighth grade. And, of course, Hunter is dating Sierra," Auntie Tan said her last statement with the most dramatic eye roll.

Trisha looked over at her brother, whose face instantly became flush. *Not this conversation again.*

Out of spite, Hunter called out, "Hi, Mrs. Jones!" Trisha flashed him a *What are you doing?* look.

Auntie Tan hated the Jones family and hated even more that Hunter was dating someone white. Auntie Tan was a strong believer in people dating within their own ethnic group, and Trisha also suspected she wanted her daughter Laura and Hunter to end up together.

"Oh, Hunter! I didn't see you there!" Mrs. Jones spotted the group sitting together and flashed a big, red, lipstick-covered smile in their direction.

HUNTER

Hunter had mixed feelings about Mrs. Jones. While she was always pleasant to him, she had also raised someone as monstrous as Paul Jones. Not only that, Sierra always hinted that her mom wasn't as sweet and gentle as she made herself out to be but refused to divulge more information beyond that.

"It's great to see you!" Hunter exclaimed. He really didn't mean to call out to her earlier, but he couldn't help pissing off Auntie Tan and his mom after they had been so unbearable all night.

"I haven't seen you in a while. You should come by more often, Hunter," Mrs. Jones said with an overly wide smile.

Hunter shifted in his seat awkwardly and looked at the other aunties at the table. *Little does she know that I've already been dating Sierra for almost a year now.*

When Hunter and Sierra first began dating his junior year and her freshman year, they both hid their relationship from the world. While Hunter didn't really care who knew about their relationship (in fact, all he wanted to do was show her off), Sierra seemed to have a lot of reservations about how her family would react. In particular, she was afraid about whether or not Paul would find out.

Needless to say, Hunter could not help but feel like Sierra was embarrassed of him, which led to him being pushy about going public, and then Sierra falsely believe Hunter just thought of her as a trophy. It took months of overanalyzing before Hunter and Sierra finally came out as official.

"Suzie, Caroline, and Phoebe! What brings you here tonight?" Mrs. Jones asked. She walked closer to the group, leaving her husband, who was talking furiously into his phone, behind.

"So good to see you, Kelsey! We're just having a little get together. This is Zi Wei, by the way. Her son, Jack Zhou, just started at Winchester. He's a junior transfer," his mom responded.

Mrs. Jones looked Auntie Xu up and down before responding, "What a pleasure to meet you in person! I don't know if you remember this, but I called you as the head of the Winchester Parents Committee some time ago to officially welcome you."

Auntie Xu stammered out a "Yes." Mrs. Jones' sudden appearance had the entire mom group switching from Mandarin to English, and Auntie Xu clearly was struggling to understand what was going on. An uncomfortable silence fell over the group.

Mrs. Jones shifted in her heels uncomfortably before breaking the silence. "Well, it was great to see you ladies. I have to get back to John before he starts getting mad from hunger. You know how men get without their food," she joked apologetically.

"Thanks, Kelsey. It was wonderful seeing you as well," Auntie Miller piped up when no one responded to her joke.

And with that, Mrs. Jones flashed Hunter another smile that reminded him of Cersei Lannister and trotted off, leaving behind the strong scent of floral perfume.

As if on cue, Jack came back through the front door from his "bathroom" break. Hunter was surprised he even returned. His face was etched with a mixture of annoyance, boredom, and suffocation. It mimicked Hunter's internal emotions, but Hunter hid it better.

"Jack, you're back! You just missed Mrs. Jones! Come sit down," Auntie Xu exclaimed in Mandarin. Her switch back to Mandarin signaled to the rest of the table to switch back as well.

"Cool," Jack responded and sat down with a thump. His long limbs drooped down toward the floor, like he was melting into the chair.

"Jack, can you please sit up straight? You look ridiculous," Auntie Xu snapped.

Jack gave an exasperated sigh and sat himself up before putting both of his arms together on the table and then dropping his head into them. Auntie Xu looked like she was about to unleash her fury when Auntie Miller turned to Auntie Tan to ask about her recent Botox treatments at the Jones Clinic, which was owned by, yes, Mr. Jones.

"Oh, don't even get me started!" Auntie Tan exclaimed. Her voice suddenly became an octave higher. "He nearly ruined my beautiful face. Seeing him just now made me want to run and tear more hair out of his receding hairline. He probably doesn't even recognize me because he thinks all Asians look the same!" Auntie Tan screeched.

Her face twisted into a menacing glare. "Remember how you didn't see me for all of June? It's because he gave me a shot on my frown line, and the next day, I had a gigantic bruise. I was too embarrassed to say anything, but seeing Kelsey all prim and proper in her blonde perfection and head-to-toe Prada got me boiling all over again. I'm never going back there. I left him a scathing review online and told all my WeChat groups about the incident."

Oh, boy. Auntie Tan must have been really agitated if she reported the incident to all her WeChat groups,[38] especially something as revealing as Botox treatments. The moms usually liked to have others think their looks were all just "natural genetics." If something juicy was blasted on a WeChat *quan*, or circle, it wouldn't be long before the entire Chinese SGV community would find out about it.

The news was going to spread like wildfire.

Hunter looked over at his sister and exchanged a glance with her right as their food arrived. *This is going to get ugly,* it said.

Hunter shook his head. They hadn't even begun fighting to pay the bill yet and it already felt like a war zone.

---

38 WeChat is the social media equivalent of Facebook, Instagram, and WhatsApp in China, except much more than that. It's also the go-to platform for monetary transactions and all things news and gossip.

WINTER

CHAPTER 15

TRISHA AND PAMELA

TRISHA

"No, stop, you're lying!" Trisha shrieked, laughing so hard it hurt her stomach. "What happened after that?"

"My brother had nowhere else to go. He apparently couldn't wait another ten minutes for me to finish, so he sprinted out to the backyard, pulled down his pants, took a squat, and let that burrito pass straight through his system," Ray proclaimed, mimicking his brother's straining position. "Apparently, a neighbor was watering their lawn and saw the whole ordeal." Ray's eyes welled up from cracking up. "I never doubted my brother again when he said he really needed to use the restroom."

Trisha wiped away her tears of laughter. "I would have been mortified! I feel so awful for your brother."

"Oh, yeah. Tommy gave me shit for weeks after that. Figuratively now, of course," Ray recalled with gleaming eyes.

It was almost halfway through the school year, and Trisha and Ray had become close friends (best friend status would always be for Pamela, of course). Today, like almost every day now, the two of them sat together on a lengthy, rustic bench near Winchester's freshly painted tennis courts after class.

Ray let out a shuddered sigh. "I miss him."

Trisha felt her heart quiver in pain for Ray. From his snippets here and there about Tommy, she knew that he passed away under tragic circumstances, but she never dug for more information. She figured Ray would tell her when he was ready.

"Ever since his death, I've felt like there has been this gigantic hole in me," Ray paused. "The weirdest part is, it didn't really hit me that he was gone until six months later. I had completely numbed out. The biggest lie about grief is that it's immediate. It isn't. Grief is like a wave that washes over you whenever and wherever it feels like it."

"Your brother sounded like a really great and funny guy," Trisha whispered, giving Ray's shoulder a gentle squeeze.

Ray stared vacantly out into the distance, all hints of mirth from minutes earlier wiped away from his face. "Tommy always wanted me to do more," he divulged. "He was working as a car mechanic to make ends meet for the family. He never even believed college was an option. He swore he never regretted the decision, but I know he always felt sad to never have the chance to pursue a higher degree."

A bright blue bird with an orange breast flitted past them as Trisha struggled to find the right words to say. The excruciating pain and longing in Ray's voice made her heart ache. *How does someone with such a beautiful soul have a life that has been so cruel?*

Ray continued, "Part of me coming to Winchester was to make Tommy proud, wherever he is. I'm going to get the college education he always wanted for me and then make a ton of bank after graduating so my mom will never have to work again."

"I'm sorry I never got to meet him, but I know he'd be so proud of you," Trisha concluded.

"You think so?" Ray said, staring at her so intently it made her heart stutter. Gentle silence hung in the air. Trisha began to feel her cheeks grow warm and averted her gaze. "Yeah," she said softly.

Trisha didn't know when, or how, it happened, but she had fallen for Ray—headfirst, wholeheartedly, passionately, *fallen* for him.

Except Trisha had no idea if he felt the same.

If only I was better at reading boys. Pamela was convinced Ray reciprocated Trisha's feelings, but then again, when it came to guys, Pamela's radar wasn't the most trustworthy either.

Ray turned over his phone to check the time. "Oh, shoot. I have to change. It's almost time for soccer practice."

"Yeah, let's go. I need to get my stuff out of my locker for Latin too." Trisha always had some sort of tutoring or afternoon activity after school. If she wasn't doing something academic-related, she was getting piano, art, or dance lessons.

"I still can't believe you take Latin classes. It's literally a *dead* language!"

"It helps for SATs," Trisha challenged, unconvincingly. In reality, her parents heard that a family friend's kid was learning Latin, so Hunter and she were enrolled into courses as well. *Everything is always a competition.*

"Does drawing help you for SATs?" Ray countered with a grin. Trisha flushed. *Not fair.* Ray knew every free minute she got, which wasn't many, Trisha drew. While her parents expected Trisha to become a lawyer or doctor one day, her real dream was to become a graphic designer.

"It helps to clear my mind in order to study for the SATs!" she declared hotly.

Ray let out a deep laugh. "You're ridiculous, Trisha Wang," he said, staring into her eyes again.

Trisha felt her face become even hotter. She hated how she couldn't control her heart rate around him. Even though they were spending every minute together these days, time felt like it was never enough when she was around him.

Trisha, unable to figure out a comeback, pleaded, "Let's go."

"Mhmm. Yep. Let's go!" Ray's eyes twinkled with bemusement. He slumped his backpack over his shoulder and the pair began to walk toward the school's student center. On their way there, they passed by a family touring the school in a golf cart with one of the junior students. *Must be admissions time for Winchester again.* Out of the corner of her eyes, Trisha suddenly spotted Pamela's red Tesla parked crookedly in one of the parking spaces.

Hmm. That's weird. I thought Pamela had left hours ago. Trisha shifted her direction toward the parking lot.

"Where are you going?" Ray asked, furrowing his eyebrows in confusion.

"That's Pamela's car. I don't know why it's still here." She got closer to the car as Ray trailed behind her. Trisha came up to the driver's seat and her eyes widened in surprise.

Inside, Pamela slumped over the wheel. If it wasn't for Pamela's signature loud snores wheezing through the windows, Trisha would have thought she was dead.

"That's weird..." Trisha commented, worry creeping up her spine. "Why didn't she just go home to nap?"

Ray nodded in agreement. "Want to see if she's okay?"

Without any hesitation, Trisha walked up to the Tesla's window and began banging.

PAMELA

Pamela woke up with a start as she felt her whole body shake back and forth. "What the—"

"Pamela! Oh my gosh, you're finally awake. You scared me! Are you okay?" Trisha shouted way too loudly into her ear.

"Trish, what's wrong with you? I was just napping. Gosh, my head hurts. Why is it so bright?" Pamela covered her eyes with her hand.

"Ray and I just shook you nonstop and you wouldn't wake up! I was about to call the cops," Trisha said, her voice filled with worry.

"Is that why my shoulder aches so much?" *Sheesh, she really shook me hard.* "Well, I'm awake now. I'm just really tired. I stayed up all night writing my AP Lang essay," Pamela grunted, rubbing her bloodshot eyes. "You can leave me in peace now." Except, Pamela hadn't been all night writing. She had been up all night doing something else.

Her heart sunk. *Ugh. I don't want to think about that right now.*

"Pam... are you sure everything is okay? The way you were passed out was not normal..." Trisha glanced past Pamela's shoulder, trailing off.

"Your glove compartment," she gasped.

Pamela didn't need to look over at the compartment to know what Trisha meant. Her glove compartment was open, and it was stuffed with bright orange pill bottles—a stash Pamela accumulated over the past year from parties, random boys, and purchases from other Winchester students.

"Oh, that's nothing. It's just my stash. You know that already, Trisha." Pamela waved it off. *I need to get out of here.*

"Yes... but... Pam, some of those bottles were completely full only a few weeks ago. How did they disappear so fast?" Her bewildered expression only fueled Pamela's growing annoyance.

"Reddy was short on drugs recently, so I sold them back to him." Pamela shrugged it off casually, giving a half truth. Pamela had been feeling less and less of the high she usually got from her pills lately, so she had been upping the dosages.

Ray and Trisha exchanged disbelieving glances.

"Okay... if you say so... do you want me to drive you home, though? You look really tired," Trisha offered.

"I said I'm fine!" Pamela snapped. She jammed her finger on the car's ignition button. It sprang to life instantly.

Ray grabbed Trisha's arm and gently pulled her away from the car. He turned to Pamela; his face filled with reproach. "Yo, Pamela, Trisha is just worried. No need to get all cranky with her."

Pamela slapped on her smudge-filled Chanel sunglasses. "Yeah, and Trisha only worries about me because she can't stop herself from being a control freak." Pamela slammed the car door and pull out swiftly from the parking space.

As she sped away, she glanced at her rearview mirror and saw Trisha begin to weep into her hands as Ray put an arm around her. She felt a wave of shame and regret for treating her best friend this way, but who was she to judge her? There was nothing wrong with her. Nothing.

But there is, a voice in the back of Pamela's mind whispered back.

Pamela tried to brush off the voice again, but it hit home this time. Tears began to flow down her cheeks, and she stopped the car next to a curb. She hit her head over and over into the steering wheel as the tears became sobs that wracked through her weakened body.

Why am I like this? Why?

Pamela squeezed her eyes shut as she thought about what happened the night before.

***

LAST NIGHT

In one of her usual frenzied, upper-dosed states, Pamela scrolled through her phone to delete mean messages from an army of girls that Reddy's girlfriend (now ex, thanks to Pamela) sent to her social media account. She deleted probably the hundredth comment with the words "slut" and "bitch" in it before a sudden wave of nausea hit her.

Almost a second too late, Pamela sprinted for her restroom and dumped the entire contents of her dinner into it. Once her heaving stopped, she sat on the cold tile ground, slumped against the toilet in disgust. *What did I eat?* She groaned and readied herself to stand back up when her eyes fell on a brightly colored box of pads[39] filled to the brim on her bathroom shelf.

A wave of nausea hit her all over again. *No... impossible.*

Pamela stumbled over to the porcelain sink and began to splash cold water against her face. She stared at herself in the mirror. A girl with sunken eyes, hollowed cheekbones, and days of unwashed hair stared back at her. Irregular periods weren't unusual for her but being over three weeks late was...

---

39 Pamela's mom, much to her annoyance, forbids Pamela from using tampons because of the taboo against them in Pakistan—it's "improper."

not normal. Her mind flashed back to the night she slept with Reddy two months ago.

Did he wear a condom? Pamela couldn't remember. She racked her brain for any memory. *Think, stupid brain.* Nothing came up from the night. It all felt like a black haze.

There's only one way to find out.

She quickly slipped downstairs, disabled her home alarm system, and swiped her car keys from the kitchen before running straight into the garage. Thanks to the monstrous size of her home, it didn't take too much work to slip in and out at night undetected.

One hour later, Pamela was back at home with a pregnancy test in hand. She squeezed her eyes shut, her heart a whirlwind of fear, as she waited for the three minutes to tick by.

Please. Please. Please. Ammi and Abba are going to kill me.

As the first rays of sunrise began to peak over the San Gabriel mountains, Pamela heard her three-minute timer go off. She slowly opened her eyes. *No. No. No!*

Two lines stared back at her.

CHAPTER 16

MATT

Matt was at a breaking point.

Ever since Jack ruthlessly called him out at the dining hall two months ago, his daily life had become a mixture of paranoia and despair. Matt was afraid that, like Jack, everyone already thought he was gay. And sure, they wouldn't be *wrong*, but Matt couldn't fathom a world where he could be free from the shame that his parents would feel and the judgement that he'd receive for being anything other than straight and narrow. As the son of a church deacon, he was always seen as a shining example of moral aptitude and spiritual strength in the church community. If he was gay, he'd be seen as the exact opposite.

I'd be a disgrace... not to mention, going to Hell.

He rubbed his sweaty palms together and leaned against his Volvo's driver seat outside of the Wang house. He sent Hunter a cryptic text about an hour ago that he was going to swing by his house and refused to give a reason why. He let out a staggered breath and got out of his car.

You deserve all the love in the world, including love for yourself. Pamela's voice rang in his head.

Thanks to her words and, begrudgingly, maybe even Jack's, the wall Matt had put up since he was eleven began forming cracks, enough cracks that he began to consider coming out to the most important person in the world to him—Hunter, his best friend, soul brother, and... longtime crush.

Matt walked up to the Wang's grandiose front porch littered with statues. It was probably already the thousandth time that he stood on this doorstep, but it felt completely foreign tonight.

Just be casual. Just be casual, Matt repeated like a mantra in his head. He shook his arms and hopped up and down.

He had first developed feelings in elementary school after Hunter stopped a kid from stealing his Korean chocolate stuffed koala bear treats. At the time, he brushed it off as extreme feelings of gratitude. After all, Matt and Hunter were the type of friends who were always attached at the hip—they swam together, commiserated over familial pressures together, and even secretly watched romantic comedies together. It wasn't until many years later, when Hunter and Sierra began dating their junior year, that Matt realized his feelings for Hunter were no longer exclusively in the friendship category.

But tonight wasn't about his romantic feelings for Hunter; it was about coming out to him—not out of bravery, but out of necessity. He was exhausted with constantly putting up an act for the world. Matt scoffed. He couldn't tell if he should hate Jack or be grateful to him. Jack's antagonism was the trigger that woke up a part of Matt he so desperately tried to bury within him. Matt was at a point where if he didn't tell *someone,* he was going to implode.

He rang the doorbell and stared at the oaken doubled door with abstract stained-glass etchings that reminded him of one of the big boss chambers in his video games.

There were a few seconds of silence before he heard light footsteps come closer. Trisha opened the door. "Oh, hey, Matt! I didn't know you were coming over tonight. Are you looking for Hunter?"

"Hey, Trisha. Yeah, I was looking for Hunter," Matt said, averting his gaze.

"He's taking a shower, I think." Trisha opened the door to let Matt in. He mumbled a "thanks," took off his shoes, and walked toward the spiraling marble staircase that led to the second floor.

Once on top of the stairs, Matt found himself dragging his feet toward Hunter's room. When he finally entered, Hunter popped out of his bathroom, gloriously half-naked and rubbing his gleaming, wet hair with a towel.

Ugh, why. Matt had seen him naked plenty of times already through locker room changes and heading to Korean saunas together, but at this moment, he wished Hunter was in a hazmat suit.

"Oh, hey Matt. I was wondering when you'd show."

Matt glanced around uncomfortably. "Yep. I wanted to talk to you about something." *I'm gay and madly in love with you and... do you think on the slightest chance you might feel the same?*

Hunter stopped rubbing his hair and tilted his head with a curious expression. "Um, yeah. Take a seat."

Matt closed the tall wooden door behind him and headed directly to the suede couch in the corner of Hunter's room and began wringing his hands. He wanted to throw up.

Hunter walked into his closet and came out with a Stanford t-shirt Matt gave him freshmen year. "Matt, is everything okay? You're acting really strange." Hunter furrowed his eyebrows in concern as he threw on the old shirt.

"Umm, yeah..." Matt said hesitantly.

Okay, you can do it. A gigantic lump sat in his throat.

"Umm, okay..." Hunter said, matching Matt's tone inflection.

"Everything is... everything is okay in the sense that nothing has happened or changed," Matt began, "but... you know you're really important to me, right?"

Hunter seemed taken aback. "Of course, Matt. You're my best friend."

"As my best friend... I... I wanted to let you know that I'm..." Matt trailed off, feeling it become harder and harder to breathe. *Why am I being so timid about this right now?* A large part of Matt just wanted to blow this off and say it was all a joke. *But I deserve this. I deserve to not live day-to-day as half of myself.*

"You're..." Hunter countered back.

Matt chewed his bottom lip and stared at Hunter. Hunter's perplexed eyes searched Matt's face.

"...gay." Matt finally muttered. He stared at Hunter intently, waiting for his face to twist into an expression of judgement, disgust, or both.

A few long, painful seconds stretched out between them as Hunter's face remained expressionless. Matt began to internally spiral. *What is Hunter thinking? Why is he not saying anything? Oh my gosh, he hates me.*

Hunter walked over to where Matt sat on the couch and put a hand on his shoulder. "Dude, thanks for sharing that."

Matt almost fell over in surprise. "What, really?" *Just like that?* He rubbed his eyes in disbelief. *No... something is off.* Matt knew that big news like this wouldn't be something that Hunter could react to so nonchalantly.

"Yeah, how else did you think I was going to react?" Hunter said with a shrug. "You're still the same person to me. The only difference is I don't have to worry about you falling in love with my baby sister now."

A feeling of ecstasy rumbled through Matt. The breath he had been holding before was suddenly released all at once.

"Was it that obvious? You don't seem surprised at all," Matt probed.

"Well..." Hunter faltered, "it's 'cause I'm not."

"Huh? Why?" Matt suddenly became all nervous again. *If I'm that obvious, does that mean everyone knows? How many people know?* He had gone out of his way to hide his sexual identity over the years and thought he had become a professional actor at this point. "I've always done the more 'masculine' things growing up. I even dated Kristie Nguyen in middle school!"

"Err..." Hunter began tapping his foot on the ground. "Remember that time in middle school when I asked to stay with you overnight? You know, when my parents started screaming at each other during your family party?"

"Yeah, of course. How could I forget?" Matt gazed at Hunter in confusion. *How is this relevant?*

"So, that night, I had a hard time falling asleep and I heard you get up at some point. I decided to get up too and use the restroom."

Matt gulped. *Oh, boy. That's how.* He suddenly remembered what he was doing that night.

Hunter continued, "The lights weren't on, but the door was cracked open enough where I could see the light on your phone screen, and I was about to knock when I saw, umm..." Hunter cleared his throat, "...the screen on your phone... and, uh... heard the sounds."

Matt felt his face turn bright red. "I thought you were fast asleep!" he insisted.

"I swear I wasn't snooping," Hunter quickly clarified. "But yeah, after that, I had my suspicions."

"So you knew since seventh grade? That was almost six years ago!" Matt exclaimed in astonishment.

"No, definitely not. I didn't *know* with absolute certainty. Not at all. Just, that, I had some suspicions after that, but I didn't want to just presume," Hunter replied, rubbing his hand behind his neck. "Do your parents know?"

"No, actually, you're the first one I've told," Matt said softly, still trying to process Hunter's generous reaction to his news.

"What! Wow, Matt, that means a lot!" Hunter exclaimed. "What can I do to help? Are you planning on telling them?"

Matt smiled. *Wow, Hunter really does care.* His thoughts then shifted toward Hunter's question about his parents and his smile dropped into a frown. "I'm not sure yet. You know how my parents are. They would never accept me. They'd probably send me straight off to some church-led conversion therapy."

"Are you sure? Your mom is so chill, though. She always has my back when my mom is raging."

"She *is* chill, but that doesn't change the fact that both my parents are very religious. I know it's harder for you to understand because you aren't religious, but Catholicism has been a core part of my life since I was born." Matt cast his gaze downward sadly. "I've literally had Sunday school sessions about how immoral the LGTBQ community is."

Hunter fell quiet for a few seconds, clearly struggling for words before responding, "Sorry, dude. This sounds so rough... I'm here for you though. I'll always have your back."

Matt felt his heart swell with gratitude and love. He was overjoyed that Hunter not only knew about his secret, but that he was also so accepting about it. Matt stared at Hunter and drew him in for a one-armed hug, breathing in the scent of Hunter's mint smelling body wash.

"Thank you," Matt said before letting go.

Hunter, clearly taken aback, chuckled, "Psh. It's nothing."

A few seconds ticked past as Matt struggled with what to do next, especially when Hunter seemed just as lost with how to continue the conversation. Matt eyed the sixty-inch flat screen TV.

"How about... Animal Crossing first, and then we can keep on chatting?" Matt suggested. "I literally pulled an all-nighter because of my nerves. I need a breather."

Hunter took a seat on the couch beside Matt and handed the controller over to him. "Sounds like a plan," he declared with a dimpled grin.

CHAPTER 17

HUNTER

———

Hunter compulsively refreshed his inbox for the twenty-second time. *Where is it?* Today was December fifteenth—the day of Stanford early action notifications.

He rubbed his bloodshot eyes. His anxiety-insomnia had kept him up all night and Hunter was impatient to relieve himself from the twisting agony of waiting. He finally refreshed the page for the twenty-third time and a new bolded email subject line appeared at the top of his inbox.

This is it.

Hunter took a deep breath and clicked on the email titled, "Early Action Decision."

"Thank you for your application to Stanford." Hunter stared at the first line of the email body. His mind twirled through the contents over and over again, desperately clinging onto some irrational hope that he was misreading the words. He finally turned away, accepting defeat.

His application had been rejected.

Hunter was crestfallen. It was only a few more days until winter break, and he thought it would have been a time for celebration.

Guess not.

His face grew hot as tears crept into his eyes. All of that work. All of those lost hours of sleep. All of the skipped events and, tragically, his strained relationship with Sierra, for nothing. The creeping tears now snaked down his face, splattering onto his keyboard.

What did I do wrong? Did I not work hard enough? Was it that A-minus I got in Spanish class? Is it because they thought I was just like any other Asian? Hunter fell deeper and deeper into an internal hole of self-doubt.

How am I supposed to face Mom and Dad now? Hunter envisioned their crushed faces with eyes that screamed "failure" at him.

Ding dong. His home's doorbell vibrated throughout his entire home. *Ugh. Not now.* He decided to ignore it.

Hunter dropped his face into his hands, relieved that his house at the moment was empty so he could wallow in his own misery.

Ding dong. The doorbell rang again. Hunter's tears of sadness quickly turned into angry ones.

There's no one home! Don't you get the message?

He waited and no one rang the doorbell again after a few seconds. *Finally.* He turned back to his laptop to delete the rejection email when an instant message notification appeared:

Laura:	Are you home?
Hunter:	Yeah. Why?
Laura:	Oh, I'm outside your house right now. Your car is in the driveway, but no one is opening the door.
Hunter:	Sry. I'm the only one home right now. Gimme a sec.

He quickly wiped away his tears and walked out of his room to open the front door for Laura.

Ugh, why does she have to show up now? he lamented. *But then again, Laura always makes me feel better.*

Hunter shuffled his way to the front door and saw Laura's image blurred through the privacy glass. He opened the door, letting the December sixty-degree winter breeze blast into his home.

"Hey, Laura. What's up?"

"Hey, Hunter!" Laura chirped. "I had this huge baking urge after school today, so I decided to make my signature lemon bars. I know they're your favorite, and you know how my mom gets when she sees me even around a gram of sugar, so I thought I'd bring them here instead."

"Oh, wow. Yeah. Thanks so much." Hunter opened the door wider. He tried his best to shield his face from her, attempting to hide any indication that he had been crying moments earlier. "You can set them on the kitchen table over there. Er, I'd ask if you'd want to stay to hang, but I'm the only one home right now. Trisha is out with Ray."

Laura's smile widened. "That's fine! If you're okay with it, I'd be down to hang out. I'm so bored home alone. Mom has been gone constantly these days. She's been stretched thin between managing her business and fighting that lawsuit against the Jones family for her botched plastic surgery."

Laura walked past him without another word, threw off her Rainbow flip flops, and marched toward the kitchen with Hunter trailing slowly after her. She set down the lemon bars on the kitchen counter before whirling around and casting a searching look over Hunter.

"Hunter, is everything okay? Do you have allergies? Your eyes look a little swollen..." Laura asked, furrowing her eyebrows.

"Nah, it's nothing. Allergies." Hunter tried to give her a reassuring smile before changing the subject. "I remember your mom mentioning that awful Botox job. I didn't think it would become a lawsuit."

"It's my mom," Laura said pointedly. "Now stop deflecting. It doesn't seem like nothing. What's going on?"

Hunter sighed. *She'll find out eventually anyway.* "I was just rejected by Stanford."

Laura's face instantly crumbled, and for a second she looked like she was about to cry as well. She quickly closed the distance between them and pulled him in for a hug.

"Oh, Hunter," Laura said softly, sympathy swirling in her tone, "I'm so sorry." Laura was so tiny her head rested right on his chest. "There are so many colleges out there anyway. Maybe this is for the best," she whispered before letting go.

"I guess..." Hunter muttered, suddenly feeling like all the years of sleep deprivation were crashing onto him all at once.

"I just don't know how to tell my parents. They barely talk these days, and the only time they really do is when they talk about college plans for Trisha and me. Early action was the best shot I had of getting into a HYSP school," Hunter paused. "My entire life, I've felt like I was never good enough for my parents. But I thought by getting into Stanford, maybe *for once*, I'd be good enough."

Laura, speechless, went back in to give Hunter a hug again. She tilted her head up from Hunter's chest and looked into his eyes as Hunter looked down at her—their faces only inches apart. "You've always been good enough. You're absolutely perfect. Anyone, any college, would want you," she insisted.

Hunter gazed into her deep and soulful brown eyes. *She really means it. She truly thinks I'm good enough.*

He wrapped his arms around her. "Thanks, Laura," Hunter murmured as he rested his chin on the top of her head. He felt Laura snuggle deeper into his arms. "Laura, I—"

A sudden clatter brought Hunter and Laura's startled eyes to the entrance of the kitchen. Sierra stood in the alcove with car keys at her feet. Her face twisted into an expression of fury and abject betrayal.

Before Hunter could even open his mouth to explain the situation, Sierra snatched her car keys and hastened toward the front door.

"Sierra!" Hunter shouted. He quickly detached himself from Laura and ran after her.

She had almost reached her car by the time Hunter got to her. He grabbed her arm. "Sierra, I know that just looked really bad, but this is a huge misunderstanding. Laura was just comforting me. I... I got rejected by Stanford less than an hour ago."

"Let. Go. Of. Me," Sierra seethed. Hunter immediately let go of her arm. Sierra opened her car door and scrambled inside. She was about to slam the door shut when her eyes landed directly on Hunter's.

"Sierra, please," he pleaded. "I can't lose you too."

"I'm sorry it didn't work out with Stanford, Hunter. I really am," Sierra said, her eyes swimming with emotions that Hunter could not comprehend. "But that doesn't excuse what I just saw. You not only turned to Laura instead of me first, but..." She shook her head. "You were completely all over each other."

"Sierra... I..." Hunter stuttered.

"It's over, Hunter."

Sierra banged the door shut, threw him a filthy look that screamed anger and disappointment, and sped away—leaving Hunter behind and utterly alone.

CHAPTER 18

THE STRANGER

LAST SPRING

After the Stranger connected with Olivia about stealing the AP tests and transferring the first $10,000 payment over, they spent weeks corresponding back and forth before the day finally came—the day to steal the AP tests. The Stranger logged onto his laptop and reentered the Dark Net.

Olivia:	I'm always ready. Why r u stealing these tests again?
The Stranger:	For revenge.
Olivia:	$$$ revenge.
The Stranger:	PPL spend more on dumber things...
Olivia:	Fair. Not gonna complain.
The Stranger:	Call u in a bit. Need to get setup first.
Olivia:	K.

The Stranger typed furiously on his laptop. It blew his mind that a fancy school like Winchester would have such weak network administration. Gaining access to Winchester's network credentials had been a piece of cake.

He pressed enter and his forty-nine-inch monitor went black before reappearing with twenty-two different camera views. The Stranger smirked. *Voila. A full view of Winchester.* He looked at one of the camera views in the bottom right corner and barely identified a petite outline dressed all in black and what looked to be a small backpack.

He looked down at his watch—2 a.m. He dialed a burner number that Olivia gave him. The phone barely rang once.

"Hi, this is Olivia," a singsong voice with traces of an Armenian accent picked up.

"Hi, it's me," the Stranger said, his voice transmitting as a robotic one to Olivia.

"Yeah, I know," she snickered. "I only give my number out to one person at a time before I toss it for a new one. Anyway, I'm out here near the football field." Olivia waved at the camera. "The school is *massive.*"

"Yup," the Stranger replied impatiently, "let's get going. There's not much time. I froze the live watch on the security feed, but I don't know how long it can stay like that before someone notices."

"Wow, you sure don't like small talk," Olivia teased into her earpiece. "Okay, let's do this."

The Stranger had barely any time to react before Olivia launched into a full sprint across the school's football field and disappeared from view. He waited for a few long minutes before anxiety began to creep in.

"Olivia? Are you there?" the Stranger asked cautiously. His words were met with silence.

Where did she go? Don't tell me she got caught already.

Suddenly, the Stranger saw her reappear onto one of the camera views in the second row. He pulled it up into full screen. *Not bad. She already made it to the library.*

"Aww, worried about me already?" Olivia cooed. She fished out a pry bar from her backpack and expertly wiggled it underneath the library's windowsill.

The Stranger opted not to respond and drummed his fingers against his desk. He minimized the view to look at all the other cameras. There was movement in camera number eight.

"Hey Olivia, heads up," he quickly delivered into his phone, "there's a security guard on a golf cart headed in your direction."

Olivia propped up the window and lifted herself up through it with ease. "Yeah," she said, "not worried." She walked over to a desk and dragged it below a vent. She took off her backpack and shuffled around before fishing out a file and screwdriver.

"I have to give it to your school." She began to unscrew the vent cover. "Despite having such an old library building, these are the cleanest vents I've ever seen!" Olivia exclaimed. "They must spend big bucks here. Also, why did I just see random backpacks laying around? Do people not steal stuff on the campus?"

"Everyone already has everything they could possibly want," the Stranger muttered. "Plus, even if someone had their stuff stolen, they could replace it easily."

Olivia whistled joyfully while slowly lifting the vent cover off. The Stranger gulped. "Olivia, are you sure you can fit through that? It's tiny."

She smiled into her earpiece. "Are you kidding me? Of course I fit." She pulled herself up into the hole and wriggled around a bit before disappearing into the vent.

The Stranger let out a sigh of relief. *That was impressive.*

Without any more camera views inside of the library, the Stranger waited in the darkness of his room until he heard the beep that signaled Olivia had turned on her earpiece again.

"Just double checking one more time—you want me to steal one exam booklet from calculus, biology, and world history? Not the rest?"

"Yep," the Stranger confirmed.

"Weird, but 'kay," Olivia responded, "I've got the exams. I'm coming back."

"Don't forget to put the vent cover back on, but loosely. We need to leave some sort of evidence of a break in behind."

"You're really playing some mind games with the school there, but okay." Olivia turned off her earpiece again.

The Stranger got out of his chair and began to pace back and forth with his eyes never veering from the computer screen.

This crazy plan might actually work.

It hadn't even been ten minutes before Olivia reappeared on camera again, sprinting across the football field away from the school. She got to the edge of the camera before he heard her victorious voice. "It's done. I'll wait for you at the cross section of Washington Boulevard and Los Robles Avenue."

"Okay," the Stranger said. He walked over to his window and lowered himself down onto a ledge carefully. *For once Mom's obsession with having the best Christmas lights on the block is useful.* The handymen conveniently left behind a long ladder next to his window.

Half an hour later, he stood on the designated cross-section, blocks away from home, when he saw a car slowly pull up next to him. A girl with dark hair and green eyes rolled down her window and tossed a backpack at his feet with a thud.

"Oh my gosh," Olivia exclaimed. "You're literally a kid!"

"Yup," the Stranger replied indifferently. He whipped out his phone and pressed a button. A *ding* ringed from Olivia's car. She pulled out her phone and smiled.

"Well, kid or not, you've got cash," she grinned. "Good luck with your revenge. See you never."

And with that, Olivia sped away into the darkness.

By the time the Stranger was back home, early rays of sunrise were beginning to shine through his window. He crashed onto his bed fully clothed and passed out in seconds. It felt like only a few minutes had passed before a loud voice shook him up with a jolt.

"Felix! Time for school! Sierra and Paul already left!" his mom shouted angrily from downstairs.

CHAPTER 19

SIERRA AND JACK

SIERRA

Sierra leaned against Winchester's big oak tree and slouched her shoulders in defeat.

When did the campus become so dreary? She stared across the unusually lifeless quad. *At least break starts tomorrow.*

Ever since the breakup with Hunter last week, Sierra felt like the beginning of winter break couldn't come soon enough. Everything reminded her of Hunter lately—the bench in front of the library where they used to meet after class, the table at the corner of the dining hall where they used to share meals, and even the cashmere sweater she put on this morning. *Hunter loves how much this sweater matches my eyes.*

She shook her head sadly. *Even when we're broken up, I still can't get away from him.*

It certainly didn't help either that the campus, despite its enormous size, felt incredibly tiny. Sierra was either hearing whispers about how the "golden couple" broke up or bumping into a profusely apologetic Hunter in-between classes.

All these moments cast self-doubt into whether or not she made the right decision.

Sierra closed her weary eyes. *All I want is one night of solid sleep.* Restful sleep no longer came to her. Instead, Sierra spent most of the night tossing and turning, fuming about, and, ultimately, missing Hunter.

"There you are!"

Sierra fluttered her eyes open as Stacy dropped her large tote next to her.

"Hey, Stacy," she weakly smiled. "How was class?"

Stacy lowered herself onto the grass and flipped over onto her stomach. "Oh, you know, the usual. I don't know how Ms. Kendrick came up with 'Thinking Like an Entrepreneur' as a class title, but I'm definitely going to miss having it next semester."

"I get that. It sounded really fun. Plus, it counts as an honors class too, right?"

"Yep, so it boosts up my weighted GPA too. I loved her 'Postcolonial Literature" class last year as well. Too bad she's leaving to teach at Cate," Stacy said in a disappointed voice.

Sierra gazed at Stacy with sympathetic eyes. Winchester was constantly trying to offer competitive benefits and incomes to faculty members in order to keep them, but it was a harsh world out there when boarding schools like Cate and private schools like Harvard Westlake offered the same, if not better, packages.

"I wish I got to take a class with her. I've only spoken with her when she led the class trip to the beach freshman year." Sierra glanced at the clock on her phone. "Why are you coming out thirty minutes later than usual though? Did Ms. Kendrick give some farewell speech?"

"I was hoping you would notice," Stacy replied with a mischievous smile. She fumbled around in her bag and pulled out a compact mirror and a golden tube of lipstick. "We actually got a lecture about privilege."

Sierra raised her eyebrows in surprise. "Privilege?"

Stacy began to apply her bright red lipstick. "Ms. Kendrick clearly bottled up a lot of Winchester stories throughout the years, and I guess she decided to unleash it all on her last day."

Stacy closed her mirror with a snap and turned to Sierra. "It was absolutely wild. She started off by ranting about how a kid questioned her authority because 'his parents paid her salary' and how she had to console a bawling freshman girl about how 'there will be another limited-edition bag from Louis Vuitton again,'" Stacy snickered. "Ms. Kendrick even said that the best thing that ever happened to Winchester was when those AP tests were stolen, because it showed that money can't buy students out of every shitty situation."

Sierra stared at Stacy in shock. "I guess I'm not surprised she had so much pent-up rage."

Stacy laughed hysterically. "These stories went on for another twenty minutes. There was the junior who tried to bribe her for a better grade, the senior who had to leave class because one of her manicured nails broke, and that new guy, I suspect she was implying Jack, who straight up tosses the dining hall's plates and silverware into the trashcan rather than clear them up in the wash station."

Sierra was floored. "I would have paid so much money to hear this rant. What happened after?"

"Ms. Kendrick just ended the whole rant with 'check your privilege' and walked out of the room. Half the class, including me, stood up and applauded after her speech and the other half looked like they were about to call up their family lawyers." Stacy made a saluting motion with her hand. "But what can they do now? Fire her? She was heading out already anyway."

"Gosh. I've always wondered what faculty here actually thought of us... guess we know what Ms. Kendrick actually thought of us now," Sierra grinned. *I wonder if I've also found my way into one of her stories...*

"Anyway, are you ready for winter break?" Stacy asked, peering over at Sierra. "You look like you need a nice, long spa day and some hot, shirtless Santa Monica guys to flirt with."

"That would be nice..." Sierra trailed off. She really just wanted one day where she didn't have to think about Hunter.

Stacy cleared her throat. "Did you bump into Hunter today?"

"Thankfully, no," Sierra answered, drawing in a shuddered breath. "I really can't deal with seeing him any longer. He's getting to me, Stacy. Slowly but surely, I'm starting to wonder if maybe I overreacted by breaking up with him."

Stacy put a reassuring hand on Sierra's arm. "Is he still blocked on social media?"

"Yeah." Sierra frowned. "But he's still trying to win me back. He left this really sweet apology letter in my locker that made my heart twist."

Stacy groaned, "Classic bro move. He clearly doesn't get you. You need time and space. I still can't believe he ended up spending time with Laura even after you explicitly told him to stay away from her."

"I know, right?" Sierra agreed. "I get that they were just hugging, but it felt like a slap in the face. He told Laura about the Stanford decision before *me*. What am I supposed to make of that? Who is *she* and who am *I* exactly to him?"

"Babe, asking these questions is gonna get you nowhere." Stacy gently squeezed Sierra's arm. "Hunter messed up, plain and simple. And you, Miss Sierra Jones, can do so much better."

"Thanks, Stacy," Sierra said softly, feeling slightly better. "I don't know what I would do without you."

"Yes you do," Stacy answered confidently with a tilt of her chin. "Your life would be much more boring."

Sierra couldn't help but flash her first genuine grin of the day.

JACK

Vroom. Vroom. Jack's Lexus LFA groaned as it tore through the 60 Freeway at one hundred miles per hour. Jack had perfected the art of not getting caught for speeding after following the advice of his best friend in Shanghai and installing a radar detector. It was incredibly cheap too—chump change at only $500.

Jack was in a particular road rage mood tonight. It was New Year's Eve and his dad just decided to push back his trip to LA for Chinese New Year in a couple of weeks. Apparently, he needed to "take care of business in Shanghai."

Jack called bullshit.

Jack's older half-brother Sam was recently featured by *Xinhua News*[40] for helping a blind elderly lady struggling with dementia find her family after she got lost in the streets of Shanghai. Apparently, the Chinese public, along with his dad, loved how Sam Zhou, with his bright orange Maserati sports car, stopped traffic on one of the busiest streets in China to give the old woman wandering in the middle of the

---

40 Xinhua News, otherwise known as New China News Agency, is the official state-run press agency for the People's Republic of China.

road a free ride home—"*Fu er dai*[41] has a Heart," the news headlines read.

Sam probably set that whole photo shoot up and paid the old women to pretend to be helpless, he thought bitterly.

Coupled with Jack's failures in the past year of getting kicked out of Exeter, he knew that in the race for who would take over his dad's multi-billion-dollar garment business, he had lost to Sam already. His dad no longer cared about him, and his mom reminded him every day about it.

"I sacrificed my life for you," she complained for the millionth time as Jack headed out the door to take his joy ride through the night. "How did I end up with a worthless son like you?"

He swore under his breath and pressed down even harder on the gas pedal and the memory. The car zoomed off of the freeway toward a shopping complex with a late-night hookah bar. He had never been so excited to meet some guys he previously knew back in the Shanghai clubbing circle. Thankfully, none of the people he was meeting were from Winchester.

He sniffed in distaste. He found his classmates to be so vile with their cheap vodka and nasty beer.

Jack and his much classier circle preferred Japanese whiskey. He leaned over and patted the four bottles of thousand-dollar Karuizawa Japanese whiskey in his passenger seat. A fifth bottle sat open in a cup holder as Jack picked it up and took a large swig. The whiskey washed down his throat, leaving a delightful burn in its wake.

---

41   Refers to the second-generation offspring of the noveau riche class in China following its late 1970s market-oriented reforms. These reforms led to dramatic gains in wealth for a new class of Chinese society, including Jack's family.

Ah, Jack thought, feeling absolutely alive. *Can't wait to finish all of these tonight.*

A red light up ahead switched from green, to yellow, and then to red. He cursed under his breath. He hated losing momentum while driving. Jack quickly swerved into an alleyway to cut across the parking lot instead.

Out of the corner of his eye, he saw the bottles of whiskey teeter on the edge of the passenger seat. *Shit.* He lunged over to catch them before they collided to the ground. With one hand pushing the bottles back, he looked up to see his car headlights illuminate the frightened face of some Asian guy.

Before Jack could react, he heard a loud *thud.*

He slammed the breaks with a screech. Like a doll, his body was flung against the car seat as his hands slipped off the wheel. The entire world spun until it crashed into a giant wall of concrete. Jack felt a sharp pain as shattered windshield glass embedded itself into his skin.

And then, darkness.

CHAPTER 20

PAMELA AND TRISHA

———

PAMELA

Ugh. Why is it so bright today? Pamela threw a long, skeletal arm over her eyes. *Why is it so cold?*

She reached for her blankets and grabbed something thin and plastic instead.

What the...? She forced her eyes open, attempting to fight the heavy grogginess overwhelming her. *What is that weird beeping noise?* A slim plastic tube lay between her fingers. Fluorescent lights beamed into her eyes, forcing her to squeeze them shut and reopen them again. Pamela's brain began to panic as her body tried to react. Flurries of white and silver flooded her blurry eyes before her vision focused on people in lab coats and scrubs quickly walking past her room.

Is that Mom and Dad? Her parents stood at the door talking to someone in a white coat holding a clipboard. *A doctor?*

"...Can you recount to me what happened last night before you received the call to come in here?" Pamela overheard the doctor ask her parents.

"We were both working late but got back home in time for the New Year's Eve meal with the kids. Pamela had cooked us all dinner by the time we returned. We all went to bed afterward," her mom answered anxiously. "It was a normal night."

"Do you know if she has a history of alcohol or substance abuse?"

"What are you talking about?" her dad blustered. "Nonsense! Our daughter doesn't do any of that."

"What exactly happened?" her mom implored.

The doctor cleared her throat. "We found traces of various drugs in her system. We believe she overdosed."

"Overdosed?" her mom asked, her voice an octave too high.

"Yes," the doctor confirmed. "I also ran an emergency ultrasound due to the heavy vaginal bleeding she experienced upon arrival. I'm sorry to inform you, but your daughter suffered from a miscarriage."

"That's absolutely impossible," her dad shouted. "All we want to know is how she got here. Not be fed lies!"

"Sir, please," the doctor responded patiently. "We have many patients on this floor and it's six a.m. Please keep your voice down." She flipped through a stack of papers on a clipboard. "A man named Calvin Reddy brought your daughter in with the ambulance. He said he found Pamela lying on the floor unconscious. He called nine-one-one from there."

"Where is this man?" her dad demanded.

"I'm not sure, sir," the doctor replied. "He dropped her off, made sure we called you, and left."

Wait. What? Fear coursed through Pamela's lethargic body. She racked her brain for what happened last night.

It was the New Year's Eve countdown rave. I was with Reddy. Pamela squeezed her eyes shut, grasping for any memory. *We kissed when it hit midnight... and then what happened?*

It was all a blur. A foggy image of her shouting at Reddy came up. *Why were we arguing?* She remembered running away and finding herself alone outside of the tent.

There was a guy... with that brownie. Right, that brownie. It felt like Pamela hit a brick wall in her brain. Nothing came up again. She looked down at her right arm that was connected to an IV. *Where is my phone?*

"Pamela?" she heard her mother's voice suddenly directed toward her.

"Oh good, my sweet *beta*,[42] you're awake!" her dad exclaimed. Pamela looked around meekly as her parents hurried over to her bedside.

"*Abba, Ammi*...?" Pamela asked.

"Tell us what happened," her mom begged. "You had us so scared. We received a call an hour ago saying you were in the hospital. Didn't you go to bed with the rest of the family last night? What happened? Were you kidnapped?"

"No, *Ammi*, I snuck out..." Pamela said hesitantly. *At least there are too many people around for them to kill me right away.*

"What? So what the doctor is saying is true? You took drugs? Are you *pregnant*?" her dad boomed.

"Apparently, not anymore..." Pamela closed her eyes. *I wish I hadn't woken up at all.* After discovering last month that she was pregnant, Pamela decided to do exactly what she always did when she felt trapped—she escaped into her own world with drugs. She was meaning to talk to Reddy about the pregnancy at some point, but... she just didn't know how.

She winced. *Guess it's not a problem now.* Maybe she should feel happy. No more worries about having to be a

---

42 Term of endearment for a child in Urdu.

teenage mom now at least, right? But Pamela only felt utter despair. Deep down, a part of her had clung onto some Hollywood notion that maybe the baby was meant to be—she'd get her act cleaned up, Reddy would love her, and her parents would support her. It would be a fairytale ending.

Besides the beeping from the machines, the room was now dead silent. Pamela opened her eyes once again. Her parents stared intently at one another across the bed. *Why am I not getting the beating of the century?* Everything felt ominous.

"*Ammi, Abbi*, please say something," Pamela whispered.

Her mom burst into tears and ran out of the room. Her dad stayed behind, staring at the wall above Pamela's head.

"*Abbi?*"

"What is there to say?" her dad choked. "I don't know who you are anymore."

Pamela's groggy eyes swam with tears. She wished she was anywhere but here. Maybe even death would be better right now. Pamela tearfully looked over at the IV pierced inside of her arm.

At least I'm pumped up with drugs here.

She wanted to laugh. Even now, all she could think about was her next high.

TRISHA

Trisha stood awkwardly at the door.

"Should we wake her up?" she whispered to Ray who was standing beside her. The two of them peered over at Pamela snoring loudly in the hospital bed.

Trisha glanced around the otherwise empty room. *Where are her parents?* Trisha knew Pamela's parents were always busy, but she figured someone would be here at least to watch over her. Pamela began to stir and then her eyes half-opened.

"Trish?"

"Hey, Pam," Trisha said gingerly, setting aside pink roses, Pamela's favorite, onto a small hospital cart. "How are you feeling?"

Pamela smiled weakly. "I feel like I got hit by a truck, but I feel more alert than I did earlier."

She made a poor attempt to pull herself up into a seated position. "How did you know I was here?"

Trisha squeezed Pamela's hand. "Anika told me that you were here after you didn't show up to our New Year's boba date."[43]

"Ah, the tattle-tell as usual."

"She didn't exactly have a choice since I was on your front doorstep when I asked her." Trisha narrowed her eyes. "Weren't you with Reddy last night? How did this happen?"

"Yeah..." Pamela turned away and became silent.

Trisha's face darkened. "I swear, if he's the reason behind this, I'm going to run over to Cal Tech and burn his dorm room down."

"Woah, there," Pamela laughed half-heartedly. "It's not his fault. He was the one who found me actually..." Pamela began to pick at her fingernails.

"So, what happened then?" Trisha pressed.

"It's all a bit of a blur, but after my parents left me this morning, I was able to get my hands on my phone and read all my missed texts from Reddy. Apparently, I ran away from him at some point, and when he finally found me, I was collapsed on the grass in my own vomit."

_____

43 Asian-owned businesses never close, even on holidays.

"Why were you running away?" Trisha took a seat on the corner of the hospital bed.

"Reddy told me... he told me he was in love with me," Pamela faltered. "I couldn't handle it, so I ran. Some stranger was selling brownies outside laced with something 'extra,' and I stupidly bought and ate it without questioning what it was laced with." A crazed laugh escaped from Pamela. "I'm a hot mess, aren't I?"

"We're all hot messes." Trisha furrowed her eyebrows. "But Pam, you're always so careful about mixing things. Why was it different this time? Why couldn't you just tell Reddy that you didn't feel the same way about him?"

Pamela sighed ruefully at the memory. "Trish, you don't get it. All I wanted to do was escape. I *do* feel the same way about Reddy. It's not exactly love, but I do like him. The problem is... I couldn't face him like that, considering..." Her throat tightened.

Pamela tilted her head downward and her long black hair fell over her face, completely masking it.

"Considering... what?"

"Considering..." She waited for her throat to relax enough to speak. "the fact that I was planning on, um, aborting his baby..."

Trisha's eyes widened in shock. She swallowed hard and looked over to the doorway where Ray still stood with a look of disbelief that mirrored hers. She titled her head. He nodded back in understanding and quietly slipped outside.

Trisha turned back toward Pamela, who began wringing her hands. Trisha scooted herself closer to her and took Pamela's hands in both of hers. "Are you pregnant?"

Tears began to fall like raindrops onto the blankets below Pamela's face. Pamela lifted her head, exposing her crumpling face.

"Not anymore, Trisha. I conveniently... killed it off when I OD'ed," Pamela wept.

"Oh, Pam," Trisha threw her arms around her. "I wish I knew. Why didn't you say anything? I could have helped you."

"What could you have done?" Pamela cried, pulling herself away from the embrace. "Helped me raise the baby? Helped me get rid of it? Helped me get therapy for depression from doctors our parents consider Western hoaxes? Trisha, we were not raised to be cliché teenage tragedies. We were raised to join the Ivy League."

Trisha felt at a loss for words. What Pamela was saying was true. What could she have done to help? *If I hadn't been spending so much time with Ray, would I have noticed before it was too late?* Trisha couldn't help but feel guilty for not being there for Pamela sooner.

"Anyway," Pamela said, wiping away her tears. "There's no point talking about this now. What's done is done." Pamela dug her nails so hard into her wrist that the skin turned white. "I killed the baby."

"You can't possibly know that, Pam," Trisha implored, trying to grab Pamela's hand again. "Did you talk to Reddy about this? Does he know?"

"No. There's no point," Pamela scoffed, swiping Trisha's hand away. "What would I even say? 'Hey Reddy, I was pregnant with your baby, had it for two months, then I lost it when I OD'ed at that rave you brought me to. Have fun studying abroad in London next semester!'"

"Well, he can at least take some of the responsibility instead of you going through this alone," Trisha pointed out. *And maybe stop feeding you drugs.*

"I've already ruined my own life," Pamela said sadly. "Why ruin another's?"

"Your life is not ruined!" Trisha shook her head in exasperation. "Who doesn't mess up in high school?"

"Pamela Shah, the perfect daughter to self-sacrificing immigrant parents, does not mess up." Pamela's eyes began to well up with tears again. "I'm probably already disowned."

"You're not disowned, Pamela," Trisha insisted.

"How would you know?" Pamela sniffed. "After my parents found out, they didn't even scream at me like they usually do. They just left without another word and haven't returned since."

A knock at the door brought their attention to the doorway. Trisha's breath caught in her throat.

It was Pamela's parents.

"Hi, Trisha," Mr. Shah said quietly. "Can we have a moment with Pamela please? We're getting her discharged soon."

Trisha glanced over at Pamela. She searched Pamela's face for any indication that maybe Trisha should stay to support her instead.

"Go, Trish," Pamela said, squeezing her hand. "I'll call you later."

"Okay," Trisha responded, still hesitant. "Just let me know when you're back home. I'll drop by any time."

She slowly walked out of the room and glanced back as Mrs. Shah placed her hand on Pamela's forehead to brush away a stray hair.

Trisha walked down the long, winding, linoleum-lined hallway of the hospital as the smell of disinfectant flooded her nostrils. *Where is Ray?* She kept on walking until she got to the elevator and saw him sipping coffee in the corner.

Something about Ray's caring expression when he looked up at Trisha made her heart melt. *I'm so lucky to have him.*

"How did it go?" he asked, concern flooding his tone.

"I'm not quite sure, to be honest. I've known Pamela since kindergarten, and I've never seen her like this before." Trisha grimaced. "I left her with her parents. I hope I didn't make the wrong decision. Pamela kept going on about how they were going to disown her."

Ray put a hand on Trisha's shoulder. "I think leaving was the best idea. Her parents and she need to talk it out based on what I heard in the room."

"Sometimes I wish we were eighteen already," Trisha heaved a sigh. "There are so many things that would just be so much easier without parents."

"True," Ray agreed, "but it's nice having someone always have your back, even if you might disagree with it."

Trisha creased her brows. "Hmm, I guess...." She tried to dig up memories of when her parents had her back, but she only winced at the recollections of when they yelled or screamed at her for being too sensitive or too weak. She suddenly felt the migraine of the century coming over her. "Let's head out. I need fresh air."

They both got to the elevator and Ray hit the down button. Trisha heard odd muffled screaming from afar, but it was getting closer. The elevator *dinged* and the doors opened, unleashing the screaming that was previously held back by the elevator doors.

"*WEI? WEI?*[44]" A lady screamed into her phone.

---

44 Mandarin for "hello."

Trisha froze in place. She recognized the woman.

"Xu *ayi*?" Trisha exclaimed, quickly switching over to Mandarin.

Auntie Xu walked out of the elevator and marched straight to Trisha. "Where is Jack?" she demanded.

"Jack? I didn't even know Jack was here. I'm visiting another friend." Trisha took a few steps back away from Auntie Xu's angry, bloodshot eyes.

Ray, bewildered, asked Trisha, "I just heard 'Jack.' Is this Jack Zhou's mom?"

His question appeared to turn Auntie Xu on him. "Yes, Jack's mom!" she hissed in English.

A voice through her phone began shouting. Auntie Xu frantically put it back to her ear and reverted to Mandarin. "Good, you're *listening* again. I'm standing in front of Jack's classmate and some random *lao wai*,[45] but they don't know where he is. I hate this country. I can't understand anything. The hospital translator said that Jack *killed* someone. She's crazy! I bet she mistranslated, and someone actually tried to run into our poor Jack." Auntie Xu burst into tears, "Apparently, he broke some bones in the car accident. What if he is disabled for life? *Can ji ren ah!*[46]" There was a click on the other line and Trisha could hear a low dial tone.

Auntie Xu's crying dissipated for a second as she processed the shock of someone hanging up on her. She released a fresh avalanche of tears and began to bawl so hard that she started hiccupping.

---

45 Mandarin for "Foreigner," or "non-Chinese." It is generally seen as a neutral term but can be viewed as impolite depending on the tone of voice. In this situation, Auntie Xu's voice sounded derogatory.

46 Mandarin for "handicapped."

"Excuse me, miss, can you please get your mom to quiet down? I can tell she's grieving but our patients really need their rest," a nurse passing through said in a disapproving voice.

Trisha immediately began to wave her hands apologetically. "I'm so sorry. She's not my mom, but actually, could you help us? We're looking for a patient. His name Jack Zhou."

"Oh, that kid. I was actually just checking in on him. He hasn't woken up yet from his surgery. He's in room 2204." The nurse glared at all of them. "I heard he killed someone."

Auntie Xu stopped crying again after hearing Jack's name leave Trisha's mouth. "What is she saying?" Auntie Xu desperately asked Trisha.

"The nurse says he's in room 2204," Trisha replied in Mandarin. *Should I tell her about the last thing the nurse said?* Trisha hesitated and looked at Auntie Xu, looking unusually disheveled in her house slippers. *Nope. Not a good idea.*

"Finally! Come with me. You're going to help me translate." Auntie Xu wrapped her bright red nails around Trisha's wrist in a painful grip and yanked her toward arrows that pointed to rooms 2200–2210.

Trisha helplessly let Auntie Xu drag her away. She waved at Ray to follow her.

The group finally arrived at room 2204. Trisha saw Jack fast asleep with monitors beeping around him and a bandaged head and leg. She noticed his wrists were tied down.

Auntie Xu began to wail all over again, "Why is my poor Jack in handcuffs?"

A police officer appeared from behind the hospital curtain. "Are you Jack Zhou's mom?" he asked in Mandarin. Trisha was taken aback. She rarely met Asian police officers, let alone Chinese ones.

Auntie Xu turned toward the officer, fuming. "Why is my son in handcuffs?" she demanded.

"Because he killed someone," the officer said bluntly.

Silence suspended the moment, like the eerie calm before the storm. Trisha felt trapped. This was clearly not a conversation she should be part of. Ray stood nearby looking absolutely lost.

"You're lying!" Auntie Xu screamed, shattering the silence.

"The victim was taking out the trash when your son hit him," the officer said firmly in Mandarin. "We believe he was driving under the influence as well. His car was littered with alcohol bottles."

It seemed like all the light in Auntie Xu's eyes extinguished as she processed the police officer's words. She staggered over to a chair and slumped down. Trisha saw her opening.

"Auntie Xu... I'm going to go now," Trisha interjected in a tiny voice.

Auntie Xu jumped. She seemed to have forgotten that Trisha and Ray were standing next to her. She regarded Trisha with a manic smile. "Of course, dear. And ignore whatever the police officer just said. *Xiao hai*⁴⁷ shouldn't be listening in on adult conversations."

Trisha got the hint and stiffly nodded. "I won't repeat what just happened."

She grabbed Ray's hand and walked briskly back to the elevators without another word.

47 Mandarin for "children."

CHAPTER 21

RAY AND TRISHA

RAY

What. Just. Happened?

Ray walked briskly toward his car with Trisha at his side. He felt like he was just dragged into a telenovela he didn't understand the language of and then violently tossed out of it in the span of minutes.

Why was Jack handcuffed to a hospital bed?

Ray felt a twinge of pity. Ray and Jack came from opposite worlds, if not universes, but Ray did feel tied to Jack as the only two new juniors at Winchester. In some ironic way, they were both outsiders. Not only that, he hated to admit it, but Ray was only at Winchester because of Jack. It was Jack's $50 million donation that helped fund his full-ride scholarship.

He stopped walking, realizing Trisha was no longer next to him.

"Trish?" Ray frowned, glancing around. His eyes eventually fell on her seated down on the ledge of a fountain they had just passed. He couldn't help but notice that Trisha, with her white t-shirt and flawless skin, seemed to be glowing in the sun. He walked over and settled down carefully beside her.

"Hey, are you okay?" Ray searched her face with concern. While from far away she had been glowing, he could tell close up now that her face was downcast.

Trisha let out a long, exasperated sigh. "Yeah, I just needed a moment of stillness after all of that."

"I don't blame you…" Ray began hesitantly. The screaming voice of Jack's mom still echoed in his ears. "What happened?"

"Oh, right…" Trisha said apologetically. "I hear Mandarin, English, and Chinglish[48] so much I don't even realize languages are constantly changing around me anymore. You have zero clue what just happened, huh?"

Ray smiled weakly. "Nope. I's okay though. I totally get the language thing. It's the same with Spanish."

"Yeah…" Trisha chewed on her bottom lip. "So, basically… I think Jack killed someone."

Ray's jaw fell open. *Jack? No-care-in-the-world Jack Zhou?* "How?"

Trisha looked away, her eyes appearing to trace the San Gabriel mountains out in the distance. "He was drunk driving and hit someone."

Ray's mind went blank. *Just like that. Another soul and family destroyed.*

Suddenly, all he could see was red as it clouded his vision. *Just like Tommy's. Just like my family.*

"Why was he driving drunk?" Ray forced out in a low voice. He gripped the edges of the concrete fountain until his knuckles turned white.

---

48 Slang for Chinese + English.

"I'm not sure…" Trisha replied, clearly oblivious to Ray's growing rage. "I'm not Jack's biggest fan, but we've had our fair share of family friend get-togethers. It's crazy for me to imagine that something like this can happen to someone like him."

"I can imagine it." Ray felt his anger begin to boil over. "He probably thought money meant that he could do anything and casually take lives without any consequences."

Trisha looked over at Ray, clearly taken aback by his sudden outburst. Realization flashed across her face. "Oh, Ray… Tommy…"

He closed his eyes. It felt just like yesterday when his mom got the call that some drunk driver hit his brother while he was jogging on the street. The driver apologized profusely to Tommy's family and even offered all of his life savings to his mom, but once she found out that the murderer had a wife and children who could not fend for themselves while he sat in jail for the next ten years, she refused the blood money. "Money won't bring Tommy back," she had painfully whispered in court.

He felt Trisha put a soothing hand on his back.

"It's fine. I'm fine," Ray sighed ruefully. "I didn't mean to come off snappy. I just… Trish, this is so ridiculous. How could he be so dumb and reckless?"

"I don't know, Ray," Trisha whispered in a broken voice. "I wish I had the answer to that."

Ray laughed bitterly. "You know what's worse? Given how screwed up the world already is, he'll probably get off without a scratch, thanks to daddy's money."

Ray already knew why Winchester had such a stellar track record for top college acceptances—it was the money and connections. Grades, SAT scores, creations of your own nonprofits even—any person could be made to look like a superhero college admit with enough time and money. While the idealist in him still believed money could not buy happiness, he was no longer surprised when things like getting out of a jail sentence could be bought too.

He got up from the ledge and began to pace.

What if I become like this one day with enough money and power? What about my kids? Will they be just as spoiled as my classmates who complain about not having a bigger beach house for parties and never know the meaning of student debt? Ray shook his head. *If only Tommy was here now. What would he think of all this?*

"Ray, are you okay?" Trisha looked at him in alarm.

"Yeah, I'm fine." Ray stopped pacing, suddenly feeling exhausted. He slowly took a seat next to Trisha again. "Sorry for being like this. I didn't mean to startle you."

"Oh my gosh, no, don't apologize! Out of anyone in the world, you have the right to be upset right now."

Ray stared at Trisha's mesmerizing dark brown eyes as a breeze swept by them, carrying her familiar scent of vanilla toward him. And just like that, his anger drained away. "What would I do without you?" he said softly.

Trisha's cheeks flushed. "I don't know what I'd do without you either."

A thought suddenly hit him.

Sure, Winchester had its fair share of nonsensical situations, and Ray clearly did not belong in this world. However, he was still grateful for being part of it because Trisha was there. He didn't know if he could ever join her world, but he would certainly try if it meant embracing every second that he could with her.

"What are you thinking about?" Trisha asked, noticing Ray's sudden stillness.

"Just thinking about us, I guess," Ray responded without thinking.

"About *us*?"

Ray smiled. He liked being her rock. He liked a lot of things about Trisha actually—how she snorted whenever she laughed too hard, how she was so clumsy she'd even trip over thin air, and her desperate, and her sometimes futile attempts to empathize with everyone around her.

He stared at her full, crimson lips and leaned in toward her.

TRISHA

Trisha sucked in her breath. *Is he about to kiss me?* She never had a real boyfriend before,[49] but everything about Ray told her that he was finally making a move on her—in front of a hospital, out of all places.

Who cares? Ray Martinez is about to kiss me! Trisha squeezed her eyes shut, puckered her lips slightly, and waited for Ray's soft, plush lips to lock onto hers as his long and lean shadow hovered over hers.

She could see it already—his broad hand reaching up to her cheek right before delicately planting his warm lips onto hers. She'd wrap her arms around his neck and sink deeper into the kiss.

This is it! Trisha felt herself stop breathing as a few seconds of silence stretched into an eternity.

Ray coughed. "Uhh Trisha, what are you doing?"

Trisha's eyes flew open. *Did I just imagine something?*

---

49 Fan Lee in middle school (whom she had only held hands with) did not count.

"Ohh, uhh," she stared at Ray, who was now standing two feet away at her. She swore she saw a flicker of remorse in his eyes.

A voice inside of Trisha's head screamed. *What in the world? He was clearly leaning in and about to make a move! Did I just imagine that?*

"Something was in my eye," Trisha frantically blurted, trying to cover up her behavior.

"Got it. Just checking because your eyes were squeezed shut," Ray awkwardly responded.

Blood flooded into Trisha's cheeks. *How could I think someone as smart and charismatic as Ray would like someone as plain and prudish as me?* Trisha's embarrassment gave way to anger, except she couldn't tell if it was directed at Ray for misleading her or at herself for making up some love story in her head.

She got up abruptly. "Let's go," she snapped.

Surprise flashed across Ray's face. "Oh, yeah, let's go. Do you want to go do anything? Boba?"

"Nope. Just home," Trisha replied stiffly. She began to blink furiously, desperately holding back shameful and angry tears.

"Umm, okay... did I do something wrong?"

Is this guy serious right now?

Trisha opened her mouth to curse obscenities at Ray, and then closed her mouth again. *It was my fault for thinking I could have been anything more than a friend.*

She pinched her lips. "No, Ray. You have done *nothing* wrong." She walked straight past him and made a beeline for the parking lot.

She heard Ray's footsteps behind her, struggling to keep up with the pace, but she didn't care anymore. *This was all my pathetic fantasy.*

Trisha quickly made it to Ray's pickup truck and waited for him to catch up and unlock the car. Wordlessly, she hopped into the passenger seat. Trisha remained silent the whole ride back home.

CHAPTER 22

MATT

———

Matt cursed under his breath. He stared at a red stain blossoming over his white t-shirt.

I look like someone just stabbed me. He threw off his t-shirt and began digging through a pile of clean clothes from his laundry basket for a new one. Music boomed again the wall, causing it to vibrate.

Maybe this party wasn't such a good idea.

His parents decided to take their annual Matt-free vacation this winter to go to Hawaii on New Year's Day, and as soon as they left the house, Matt did what any brilliant teenager would do—he decided to throw a New Year's party. Half of the senior class made their way into Matt's contemporary home with an outdoor waterfall and private rooftop garden. He knew the majority of his party guests were only there for the free booze Sebastian from the water polo team had come with, but he didn't care as long as everyone was having a good time and not trashing his home.

That lasted for two hours before the night descended into debauchery and more of his classmates, himself included, began to loosen up. When someone accidentally spilled Sebastian's Moet all over his mom's Steinway piano, Matt drunkenly sprinted to clean up the mess (he may or may not have taken four peach soju shots in a row prior to that) before crashing into Hunter. The entire contents of Hunter's wine glass splattered onto Matt before dripping onto the white carpet.

Now, Matt was trying to slap himself awake, back to a clear head, so he could return downstairs and kick everyone out.

It's like karma came back to haunt me after I spilled jelly on Jack. Matt shuddered. *I wonder where he is now.*

A knock brought Matt's attention to his bedroom door as he threw on a new shirt.

"Hey, man, sorry about the shirt," Hunter said apologetically. His eyes shined too bright and his entire face flushed a deep red. "I tried cleaning as much wine as I could from the carpet."

"All good," Matt quickly responded, trying not to slur his words himself. "I'm an idiot for throwing this party in the first place. I thought it would be a good way to celebrate the beginning of our final semester together."

Hunter closed the door behind him, blocking out the screaming music outside. He stumbled over to Matt's bed and sat down. "Yeah. Dude, time went by so fast."

"You bet." Matt took a seat next to Hunter. "I can't imagine not being in the same location next year."

"I know, right?" Hunter extended a hand to pat Matt's shoulder. "We'll love college though, especially without your parents around. You can just be you."

"Agreed." Matt frowned. After coming out to Hunter, he felt like a monstrous burden had been lifted off of his shoulders, but he knew it would be awhile before he told his extremely Catholic parents that he was, in their eyes, a "sinner."

"Hey," Hunter looked at Matt sympathetically, as if reading his mind. "They're your parents, dude. Being gay may surprise them, but they'll come around."

"Hopefully…" Matt's breath hitched. Hunter was leaning really, really close to him. He could even smell the aftershave. The scent was addicting. Matt leaned in closer and found himself staring straight at Hunter's full, sensual lips.

His mouth became dry.

"Matt, what are you—"

He didn't even register what his body was doing. He felt his hungry lips meet Hunter's. Hunter's eyes widened in shock and shoved Matt back. The force of being thrown backward instantly jolted Matt into realizing what he had just done.

"Hunter," Matt breathed, "I... I'm so sorry... I—"

"*Matt,*" a whisper hissed into the room.

Matt felt the air leave his body. "Shit."

I'm doomed. His parents stood at the front of the room, looking murderous.

***

Matt sat on the living room couch, staring at his stone-faced parents.

After the airline delayed their flight to Hawaii until the next day, his parents returned home to find the living room trashed and drunk teenagers passed out by the fireplace before walking upstairs and finding Matt kissing Hunter.

It was a shit-show.

His parents stared at Matt with raging eyes, surrounded by the mess left behind after they kicked everyone, including

Hunter, out of the house. Matt stared at a crushed beer can lying on the carpet near his feet.

"Matthew Lee Miller," his mom hissed, her voice laced with anger. "Do you have anything to say for yourself?"

"I... uh..." Matt stammered.

His mom's phone began to ring, saving him from responding.

"Who is calling at this hour?" his dad asked as his mom fumbled for her phone in her purse. The high-pitched ringing grew louder as she fished it out and looked at the caller ID.

Her eyes widened before she swiped the screen. "Hi, Phoebe?"

Why is Hunter's mom calling right now? Did something happen to Hunter on his uber ride home?

A confused silence fell over the room as his mom pressed the phone to her ear. Her face twisted in wide-eyed concern.

What is going on?

"That's outrageous!" his mom finally exclaimed. "Where did this woman even come from?"

His mom promptly got off the couch and walked into the kitchen, leaving his dad and him awkwardly avoiding eye contact with one another in the living room.

Matt couldn't help it, but he strained himself to eavesdrop on whatever was going on. He still desperately needed to explain to Hunter what had happened earlier in his bedroom.

"Badminton partner? What did he do, see her do too many birdie hits in Lululemon? I'm so sorry to hear that, Phoebe. That's the worst way to find out. To catch them in your own bedroom too! Do Hunter and Trisha know?"

Badminton partner?

"I see," his mom began talking into the phone again. "That makes sense. I know your relationship has been rocky lately, but cheating was the last thing I thought would happen, especially given how full of pride Hector is. I'm so, so sorry. Where are you now?"

Matt felt numb all over. *Tonight is just getting worse and worse.*

"I see. It's good to be with your brother during this time."

Some mumbling continued before his mom sadly said, "Yes, that makes sense. Get some sleep, Phoebe. You've had a really long day. I'll see you first thing tomorrow." The phone clicked off before his mom let out a heavy sigh.

"What a night," she walked back into the living room with exhaustion written all over her face. "Here I thought we'd be blissfully on our way to Hawaii right now." His dad reached over and gave his mom's hand a gentle squeeze as she sat back down onto the couch.

Matt fidgeted with his hands, trying to make sense of the information that he just overheard. "Mom," he began hesitantly, "...what is going on?"

She looked over at Matt. "How much of that did you hear?"

Matt everted his gaze. "Everything."

His mom let out a deep exhale. "Don't say *anything* to Hunter. Auntie Wang wants to keep this a secret from him and Trisha."

"But why, Mom? Don't they have a right to know that their dad is *cheating* on their mom?"

"You know how families are in this area. They have their *mian zi*. Auntie Wang does not want to lose face." His mom sighed, "In the end, she wants to protect her kids from the brutal truth."

"Okay…" Matt said hesitantly. "Are Auntie and Uncle Wang going to get a divorce?"

His mom paused for a moment, contemplating the question. "I'm not sure. You know how stigmatized divorce is in our culture. Hunter and Trisha are already grown though… maybe your Auntie Wang will feel less pressure knowing that."

"Yeah, that's fair…" Matt trailed off, wondering how to end the conversation. Maybe this was the distraction for the night that would get him off the hook.

Seeing Matt become visibly relieved, his dad interjected. "You're not off the hook, Matt. Besides having your classmates trash the home, what were you doing with Hunter in your room?"

Every particle in Matt wanted to sprint back to his room. If only he could rewind time right now. He closed his eyes and remembered Hunter's confusion and judgement as he scrambled away from Matt upon seeing his parents. Should he lie to them? Would they even believe him if he lied?

"Matt…" his mom's voice prodded.

His eyes flew open, and before it truly registered in his brain, he blurted out, "I'm gay."

His parents stared at him, stunned.

"Are you sure you're…" his mom lowered her voice, "… you're *gay*?"

Matt tried not to roll his eyes. *Ugh. Of course they would just think it's some "phase."*

"Mom, I've known for a while now. I *am* gay. It's not a decision. This is just how I was born."

His mom turned to his dad nervously. Matt felt his hands begin to shake. *What have I done? They weren't supposed to find out this way.*

His dad looked at his mom and then at him. Matt swore his dad had stopped breathing. His dad shot straight up from the couch, startling him and his mom. He stood like a stone pillar in the middle of the room, barely breathing. Matt opened his mouth to say something when his dad finally spoke.

"Genesis nineteen..."[50] his dad said softly, and he staggered out of the room without another word.

Matt felt a carousel of fear and regret rotate within him as he watched his dad leave. *Of course he'd bring up the destruction of Sodom and Gomorrah. Does Dad think I'm going to destroy us all for being gay, or would it just be me who goes to Hell?*

He wanted to scream.

His mom burst into tears. "This isn't what God wants for your life, honey," she cried. "I love you so much and I want what's best for you. How are you going to have kids?"

Matt, distraught at his mom's reaction but also disappointed by it, helplessly watched her weep.

Matt finally walked over to her and put an arm around her. "Mom, it's going to be okay. I can still have kids. Please, you're making me feel bad."

His mom looked at him with swollen eyes. "Matt, I don't want to go to Heaven if you're not there with me."

The light airy feeling Matt felt while coming out to Hunter was now eclipsed by a black hole. Tears began to stream down his face as well. In one night, he lost everyone who mattered to him.

---

50 Genesis 19 is a story in the Bible that tells of the destruction of the cities, Sodom and Gomorrah, and has been used in some cases as a condemnation of same-sex love in the Christian community.

CHAPTER 23

JACK

—

Why does everything hurt?

Jack tried to rub his eyes with his hands. *What the...?* He couldn't lift his wrists. Something was tying him down. He shot his eyes wide open.

What happened to me?

He heard beeping next to him as he stared at his right leg wrapped up and raised on the bed.

Why am I laying on such a lousy bed?

"Hello? *Wei?* Anyone?" Jack croaked. "I'm thirsty." A figure sitting in the corner of the room stirred. A chill went down his spine.

"*Lao ba?*"

It was his dad.

"*Er zi*, you're awake," his dad said tiredly in Mandarin. "Your mother and I have been worried sick about you."

"What happened? Why are you here? Where's mom?" Jack demanded, shifting around uncomfortably. *Wo kao,*[51] *everything hurts.*

---

51 Mandarin slang for "crap."

"I flew overnight from Shanghai. I told your mom to go back home. She wouldn't stop screaming at all the nurses and was on the verge of getting banned from the hospital. Do you remember anything from last night?" his dad asked, eerily stern.

"Hmm, I was driving to Four Seasons Plaza... and then..." Jack scrunched up his face, "I remember a weird noise, like my car hit something, and then I just woke up here."

His dad stayed silent.

"Why are you quiet? What happened?" Jack noticed his dad's bloodshot eyes and his uncharacteristically wrinkled Brioni shirt.

Is that a stain on this shirt? Isn't Dad supposed to be in Shanghai buying out some new e-commerce startup? What is going on?

"Son..." his father began to tear up, "you hit someone with your car."

Jack's jaw went slack. *Hit... someone? Huh.*

"Oh..." Jack tried to shake off the giant fog in his brain. "Well, that explains why I'm in the hospital." The thirst in Jack's throat began to get more and more desperate. "Dad, can I get some sparkling water?"

His dad began to sob.

"*Ba*, why are you crying? You're acting really weird." Jack had never seen or even heard about his dad shedding tears before.

"Do you not even care about that boy you hit? Aren't you even worried about how he's doing?" his dad responded between sobs.

"Umm, sure, I guess, but we'll just give him a ton of money, right? He'll probably never have to work again for the rest of his life." Jack shrugged. "He's probably feeling lucky that he got hit."

"You're right... he isn't ever going to work again..." Jack's dad began to sob harder. "You killed him."

Jack's mouth dropped open. *Killed... him?*

"You killed him!" Jack's dad yelled. "This nineteen-year-old boy had been working extra shifts to pay for college, and because a stupid kid like you decided to drive while drunk, he died underneath your car!"

Jack was speechless. His memories from the night before all came flying back—the flash of car lights on a guy holding a trash bag, the thump beneath his car, pure concrete flying before the car crashed, the burst of smoke before passing out.

He killed someone.

Is this why I'm handcuffed to the bed? He glanced down at his chained wrists. A sudden sense of panic overwhelmed him.

"Dad, am I going to jail?" he cried.

His dad's sobs suddenly became silent as he brushed away his tears.

Jack felt like the room was shrinking in on him. "Dad, you can't let me go to jail. You can pay them to let me out." He struggled to breathe. "We can pay the guy's family whatever they want and then everything will be okay."

"Do you not feel guilty at all? Do you think paying the family will bring their son back? Do you know their son was from China too?" His dad looked out the window in the room, eyes glazing over. "He was sending money back home to his village on top of trying to make ends meet for his studies. He worked harder in one day than you have in your entire life."

"Of course I feel bad. It sucks, but he's dead while I'm still alive. We can make it a win-win situation by compensating the family and then I won't have to go to jail," Jack pleaded.

His dad turned his gaze away from the window and stared at Jack. The wrinkles on his face had never looked deeper and graver. "Jack, I'm sorry. I have failed you as a father. I never taught you right from wrong. I never gave you consequences. I never set limits for you." His dad's eyes welled up with tears. "Now, you've become a... a monster."

"Dad, what are you saying?" Jack shouted, pulling against the handcuffs. "I'm your son! I know you're angry, but you can't abandon me!" Cold sweat dripped down his forehead. *This is not happening. It can't.*

His dad got up from the corner and walked toward the room's door. "You have no shame. I will provide you with the best lawyers, but after this, no more money. This..." His dad waved up and down in his direction, "...can't be the same anymore."

He pulled the door open and began to walk out.

"Dad, don't leave me here! Where am I supposed to go?" Jack screamed after him.

His dad paused halfway out the door. "Straight to jail is where you'll go," he responded without turning around. "I've tried paying bail for you, but as a Chinese citizen, they won't release you—not until you have been tried. You'll have the best lawyers, son, but... I'm going back to China. I can't see my own blood be like this. I'm sorry." And with that, his dad, the dad Jack tried so hard to prove his worth to since he was born, disappeared.

Jack laid his head down on the hospital pillow and, for the first time in a long time, began to weep.

CHAPTER 24

PAUL AND FELIX

———

PAUL

LAST SPRING

Paul glanced at his phone. *Shit, 10 p.m. already? I need to get out of here.* It was the week of AP exams, and he hadn't exactly been studying for any of them.

He got up from his seat on the couch and announced he was leaving the mansion. Everyone immediately waved him back down.

"*Live a little,*" the crowd of rowdy, drunk voices demanded in jumbled unison. Unlike Paul, they didn't care about the AP exams. The invite tonight came from Paul's friend and Winchester alum, Johnny, a freshman at Pitzer College.

Not wanting to seem like a buzzkill in front of the college crowd, Paul put his hands up in the air and said, "One more beer," and then snatched someone's joint to take a huge puff.

He cracked open a can of Chimay and poured the cold, crisp beer down his throat. *Just one more to loosen up...*

Five beers and three joints later, Paul's breathing grew heavy and his eyes began to droop.

Shit. I need to get back home. Now. I can't afford to flunk the APs. It will look so bad on my USC application.

"Ima go." Paul stumbled away from the group and up the basement stairs, ignoring the groans and swearing that echoed behind him. He fumbled in his pocket for his phone to order an Uber Black. Paul used to regularly drive drunk in his Range Rover, but that quickly came to a halt when he accidentally hit a stop sign while completely high.

Paul winced at the memory. He received the beating of his lifetime when his dad found out.

By the time he got home, it was already 1 a.m. *All-nighter. Here I come.* Paul heavily stomped up the stairs, mentally kicking himself for staying out so late. He saw that his little brother's light was still on through the crack underneath the door.

What a freak.

He lumbered past the door and slid into his room, passing his water polo trophies and a large Trojan pennant nailed to the wall. He collapsed onto his bed and stared into the darkness.

He tried to slow down (or was it speed up?) his heart. He felt all over the place. He still remembered how Grandpa Jones taught him a breathing technique as a kid on a visit to his nursing home. *Close your eyes. Breathe in through your nose for three counts, breathe out through your mouth for three counts. Repeat.*

Paul never did this trick in front of anyone, lest they thought he was some yoga-loving hippie. These days, however, he found himself turning to Grandpa Jones's breathing trick more and more.

Shit, I miss Gramps. Grandpa Jones was the only person who ever let Paul cry in front of him without consequences.

Paul woozily dragged himself off the bed and shook his head in quick succession.

Wake. Up.

He clapped his hands and the lights in his room automatically turned on. He trudged over to his desk and reached underneath it to pick up his black leather backpack.

Weird. Where is it?

Paul could have sworn he brought it out of his car when he returned back from school earlier. *It must still be in the car.* He stretched out his arms and, like a sloth, trudged his way back downstairs.

A breeze smacked him in the face as he opened the front door. He hated going out at night. He never showed it, but Paul Jones was terrified of the dark. Paul popped open his trunk and, as expected, his backpack was nested underneath his water polo duffle. He heaved it up and swung it over his right shoulder.

He released a string of curse words. *Why is this so heavy? Ugh. Whatever. Must be the pot and beer messing with me.*

Paul made his way back to his room, passing by his little brother's room again on the way back. The light was off.

Probably done playing his dumb online games.

He shut the door behind him with a slam. Sierra had told him repeatedly to be more quiet when he got home, but it was just Sierra. She knew she could never command him to do anything.

Paul peered at his phone again—1:18 a.m. He was supposed to begin studying at 9 p.m. Regret washed over him. USC was never going to accept him if he flunked his AP exams junior year. He threw his backpack onto the desk and ripped it open.

A stack of AP booklets that were definitely not his were stuffed into his backpack.

"What the fuck?" Paul exclaimed out loud.

What idiotic person mixed up our backpacks and shoved this in? Paul picked up the stack to toss them into the trash bin and paused. *Why is there plastic wrap all over the booklets?* His eyes widened. *Is this the AP biology exam for tomorrow?* He squeezed his eyes closed and then reopened them. *What was in that weed tonight?*

Paul quickly began flipping through the other booklets. Sure enough, there was also the AP world history and AP calculus exam booklets in the pile.

Paul quickly walked over to his restroom, splashed cold water on his face, and then returned. The test booklets were still there.

This must be some shitty prank.

Paul placed the booklets down with a *thunk* on his desk and flung open his door. He glanced left and right into the dark hallway. The house was as silent as a graveyard.

Paul turned back into his room and quietly shut the door behind him. His brain felt like it was on fire. *Should I be fist pumping right now or burning these booklets?* Whatever wooziness he felt was now replaced with a mixture of intense fear and glee.

How did these exams get into my backpack? Who put them there? Does the person know I have them? And... can I get away with studying them without getting caught? Question after question shot itself through Paul's throbbing head.

He began combing his room in a paranoid frenzy for any hidden cameras, tripping over his own feet, exercise equipment, and a pile of dirty clothes in the process.

He found nothing.

Paul glanced at the time again. It was already well past 2 a.m.

Screw it. I don't have time anymore. Since when did I ever get in trouble for doing what I wanted anyway?

He proceeded to tear off the rest of the plastic wrap, flipped open his laptop, and began to google all of the answers to the questions.

FELIX

MEANWHILE, A FEW DOORS AWAY…

Felix smirked as he watched Paul studying the stolen AP exams through live hidden camera footage. *Planting the AP tests into his backpack was too easy.*

As soon as Paul left the house earlier in the day in their dad's car to play golf, Felix casually walked downstairs with his backpack full of the stolen AP exams. With a quick snatch, Felix swiped Paul's car keys from the kitchen table and slipped into the garage to make the drop-off. After stuffing Paul's backpack full of AP tests, Felix attached a ridiculously expensive micro camera the size of a fly, courtesy of Dark Net shopping, onto Paul's USC keychain.

The only hiccup that happened was bumping into Sierra on his way back from the garage.

While all the years of bullying he'd experienced from Paul had taught Felix how to feign indifference when needed, Sierra was the one person he couldn't lie to. She seemed to see through all of his lies, and so when she asked Felix what he was doing with Paul's car keys in hand and a backpack in another, Felix lied through his teeth with some bullshit excuse about needing to grab a water bottle from Paul's car before going for a run.

She's definitely onto me, Felix had thought to himself at the time, while gazing into Sierra's piercing and skeptical eyes. He had almost fumbled up some other excuse, but she eventually let him go upstairs without another word.

Hours later, Felix felt his paranoia about Sierra knowing something was up was just that—paranoia. *There's no way she could have known what I was doing.* He closed his laptop, satisfied he recorded enough of Paul studying the AP tests for evidence.

Now all I have to do is wait. Felix planned to release all the evidence pointing to Paul right when it hurt the most—next year on April 1, the day of college decisions. Paul would be basking in glory after getting into USC, likely after his parents had pulled the strings to get him in, and then would be immediately arrested.

Felix smiled triumphantly.

PAUL
PRESENT DAY
Shit!

Some scum on the water polo team had decided to reveal to Paul's go-to hookup, Jessica Roberts from Flintridge, that he was also sleeping with Becky Jacobs from St. Lucy's, and then his ex-hookup, Felicity Warner from Brentwood, connected with both of them over social media to create a new hashtag—#DeletePaulJones.

Paul now faced the wrath of crazy girls on social media who wanted him destroyed.

Damn. This is what happens when you try to juggle too many girls.

Paul heard his brother's door squeak open a few doors away. He smiled sardonically. *I know what will make this day better.*

"Oh, *Felix*!" Paul shouted in a singsong voice. He flung open his door. "Whatcha doing right now?" Paul stuck his head out into the hallway, locking eyes with his weird-ass little brother.

"Uh, I was about to head out for a run," Felix replied suspiciously.

"How about you hang with your older bro instead?" Paul asked with a glint in his eye.

"Why on earth would I do that?" Felix muttered, beginning to walk down the stairs.

Anger flashed through him at his little brother's words. "What'd you say?" he shouted, stomping toward the stairs.

Felix looked up from the lower flight, shrugged, and ignored him.

All he could see was red. Paul sprinted toward the stairs in blind rage and kicked his brother in the back. Felix's body dove face-first into the tiled floors at the bottom of the stairwell. A small pool of blood began to form underneath Felix's face as he whimpered in pain.

Paul digested what he had just done for a few seconds before the garage door opened and Sierra walked inside the house. She immediately spotted Felix lying on the floor.

"Oh my gosh, Felix!" She ran toward him and began to help him flip over.

"He had a small accident," Paul said, feeling the anger drain away at the sight of Felix's pooling blood.

Sierra glared at him. "*Small* accident?" she screamed. "Paul, don't give me your bullshit." She looked down at Felix and brushed back his moppy hair. "Felix, what happened?"

Felix clutched his nose, flinching in pain. "Paul pushed me down the stairs."

"Tattletale," Paul mumbled. He was about to say more when he saw his sister's livid face. She looked like she was about to kick *him* down the stairs. Sierra moved quickly and grabbed a blanket sitting on the sofa.

"That's mom's favorite Valentino vintage throw, you know," Paul pointed out.

"I don't care," Sierra seethed. She bundled the throw into a ball and pressed it against Felix's nose. "Felix, let's take you to urgent care."

Felix nodded, and the two of them got up, moving toward the garage. "Yo, sibs," Paul shouted as he began to see them walking away from him. "Clean up the blood first. It's spreading closer to the white carpet in the living room."

"Clean it up yourself!" Sierra screeched, hurting his ears. "Paul, you're an absolute nightmare. I swear, you should be in jail!"

He heard the garage door swing shut. Paul was left alone in a thick and heavy silence with a pool of blood standing in between him and his sudden need for some leftover chicken tenders in the fridge.

"They're both *so* dramatic," he declared to the empty air. He walked down the remaining steps, leapt over Felix's leftover blood, and strolled into the kitchen to make his well-deserved snack.

CHAPTER 25

TRISHA AND HUNTER

TRISHA

Ding dong.

"Trisha, can you get the door?" her mom yelled from downstairs. Trisha looked up from her easel where she had just finished mixing the perfect shade of lavender oil paint for her impressionism-inspired painting. She groaned.

Why does Hunter never get the door?

She got up and prayed the color wouldn't dry too much by the time she got back. It was Chinese New Year, after all, and there was no time for a break once the festivities began. *What was I thinking for even trying to paint on a day like today?*

"Trisha, did you hear me?" Annoyance was now mixed in with her mom's high-pitched voice.

"Coming, Mom!" Trisha hollered back. She walked over to her home's touch screen security system and pressed a button. She watched as her home's iron gate opened to reveal a Bentley followed by a Porsche on the winding driveway. They quickly jolted alive and sped toward her house sitting on top of the winding hill.

Must be the Tans and Lus. Trisha walked over to Hunter's door and banged on it. "Hunter, the Tans are here!" Trisha shouted, knowing he probably couldn't hear anything at the moment as he played rock music through his noise-canceling headphones. Trisha walked downstairs and passed by her mom expertly rolling wads of dough into perfectly round dumpling skins.

"Finally," her mom barked. "Hurry and get the door. You know how rude it is to leave them waiting." She reached over to a big bowl filled with raw pork, Chinese cabbage, shallots, chives, and seasonings.

"Mike! This dumpling filling needs more soy sauce!" her mom hollered.

"Sheesh, *jie*, I'm right behind you," Uncle Mike snapped back. He left his too-pregnant-to-travel wife at home to make the three hour drive from San Diego in order to help his sister out with the party.

Trisha had a love-hate relationship with Chinese New Year, a holiday that celebrates the beginning of a new lunar year and also the biggest holiday of the lunar calendar. On the one hand, she got to see extended family like Uncle Mike come over, but the day was also exhausting and filled with drama. She used to get red envelopes stuffed with cash, but as Hunter and Trisha had gotten older, that didn't happen as often anymore. This year, the Tans, Lus, and Millers were joining them for a Chinese New Year party.

The Zhou family used to be on the invite list... until Jack landed himself in jail. Trisha flinched at the memory of the hospital. Once everyone returned to campus after winter break and the notorious Jack Zhou, with his flamboyant style choices and alternating luxury cars, was nowhere to be found, rumors quickly spread about his predicament. One rumor even suggested Jack's fortune was all based on mafia money and that his family was now on the run from the Chinese government. Eventually, the entire story of how he killed someone in a DUI was leaked when Stacy Williams overheard her dad talking to a gossiping faculty member. The truth only heightened the rumors.

Trisha got to the floor-to-ceiling front door and opened it with her widest smile. "*Xin nian kuai le*[52] Auntie Tan, Auntie Lu, and Uncle Lu!" she exclaimed. "Everyone is so timely! You even arrived together."

Auntie Tan and Laura stood on the doorstep with a box of Longjing tea,[53] and Uncle and Auntie Lu, with their recently returned twins from NorCal and Boston right next to them.

"Of course," Auntie Tan replied in snippy Mandarin. "We didn't want to be late. Is that your new Porsche, Tina? I saw how much it glowed after it pulled up *behind me*."

Trisha tried not to roll her eyes. Auntie Tan was always competing with Auntie Lu, even when it came to arrival times. The jealousy antics had escalated last year once Auntie Lu's twins, Chris and Fiona, were accepted into Harvard and Stanford.

"Hi, Trisha! Long time no see," Fiona swept up Trisha into her long, graceful arms. Trisha felt like she was hugging a celebrity. Blessed with a model-like figure and high cheekbones, Fiona Lu had a way of making every person gravitate toward her. Tonight, in her tight, red turtleneck, bleached

---

52 Mandarin for "Happy New Year!"

53 Longjing tea, otherwise known as Dragon Well tea, originates from China's Zhejiang province and is well known for its high quality. The tea is largely produced by hand and can cost more per gram than the price of gold. Tonight, Auntie Tan brought Longjing number forty-three, which was not the most expensive variety. The twenty-eight-gram bottle only cost $546.

ash gray hair, and exquisite jewelry that sparkled against her glowing skin, Fiona was stunning as usual.

"Fiona! I've missed you! I thought you'd be in NorCal for Chinese New Year. Isn't school still going on?" Trisha asked as Fiona released her, leaving an intoxicating scent of floral and sandalwood behind.

"Oh, yeah," Fiona said with a hint of mischief in her voice. "We got special permission to skip class and come home this weekend, just for Chinese New Year!"

"Wow, that's awesome!" Trisha said in surprise. She turned her attention toward Fiona's twin Chris, the spitting image of Fiona but taller, more masculine, and chiseled.

"Chris! It's been too long as well." Trisha couldn't help but blush a little. After having her heart torn into bits by Ray outside of the hospital, Trisha didn't mind a little bit of eye candy for the evening.

Chris flashed a sparkling white smile, "Yes, it's been way too long. I think the last time I saw you was, what? Last year during our graduation?"

Trisha cringed. *Oh yes, how could I forget? You and your mom began to argue right before the ceremony about how you wanted to take a senior trip to Southeast Asia rather than do a summer internship at Stanford Hospital with a family friend.*

"Yes, last year," Trisha replied awkwardly. Chris handed a box of wild ginseng[54] to Trisha. "Anyway, Happy New Year! Where's Hunter?"

As if on cue, Hunter appeared right beside her.

"Hey man, long time no see," Hunter grinned from ear to ear. "How is the East coast? Missing the Cali sunshine yet?"

---

54 Costing on average $500 per pound, wild ginseng is highly valued by Chinese people for having powerful medicinal benefits. Given the weight of the bag, Trisha guessed it cost at least $1,500. Auntie Tan was not happy.

"You bet," Chris frowned. "Not even my Canada Goose protects me from the Boston chill. It's awful."

"The kids clearly have plenty to chat about," said Uncle Lu, dressed in a neon colored silk shirt and neatly ironed pants.

One of China's biggest real estate developers, Uncle Lu grew up basking in the luxury lifestyle, including buying items like Apple Watches and gold chains for his miniature Schnauzer, Scruffy. After meeting Tina Lu, the daughter of a well-known senior Chinese Communist Party official in the Zhejiang province, through a professional matchmaker who specialized in fortune telling based on birth dates, the pair were engaged and married within six months. Once China began its crackdown on corruption (which Uncle Lu swore he was not part of), he decided it was time to leave China for better horizons. Under the US's EB-5 investment visa, Uncle and Auntie Lu immigrated to the US with their then six-year-old twins in tow.

"Please come in!" Hunter opened the door wide, giving Laura an awkward glance. Trisha caught the look almost immediately. *Huh, wonder what that's all about?*

It was incredibly obvious to Trisha how much Laura liked Hunter. That had been the case since they were little kids when Laura would play wedding with Hunter using Trisha's stuffed animals as wedding guests.

Trisha shot a questioning look at Hunter, who refused to make eye contact with her.

The group walked in, taking off their shoes and switching into memory foam slippers before making their way into the home's one-thousand-square-foot living room.

"Tina! Caroline! Jim! You're all here!" her mom's voice echoed from the kitchen. "Give me one second! I'm almost done wrapping these dumplings! *Hector*!"

Trisha startled at hearing her dad's name come out of her mom's mouth. Her dad had quietly moved out of the house to an undisclosed location last month. Trisha and Hunter were both stumped as to why he disappeared, and both of their parents stayed mute on the details. It didn't surprise Trisha and Hunter. Their parents' marriage had been declining for years now. To them, this new separate living situation wasn't so different than when they were both at home ignoring one another.

Surprisingly, Trisha's dad suddenly turned up this morning. She had thought for a brief second he was back to reconcile with her mom. Unfortunately, that was not the case. It was all just for show.

"Good to see everyone! It has been awhile!" Trisha's dad declared, appearing from the home office. As soon as Trisha's dad arrived that morning, he briefly exchanged pleasantries with Hunter and Trisha before disappearing into a room. That's when it was obvious he was only home to keep up appearances for the party.

I'm so over all of these fake pleasantries.

Hunter appeared to be in the same boat when he suddenly turned to Fiona, Chris, and Laura and asked, "Hey, want to go hang out in the home theater?" All of them nodded their heads enthusiastically. Everyone knew there would be superficial updates on everyone's lives and parents humble-bragging about their kids for the next hour.

Suddenly, a loud knock was heard at the front door before it popped open to reveal Matt and Auntie Miller. "Hey, everyone," Matt greeted. "*Xin nian kuai... le?*" Trisha giggled. No matter how hard Matt tried to learn Chinese, it never sounded right.

"Hi, Auntie Miller. Hi, Matt..." Hunter said, awkwardly waving. "How did you get in? We never opened the gate."

Matt brushed away a bead of sweat trickling down his forehead and looked down at his hands. "Mom and I wanted to work up our appetite for dinner tonight, so we decided to hike up the hill." Matt avoided eye contact with Hunter.

Trisha furrowed her eyebrows. *First Laura was acting weird, now Matt. What has Hunter been up to?*

"Ah, good idea," Hunter mumbled, rubbing the back of his neck. "My mom and aunts have whipped up a storm. There's a whole fish, braised pork, lobster noodles, Wagyu steak, abalone porridge, rice cake, *tang yuan*, dumplings, of course, and bird's nest. We've also got eight treasured sticky rice for dessert."

"And cake!" Matt's mom chimed in, holding up a see-through cake box.

Trisha's eyes widened in astonishment. "Wow, that looks so real!" Inside the box was an intricately made 3-D pig with fat rolls and little hairs etched in detail. If it wasn't for the surrounding frosting, Trisha would have thought it was a real sleeping piglet.

"Thanks!" Auntie Miller beamed proudly. "I made it myself in honor of the year of the pig."[55]

The whole group crowded around the cake exclaiming at the detail. After ten minutes of oohing and ahhing, Trisha felt like it was time to disperse from the adults.

"*So*, home theater anyone? Take two?" Trisha said expectantly.

---

55 For every new Lunar New Year, there is a new Chinese zodiac sign, repeating in a twelve-year cycle. Each Chinese zodiac sign is tied to different superstitions, like luck for the year, based on your zodiac sign.

All the non-adults looked back at her in relief and nodded in unison.

HUNTER

"How has senior year been, Hunter? Has senioritis set in yet?"

Hunter hit a billiard ball and watched it roll into a pocket before looking up to respond to Chris's question.

"It's been alright, I guess," he grimaced. "It hasn't been what I imagined it would be like."

"What do you mean?"

Hunter debated how much he wanted to reveal, given how Matt and Laura were also in the room. Hunter settled with giving most of the truth.

"Well, just to start off, I became a Stanford reject and also lost the love of my life in one swoop." *And then Matt kissed me, so now it's super awkward, oh, and Laura over there, she helped me get dumped.* Hunter tried to muzzle the other comments in his head fighting to get out.

Chris whistled. "That does sound pretty, uh, crappy. I thought Sierra and you were going to get married."

"Apparently not," Hunter grumbled before hitting another billiard ball.

Everyone in the room exchanged awkward glances with one another. Hunter ignored it.

"It was all my fault!" Laura abruptly wailed. The room fell quiet. Hunter silently cursed. Guess one of his secrets was about to come out.

Fiona spoke up, "Uh, wow, Chris and I go away for one semester and now our sweet, innocent Laura has gone and broken up the Hollywood couple?"

Trisha weighed in too, just as clueless. "What's going on, Hunter? You never told me why Sierra and you broke up."

"Stop, everyone. Sheesh," Hunter snapped. He turned to Laura, "Look, Laura, I already told you multiple times already. It's not your fault, okay? Sierra and I already had a mountain of problems, and apparently hugging you was the final straw."

"But Hunter... I feel *so*..." Laura began to say.

Matt burst out laughing.

Everyone turned to Matt in confusion.

"Sorry," Matt continued laughing. "It's just... I..." He gasped for air. "I *kissed* Hunter, and Laura here looks like she is about to be excommunicated for *hugging* Hunter."

Hunter facepalmed. *Okay, guess everything is out now.*

"Oh my gosh, Mattie! I'm so happy for you! You finally came out!" Fiona cooed.

"Uh, wait, you already knew?" Matt said in surprise.

"Everyone knew. We were just waiting for you," Fiona replied with a wave of her hand.

"Huh..." An expression of relief and confusion washed over Matt's face.

"This kiss though... sounds scandalous," Fiona added with a wink.

Hunter groaned. "Please, Fiona, stop digging. Matt just had a bit too much to drink and fell onto me by accident when it happened. Right, Matt?" *Please actually be the case.*

"Right. Yeah, exactly," Matt nodded stiffly. Hunter let out a breath of relief. A part of him felt like Matt was lying, but he couldn't deal with what the alternative might be.

"That's it?" Chris exclaimed in disbelief. "Boring."

"Yup. It was a very embarrassing fall," Matt replied half-heartedly. "Anyway, how has college been? You literally have been the talk of all the Asian moms since leaving. Suddenly no one's kids could compare to Chris and Fiona Lu."

The twins exchanged looks and burst out laughing simultaneously. The entire room stared at the twins, deeply confused.

Fiona, still giggling, began, "Ah, friends, you'll never guess what we've been up to..."

"We have the craziest story you're all going to judge us hard for," Chris finished her thought.

Hunter was so confused. Trisha spoke up, "Okay, you're confusing all of us now. What is going on?"

Chris looked over at Fiona and grinned from ear to ear.

"We dropped out of college!" the twins shouted together.

The room fell silent. Hunter was dumbstruck. *What?* Every parent's dream kids are doing the complete opposite of what everyone else thinks they're doing?

Matt jumped up from the bar stool that he was sitting on, looking grateful he was no longer the center of attention. "Lu twins, spill."

"I guess I'll go first then. Mine is the more boring story," Chris said with a playful smile. He was clearly getting a kick out of building the suspense.

"The first semester of Harvard was incredibly suffocating," he began. "It was all these WASPs[56] along with Asian kids like us who have grinded their entire youth away for the '*Ha fu*'[57] stamp of approval. My international Chinese friend group revealed to me we have nothing compared to them. If we're the top one percent, they are the top point-zero-one percent."

---

56 Slang term standing for "White Anglo-Saxon Protestants," which refers to upper-class, white, and preppy people from New England. Universities, especially private ones, can have a reputation for being "WASPy."

57 Mandarin for "Harvard." Apparently, one of the Wang's family friends named their newborn son *Hafu*.

"Reminds me of Jack Zhou," Trisha mumbled.

"Who's that?" Fiona asked.

"He's this super wealthy guy who transferred to Winchester this year, but is, um, in jail right now," Matt responded.

Fiona's jaw dropped. "Damn, I miss Winchester drama."

"*Hello*, I was telling my epic story!" Chris made a melodramatic "look at me" wave.

Hunter rolled his eyes. "Back to you, Chris."

"Anyway, this one other guy, Bob, decided he wanted to build a startup that would cut out the realtor in real estate transactions. I decided it was a great idea, so now I'm living in his Newton mansion coding away like a stallion while we apply to be part of an accelerator."

"But... what about college? *Harvard*?" Trisha exclaimed.

"It's just a piece of paper. Plenty of famous people have dropped out of college. Just look at Mark Zuckerberg," Chris shrugged. "Plus, if everything blows up in my face, I'll just come back and work for the family business. Who would ever question I didn't graduate from Harvard? Everyone already knows I got in and my parents are certainly never going to admit it."

"Wait. Do your parents even know? Wouldn't they still be expecting the tuition bill?" Laura said, looking bewildered.

"Sort of?"

"What do you mean by 'sort of?'" Hunter asked.

"Well, we tried to tell them, but they just hung up on us and we never spoke about it again. They're still going through all the motions as if we're still attending Harvard and Stanford. They've even received emails about our withdrawals but still haven't said anything. Fiona and I are just happy we haven't been cut off for life, so we've let this charade continue."

Hunter shook his head in disbelief. "Damn, Chris, you've always been the most daring out of us, but this is... something else. You completely went above and beyond like you always do, but in the most ironic way."

"Yeah..." Chris said with a smirk. "Honestly, this is just me chasing my dreams. I'm done being my parents' puppet."

"Pst," Fiona whispered loudly. "Can I have my turn to explain how I blew up my life now?"

"The stage is yours," Chris bowed dramatically.

Hunter chuckled as Fiona flashed a wide smile from her seat on the bar counter, swinging her legs like a little girl. The twins never ceased to entertain.

Fiona launched straight into her story. "So, I went to Stanford last fall with these fake, empty dreams to be a doctor one day. That lasted for all of one day once I got to Palo Alto."

Fiona hopped off of the bar table and began to pace around the room passionately. "As you know, I've been interested in music since I could talk."

"Duh," Matt stated. Everyone in the room knew Fiona had amassed five million followers through her videos of pop song medleys on her ukulele.

"At Palo Alto, I began to take up gigs at local coffee shops," Fiona continued. "Around two months into the school year, another Stanford classmate was sitting in the coffee shop while I was singing and sent a video of it to his dad. Turns out, his dad is a major recording executive."

Fiona's expression became wistful. "It's been a whirlwind ever since, but my demo has been passed around everywhere. My first album is going to come out this summer. There's no way I have time for pointless classes like organic chemistry anymore. When am I ever going to use that in my singing career?"

Hunter was dumbfounded. *These twins really have guts.*

"Wait. So where are you staying if you're no longer in a Stanford dorm?" Trisha asked.

"Oh, I'm now dating the guy who discovered me," Fiona replied nonchalantly. "We live together. He's part of the whirlwind."

"You mean your classmate from the coffee shop? Wouldn't he be in a dorm too?" Laura chimed in.

"No, no, I'm dating his *dad*. Not the son. His dad, Robert, is my boyfriend." Fiona sighed whimsically, "I call him Robbie."

Chris buried his head in his hands and groaned loudly. "This is the part of her story I don't agree with. I'm not going to have the girl version of me walking around dating a guy who is twenty-one years older. It's wild."

Hunter's mouth fell open. Fiona had always struck Hunter as someone who would date older—she always gave off this mature and worldly vibe that was beyond her years—but not *that* much older.

"Before you all go judging me, age is just a number," Fiona huffed. "Robbie is the best guy I've ever dated and treats me right. He showers me in Van Cleef and knows how to wine and dine me. The cherry on top is that he knows how to move my music career forward."

Everyone in the room seemed to give one another skeptical glances, but no one said a word.

Hunter felt his phone vibrate. It was a one-word message from his mom—"food."

"Storytime is over," Hunter announced. "Dinner time."

As if on cue, Matt's stomach grumbled loudly.

CHAPTER 26

TRISHA

———

"Trish, go help set the table!" her mom yelled as soon as Trisha walked back into the house. *Ugh*. Trisha marched over to the kitchen cabinets and began taking out colorful, gold encrusted plates.

"No! *Zhen chun*![58] Take out the nicer ones," her mom snapped while pouring abalone soup into a large bowl with fuchsia and coral hues.

All of the plates are nice. What is she talking about? Trisha dug back deeper into the cabinet. She saw a collection of unfamiliar porcelain. *Must be these.*

Trisha pulled out the stack of mosaic porcelain plates with silvery spirals adorning the edges. She picked them up and walked over to the large round table where everyone had taken their seats. The family friends were spinning around the lazy Susan as they enjoyed nicely plated fruit platters stacked with tangerines, dragon fruit, kiwis, and peeled apple slices.

Her mom followed closely behind with a piping hot bowl of soup. "Dinner time!" she shouted, despite the fact everyone

---

58 Mandarin for "so stupid."

was only a few feet away from her. Trisha began to set down plates in front of everyone.

"Wow, Phoebe, are these new? They're so pretty," Auntie Lu exclaimed as she held up her plate to the glass chandelier lighting.

"Yes," her mom said with a coy smile. "It's just something small I picked up the other day while shopping in South Coast Plaza."

"It's absolutely exquisite. The engravings especially," Auntie Miller remarked. "What is it?"

"Oh, just platinum," her mom quickly replied. "You know me, I'm not the biggest fan of being flashy. I thought Hermés was going overboard by putting platinum on porcelain, but they were on such a great discount you know I just had to get them. Just two hundred and fifty dollars per plate!"

Trisha stifled a laugh as Hunter made a dramatic eye roll from across the table. Her mom had a wide array of skills, including professional humble bragger.

While Trisha passed around the remaining plates, Uncle Mike and her dad appeared with large plates in each hand. "That must be the Wagyu beef!" Chris exclaimed in excitement as he tunnel-visioned onto a slab of meat.

"Yes, I expedited the shipping from Japan just to get it here in time for Chinese New Year," her mom declared proudly. "The lobsters are also freshly shipped from Boston."

Her mom turned toward the kitchen again. "There are a few more dishes. I'll be right out with it. Hunter, come help us in the kitchen!"

"Fine," Hunter grumbled as he reluctantly got up from his chair and followed after her.

"Chris, you probably get plenty of lobster at Harvard, right?" Auntie Miller turned to him, trying to make conversation.

Chris didn't even miss a beat before responding casually, "Yes, of course. Cambridge is full of lobster restaurants. I go there with my friends all the time, especially after a long day of studying in the library."

Auntie Lu smiled at her son's perfect response. "Ah, I'm so lucky to have such a hardworking son, but I worry he works too hard!"

Auntie Tan jumped in. "You must tell us your secret for getting a son like yours. I saw on your WeChat moments you recently opened up *Hafu Excellence* for college counseling? I love how your logo includes the twins with Harvard and Stanford stamped over it."

"What? You opened up a college counseling business?" Fiona turned to her mom, confused.

Trisha quickly realized the twins had no idea what their mom had been up to. *That's why their parents ignored the fact that they dropped out.*

"Oh yes, honey. I wanted to help other kids get into the colleges of their dreams too, especially after *we* worked so hard to get into college," Auntie Lu replied nonchalantly.

Trisha smirked. *Classic. Another parent trying to live out their hopes and dreams through their kids.* While her own parents could be overbearing and overly college-focused as well, at least they would never paste Hunter and Trisha's faces on a logo and call out to the world how successful they were as parents.

Has there ever been a successful parent in the world?

"Mom, first of all, it was *me,* not *us,* and certainly not *you,* who slaved away pulling all-nighters and juggling academics, clubs, competitions, and standardized tests." Fiona's face darkened. "Also, you can't just use pictures of us on a business logo without our permission!"

Auntie Lu smiled menacingly at her daughter. "Fiona, we're in front of guests right now. Don't ever speak to me that way."

"Why not?" Fiona shouted back. "I'm not the one being ridiculous."

"I gave birth to you and Chris and gave up so much for both of you. I *own you,* so I can do whatever I want with you," Auntie Lu seethed, her voice lowering into a hiss.

Fiona glared at her mom, looking as if she were torn between lunging at her or just letting it go. Auntie Tan, across the table, looked absolutely giddy at her friend's "perfect" children being not so perfect after all.

Chris, who was sitting beside Fiona, placed his hand on his sister's. He whispered something into her ear before Fiona glared at her mom one more time. Her shoulders slumped down in defeat, clearly choosing to let this argument go.

Trisha drew in a long breath. *We haven't even begun dinner yet and we're already at each other's throats. If only Pam was here. She'd be eating up the drama like dessert. Speaking of Pam...*

Trisha furrowed her face. Pamela had been MIA ever since the hospital incident. Trisha still saw her at school, of course, but otherwise Pamela had all but disappeared. There was always some excuse about needing to drive her siblings around or study for a test whenever Trisha tried to dive deeper into what happened.

Trisha brushed away her thoughts. *It's Chinese New Year. I'll think about it later.* She looked up and realized an unsettling silence had fallen over the table.

As if on cue, Hunter, her parents, and Uncle Mike came out of the kitchen with an array of dishes.

"Why is everyone so quiet?" Her dad asked, placing two plates of pork and vegetable dumplings onto the lazy Susan.

Matt let out a forced chuckle and exclaimed, "Uncle Wang, that looks delicious!"

In a span of minutes, the fruit platters were replaced with an array of food bursting with color and flavor. There was a round of pushing the lazy Susan back and forth insisting someone else should eat or try a dish first before it was replaced with a symphony of munching sounds.

"Uncle and Auntie Wang, the dumplings are so good," Laura said with a sweet smile as she dipped her dumpling in a mixture of vinegar and *lao gan ma*.[59]

"Thanks, Laura," Trisha's mom beamed.

"Laura, it's been awhile since I've seen you. The older you get the more you look like your mom, except maybe a bit chubbier," Auntie Lu commented in between bites of stir-fried Chinese broccoli.

Auntie Tan scoffed. "Yes, it's all that American food. I certainly did not have thighs like hers when I was younger."

Laura's face blushed crimson red as she put down a half-eaten dumpling. Trisha immediately swooped in to back her up. "I think they're perfect," she said firmly.

"Hmm. Maybe for Westerners," Auntie Tan mumbled.

Laura mouthed a silent "thank you" to Trisha but did not pick up her dumpling again. Instead, she put down her chopsticks and began to sip tea.

Auntie Tan, ignoring what Trisha said about her daughter, launched into her usual probing questions. "Kids, I heard

---

59 *Lao Gan Ma* is an incredibly popular chili sauce from China. The founder, Tao Huabi, who started off as a street vendor, is estimated to have a $1 billion net worth and is also well known for her fleet of luxury cars.

during the Winchester parent meeting that there still hasn't been any progress on the AP exam case?"

"Yeah, not at all," Hunter said with his mouth full of noodles. "I honestly don't care anymore. It's already been over a year."

"It's the *principle* of it," Auntie Tan explained. "I can't have kids thinking they can get away with cheating while my poor daughter is doing everything by the book to get into college. I've been nagging the police department to get a move on it."

Everything by the book, including having access to the best college counselors, tutors, and opportunities money can buy, Trisha thought silently.

"Also," Auntie Tan continued. "I heard the international students have been speaking too much in their native tongue again on campus. That is unacceptable!"

"I don't see anything wrong with that," Auntie Miller said. "They miss home. A lot of these students have to stay with host families while their parents are all the way across the sea. The least they can do is hold onto their language."

"Well, they're in America now. They should learn English, like how I learned English," Auntie Tan huffed.

"Yet you speak only Mandarin ninety-nine percent of the time," Trisha's dad said in a low voice. Trisha tried to hold back a giggle. *Go Dad!*

She saw her mom elbow him for his blunt remark before her mom quickly covered up her dad's comment. "And as you should, given how it's more useful to speak Mandarin in our area these days."

Her mom paused before changing the topic. "Has anyone heard from Zi Wei lately, by the way? She stopped responding to my messages after... you know..."

"After her son ran over another kid?" Auntie Tan said with no hesitation. "No, and I don't care. Her son was so spoiled. I only tolerated her because she gave me that Xinjiang jade for Christmas. Looking back, though, that was so stingy of her; she probably gave me the smallest one she owned after I helped her with her move and settling in." Auntie Tan sniffed in distaste.

"I think what happened to her was awful," Auntie Miller said. "She must feel so alone. We should keep trying to reach out. She needs all the support she can get right now."

"I am certainly not. I was only friends with her so I could get some business done with Mr. Zhou. She's not *that* rich anyway. She's only a mistress." Auntie Tan rolled her shoulders back haughtily.

An awkward silence fell over the room as the dinner guests were clearly disconcerted with Auntie Tan's statement but also not brave enough to go face to face against her.

Finally, Uncle Mike cleared his throat, "Who is excited for watching the CCTV New Year's Gala[60] tonight? I heard they spent a tiny fortune on it this year."

Conversation began to liven up again. Hunter and Trisha's eyes connected across the table.

Just another night at the Wang house.

---

60 The CCTV New Year's Gala is an annual, three-hour event held on Chinese New Year. It has the largest audience in the world during this time frame, attracting more than one billion viewers in 2018. Given time zone differences, families will stay up watching the show into early morning hours.

SPRING

CHAPTER 27

PAMELA

"*Ammi*, an arranged marriage is *not* going to fix my issues!" Pamela dropped the clean plate in her hands into the dishwasher[61] with a *clang*. "This is the twenty-first century!"

"You don't know what you're talking about, Pamela," her mom said sharply in Urdu. "If we don't find you a good match now after all the things you did earlier this year, I'm afraid no one will ever want you in the future. At least now you still have your youth."

"Maybe I don't want to be with anyone in the future then!" Pamela screamed while reaching for another dirty plate in the sink. "I'm not some cow you can just sell off to the highest bidder. Is what *Abba* said true? You found some old divorcé in Karachi to marry me off to? You know I'm sixteen, right? It's illegal in the US!"

"But it's legal in Pakistan," her mom replied calmly. "Also, stop making Abdul sound like a horrible choice. The fact that he's rich, a doctor, and willing to still take you as a wife

---

61 Even though the Shah family could certainly afford running dishwashers, they always preferred their own habit of washing it themselves and using the dishwasher as a drying rack.

despite the fact that your flower has been plucked is already extremely generous of him."

Her mom lowered her voice. "He even knows about your... hospital incident. It's a miracle he agreed."

Pamela felt like her ears were bleeding. "This is *not* happening to me. I will run away if you try to do this."

"And where will you run off to? How will you make money? Sell yourself?" Her mom gave her a withering glance. "I guess you're not too far from doing that based upon what you told us at the hospital."

Crash. Pamela threw a new plate she was holding into the sink, breaking it instantly.

"Throwing a temper tantrum is not going to work, Pamela." Her mom continued peeling the apple in her hand with a knife, unfazed. "Just think about it. We're not forcing you."

"But you basically are by threatening to disown me!" Pamela shouted as she stormed out of the kitchen. "I *hate* this family!"

What is the point of life if I'm just someone's doll to play with? Pamela ran into her room, wiping away tears, leaving streaks behind on her face with her still greasy hands. She made a beeline for her walk-in closet and dragged open a drawer full of socks.

After Pamela got home from the hospital following her New Year's fiasco, her parents had put her in a makeshift prison. Pamela's driving privileges had been taken away, she was only allowed at home or in school, and, worst of all, her phone and laptop had been confiscated. She could only access the internet now with the computer in the kitchen—in full view of everyone.

That being said, it wasn't like Pamela wanted to go out anymore either. All she wanted to do was wallow in her own grief. *Especially after...*

Pamela's throat tightened. She still couldn't think about what had happened at the hospital. *My baby. I killed my baby.* Pamela's sleep was drenched with nightmares of her unborn child while, when she was awake, voices in her head screamed at her to take her own life.

Life was becoming too painful to keep on living. Drugs were now the only thing that she could look forward to.

Pamela dug underneath the socks in the drawer until she hit the bottom and fished out one long stocking. She pulled out a variety of pills in plastic bags and popped a light blue pill into her mouth.

Her parents had wrongly believed that by becoming even stricter with her, Pamela would no longer have access to drugs. They were so wrong. Even with Reddy now on a study abroad program for the semester in London (still clueless to the fact that Pamela lost their baby, or that it existed in the first place), Pamela still managed to amass a sizable stash of drugs from various classmates at Winchester.

She crawled underneath her covers, fully clothed, and closed her eyes.

All I want to do is sleep forever.

***

Pamela woke up with a jolt.

"Pamela?" Anika whispered.

"Hm? What?" Pamela tried to shake off the grogginess. "What time is it?" She looked over at the clock. "Anika, it's three a.m. Are you serious right now?" Pamela groaned. She turned away from her little sister and threw the covers over her head.

"Pamela, please. I'm scared." Anika began to shake her. "It's hard to breathe."

Pamela's eyes fluttered open. "What? What are you talking about? Did you watch a scary movie again?"

She heard her sister make gasping noises. Pamela reached over and switched on the lamp in her room and turned her annoyed gaze onto Anika.

"Anika, will you stop being—Anika?"

Tears streamed down Anika's face as she fidgeted with Pamela's blanket. Pamela bolted out of bed. There was something about her sister's restless, agitated look that felt familiar to her.

"Anika, what's going on?"

"I'm sorry. I didn't mean to," Anika whispered nervously. "I was just so curious. It seemed so special."

"What seemed so special?" Pamela demanded. She felt a wave of unease wash over her.

"I... I took some of those pills from your sock drawer. You're always guarding it, so I thought there had to be something special about them."

"No, no, no, Anika, how many did you take?" Pamela quickly went into her closet and scoured through the socks. In the corner of the drawer, an empty Ziploc bag labeled with an "A" lay empty.

Pamela turned around and rushed back to Anika. "Anika, you took Adderall, okay? It looks like you took more than a kid should have, but not so much where it's dangerous." Pamela breathed a sigh of relief before feeling anger quickly replace it. "What were you thinking?"

"I'm... I'm sorry..." Anika blubbered as fat tears began to roll down her chubby cheeks.

Pamela reached for her phone on her nightstand and quickly Googled the effects of having too much Adderall, even though she already knew what the answer would be.

Confusion, rapid breathing, insomnia, panic. She began to pace.

"You're probably super wired up from the pills right now and going to stay up the whole night. The reason why you feel like you can't breathe is because you're having a panic attack," she said out loud, more to herself than to Anika.

"Stop pacing, Pamela. It's making me dizzy. My heart is about to pop out of my chest." Anika curled into a fetal position on Pamela's bed.

Pamela quickly grabbed a water bottle sitting on her desk and swiped an old paper bag from a convenience store on her cluttered floor. She hurried over to Anika.

"Anika, get up," Pamela instructed, hoisting her sister upright. "Breathe into this bag. Big, deep breaths."

Anika began to take large, shaky breaths. Pamela nodded, feeling the sickening pain of worry that almost paralyzed her minutes earlier begin to subside.

"Okay, once you're done, chug this water bottle." Pamela placed the bottle next to Anika. She reached over and gently placed Anika's head onto her lap.

Pamela held her sister silently for fifteen minutes as her panic attack abated. When she felt like her sister was normal again, Pamela felt her concern turn into pure sadness.

This can't continue anymore. I can't transfer my issues onto my siblings' lives as well.

But what could Pamela do? If she felt trapped before, she felt suffocated now. Her parents didn't even look at her like she was human.

She gazed down at her sister, who was now cuddling next to her, eyes wide open.

But I have to at least try. I've already ruined my own life, but I can't be the reason why Anika's life is ruined. Pamela rummaged through all her memories of her parents rejecting her pleas for therapy, believing that it was a fake practice made up by Westerners.

Could I actually convince Ammi and Abba? Pamela almost laughed out loud. How could they listen if they didn't even care in the first place?

She looked down at Anika, who now gulped down the water bottle like her life depended on it. *I will try one more time. One chance to get help. If not....* Pamela flinched. She could only see darkness beyond that.

Pamela kept Anika company for the rest of the night streaming trashy reality television while waiting for the wiring effects of the drug to die down. It wasn't until 6:30 a.m. before Anika fell fast asleep next to her. Pamela gently shifted herself away from her sister and quietly left the room. She crept downstairs, her hand shaking as it slid down the bannister.

The strong smell of coffee hit her before Pamela even entered the kitchen. Her mom, pouring a cup of hazelnut coffee, and her dad, wolfing down a paratha, looked up at her in surprise.

"You're up early," her dad commented.

Pamela stood at the kitchen entryway, frozen. Her heart beat so rapidly it made her wonder if maybe she had been the one that took too much Adderall instead.

"*Abba, Ammi,* I need help," Pamela croaked.

Her dad put down his paratha mid-bite and stared at her. Her mom, unfazed, sipped her coffee and looked at Pamela skeptically.

"Are you being dramatic again?" her mom demanded. "An arranged marriage is not the end of the world."

Pamela collapsed onto the floor and began to sob.

"Ayesha," her dad snapped, "let her talk." He walked over to Pamela on the floor and squatted down next to her. *"Bay-ti,*[62] what is wrong?"

For the next hour, Pamela's parents listened as she recounted her drug addiction beginning from freshman year. She spoke about how the drug usage started off innocently, but then it grew into something more as she began using it for parties as well. Pamela also reluctantly revealed that she was trapped in a cycle of needing drugs to survive. She no longer had control over her own actions. By the end of the hour, her parents sat on their chairs grim and speechless.

Her dad silenced his phone as it rang for the fourth time that morning. It was a weekend, but it never stopped ringing anyway.

"Pamela, why have you never said anything to us?" Her mom's voice broke as she spoke.

"I've tried, *Ammi.* I've tried so many times. Remember when I told you both I had depression freshman year? You told me it was just the evil *jinns.*[63] Every time there is something wrong in my life, you just dismiss it. Anything that is outside of what you think is the 'perfect daughter,' you just blame on not being strict enough with me," Pamela blinked back tears. "Honestly, if it wasn't for drugs, I would have left this earth long ago. This family sucks the life out of me."

Her parents exchanged solemn glances with one another.

"All we've ever wanted is the best for you, Pamela. You just don't trust us enough to believe we know exactly what is best for you," her dad murmured.

---

62 Urdu for "daughter."

63 Supernatural beings in Islamic mythology that can be denoted as demonic in nature.

"Do you actually though, *Abba*?" Pamela shook her head. "You know nothing about my life. If you did, would we be having this conversation right now? I can't believe even during a conversation like this, even with me *telling you* I'm addicted to drugs, you're still in denial."

She threw her hands up in the air. *This is impossible. I'm so stupid for even trying.*

Pamela got up to walk away. "I'm so done."

"Pamela, please," her dad begged, getting up from his chair. "Let's talk. You can't expect us to be perfect parents either."

She paused at the foot of the stairs.

"If I talk, will you listen?" Pamela implored, refusing to turn around. "And will you stop bringing up this arranged marriage nonsense?"

"What have we been doing for the past hour?" her mom pointed out. "As for the marriage... we can discuss..."

Out of the corner of her eye, Pamela saw her little brother Nirav peeking through the second floor bannister at all of them. She made direct eye contact with him and his eyes widened in surprise and terror.

She dropped her gaze, ashamed at herself. *Even my little brother is scared of me now.* She turned around toward the kitchen again and faced her parents. *I can't keep on running anymore.*

Pamela stared at her parents, who suddenly looked so tired and broken. She couldn't help it, but their defeated gazes also gave her hope that they were finally realizing the status quo of dismissing everything away was no longer going to work this time around.

Last chance. Please, please, let them listen to me.

CHAPTER 28

MATT

—

Matt switched on his bathroom lights and stared into the mirror. The glare hurt his head, which seemed to have a permanent migraine from sleep deprivation these days.

He gingerly touched the dark circles highlighting his gaunt face.

I look like a ghostly raccoon.

Ever since exploding his life on New Year's Day, his parents had been desperately praying with the church pastor to "get rid of his sinful thoughts." Matt tolerated it at first out of guilt (his classmates did trash the house after all), but when the pastor recommended Matt go to a conversion therapy camp for the summer, Matt promptly told him to go "fuck himself." After that, the pastor never came around again and his parents began to avoid him completely.

He felt like an idiot. *Why did I confess to them?* He knew how conservative and Catholic they were. Yet, he thought, maybe, just *maybe*, they'd love him enough to overcome their beliefs.

He was wrong.

Now, his family was in a cold war... and his friendship with Hunter...

Matt furiously rubbed his limp hair. After the New Year's party, Hunter had gone about like nothing happened between them, as if the kiss was just some unfortunate accident. Matt knew Hunter was either too weirded or grossed out by the encounter to admit Matt had deliberately kissed him.

Hunter was acting like everything was completely normal, so Matt decided to go along with Hunter's charade. Yet, every so often after water polo practice or during AYCE sessions, Matt saw Hunter flush awkwardly whenever he got too close or said anything remotely bromance-y.

It was better than never speaking again at least.

Matt heard a gentle knock at his door. He walked out of the bathroom and glanced at the clock. *Who is knocking at my door at eight a.m. on a Saturday?* He walked over to his bedroom door. *Must be Mom, only she would be up this early.* Sure enough, he heard the sound of his mom's voice.

"Honey? Are you awake?"

Matt took in a sharp breath. *Not another camp convo.* He walked over to his door to open it. His eyes widened in shock as his mom grinned at him from ear to ear. "Congratulations on BU!"

She rushed into the room and pulled him into her embrace. He froze in place. It had been so long since he had interacted with his mom, let alone received a hug from her.

"Uh, thanks," Matt mumbled, pulling away. "I found out through email yesterday, actually. I guess they sent that gigantic scarlet acceptance folder through the snail mail?"

"I just pulled it out of the mailbox and knew immediately by the size that it had to be an acceptance." His mom held up a large envelope that he hadn't noticed in her hand earlier. "I haven't opened it yet."

"Oh, yeah, thanks." Matt reached over for the thick folder. He felt a swell of pride overwhelm him, but then it quickly faded again as he looked at his mom.

"Can we talk for a little bit, Matt?" his mom looked at him imploringly.

"Uh, sure." Matt emotionally prepared himself for a "pray the gay away" session.

They took a seat on his unmade Star Wars-themed bedding. "I know it has been a tense couple of months at home," his mom began, "and I... I want to try to work this... new... identity situation out."

Mat sat motionless. His mom was stammering so hard he didn't know if he heard her correctly.

"What do you mean 'work this out?'" Matt replied, using air quotes with his fingers.

His mom took a deep breath. "It caught me by surprise when you told us that you were... that you were... not straight… after we got back from the airport." His mom looked down at her feet. "I think I've known all along deep down in my heart, but... I... I just didn't want to face the truth."

Are Mom's hands shaking? His eyes darted around the room, not sure where to look.

His mom waited for Matt to say something. He didn't. "I just want you to know that I love you unconditionally."

Matt stared at her with incredulous eyes. *This still doesn't make sense. What is with this sudden change of heart?* He shook his head.

"Mom, I really appreciate that you're telling me this, but I don't understand why you couldn't have said this originally." Matt struggled for words. "It's... it's... honestly kind of hard to believe what you're saying... is this only because I got into BU?"

"No! Of course not!" She exclaimed, horrified. "College has nothing to do with this. I just thought we could try figuring this out together. I can't stand the silence in this house anymore."

"But Mom, still," Matt narrowed his eyes skeptically, "what changed? You can't just be like, 'Oh my God, you're going to Hell' one second and then be like, 'I love you for who you are' another second."

"It's not sudden... and to be honest, I'm still processing it. I still need time to come to terms with this situation. You know what our community says about homosexuality, but I've begun emailing back and forth with an LGBTQ-friendly pastor who is really opening my eyes to the situation." Matt's mom paused. "I'm not sure how we'll tell everyone at church, or how to even tell your grandma, but one thing for certain is that you are my son. I don't understand you... but I want to at least try."

Tears began to sting Matt's eyes as a jolt of hope coursed through his body.

Is Mom actually coming around?

Matt was afraid to get his hopes up, especially given how uncomfortable his mom seemed at the moment. *But this is still progress.*

He nodded stiffly at his mom. "What about Dad? Is this what he thinks too?"

His mom silently shook her head. "I'm sorry, honey. He needs more time."

A part of his hope collapsed inside of him. "What if he never gets there?"

"Let's take this one step at a time," she said softly. "For now, he wants to be left alone... he doesn't want to talk."

Matt wasn't surprised that his dad was still in denial, but it still didn't make his throbbing heart feel any better. His dad was rejecting a core part of him.

His mom awkwardly looked up at Matt and searched his face. Matt blinked at her, simultaneously trying to reconcile the shadow of his dad's dismissal with his mom's candid and expectant expression.

"So... honey... Matt... do you want to go celebrate? I can take you to *Din Tai Fung* for some of your favorite soup dumplings. I'll order whatever you want," his mom asked hesitantly. "That's what you do, right? Celebrate? I read online that it's good to throw a coming out party..."

Matt managed to choke out a laugh. "Is that why your responses sounded so rehearsed?" He patted his mom's shoulder. "Thanks for the effort, Mom."

She blushed. "I just didn't want to say the wrong thing, especially given my reaction last time."

Matt's laugh flowed freely now as he clasped his acceptance envelope to his chest. *Life still sucks, but for today, it's okay.*

"*Din Tai Fung* sounds perfect, Mom."

CHAPTER 29

JACK

———

"I suspect your trial will not conclude until mid-May," the white-haired man named Mr. Jenkins said to Jack.

"May? That's another two months away!" Jack clenched his shackled fists angrily. "I can't sit in here anymore!" he shouted.

He despised this frail man with a balding head and ugly, thin lips. Jack had not heard from his father since he said goodbye to him on New Year's Day. However, one of the last things Jack's father had done for him was hire Mr. Jenkins to represent Jack in court.

While Mr. Jenkins initially refused this strange Chinese man who mysteriously called him through a translator, he certainly understood dollar signs and zeros and was easy to persuade. Mr. Jenkins, one of the best lawyers in the Los Angeles region with distant ties to O.J. Simpsons's "Dream Team," was paid $2 million upfront to help Jack fight his case, plus an additional $2.5 million if Jack was given no jail time.

Now they were stuck with one another.

"There is no normal timeframe for trials in the US, and the police department took a month to conduct a comprehensive investigation. You also have a complex case that requires significant amounts of paperwork and preparation," Mr. Jenkins said in a matter-of-fact voice. "As an international student, you cannot be released on bail, and I had to pull more than a few strings before the judge agreed to not send you off to a grand jury. At least in the juvenile system, you'll have a more lenient sentence."

Jack pursed his lips. "How do I even know you're doing your job correctly?"

"By the very fact that I saved you from almost destroying the case during your preliminary hearing." Mr. Jenkins looked over his spectacles disapprovingly. "Your stubborn refusal to respond to any of the judge's questions did not set a good tone. You should be grateful."

"So, what do I do now, old man?"

"I would appreciate it if you would be patient and wait until the trial," Mr. Jenkins responded in a flat voice, ignoring Jack's name-calling.

"And what exactly are my charges at the hearing?"

"Vehicular manslaughter, a DUI, and minor in possession of alcohol."

Jack stared at him dumbfounded. "That's stupid. Yeah, I wasn't in the right headspace while driving, but that dude should have seen me speeding toward him from a mile away. I barely drank anything."

Mr. Jenkins listed off all of his points like they were part of an instructional manual. "Number one—your alcohol blood level was three times above the legal limit. Number two—you're under twenty-one and, therefore, not within the legal confines to drink in this country. Number three—if you continue to show no remorse for the victim, the judge is surely handing you the maximum sentence for vehicular manslaughter."

"Ugh!" Jack dropped his head between his handcuffed hands. He hated this ugly polyester uniform. *I can't stand these peasant clothes anymore.*

"Promise me now that I'm not going to end up locked away here forever," he demanded.

"I'm a lawyer, Jack. I never guarantee anything." Mr. Jenkins stroked his stubbled chin. "However, I do think I can build a strong defense case based on another car accident by Ethan Couch in 2015."[64]

"What happened to Ethan Couch?" Jack asked, his curiosity momentarily overriding the itchiness of his polyester orange jumpsuit.

"Well, something very similar to your case. When Ethan was a teenager, he was driving drunk and killed four people while seriously injuring two others. The prosecutors at the time sought twenty years in jail time. At least the prosecutors on your case are only seeking six years."

"Wait, they're seeking *six years*? Can't they just deport me back to China?" Jack began to knock his forehead against the cold, metal table.

"Not unless you happen to know the President of China."

"Well, I technically went to elementary school with his niece..." Jack began.

Mr. Jenkins interjected. "No, I mean if the president is actually your dad. Wealth only gets you so far. This applies across all countries and cultures. You need power as well."

"Whatever," Jack half-waved his shackled hand in a dismissing motion, understanding he wasn't going to get out

---

64 Madison Park, "Ethan Couch of 'affluenza' case released from jail," *CNN*, April 2, 2018.

through connections. "Finish your story. What happened to Ethan?"

"The prosecutors claimed that Ethan was the victim of 'affluenza.'"[65] A flash of ridicule glowed in Mr. Jenkins' eyes when he said 'affluenza,' but it was so fast Jack couldn't tell if he imagined it.

"Affluenza? What is that?"

"Like I was about to explain, affluenza applies to very wealthy and privileged children like yourself..."

Jack nodded furiously.

"...because these privileged kids never had anyone set limits for them, they end up having a lack of motivation in life, sense of isolation, and a blatant disregard for rules and consequences."

"Uh, yeah, lost you there. I have a perfect GPA on top of several championship award. I have a best friend back in China, and I only bend rules when I feel like they're stupid," Jack shot back. *This whole situation is stupid.*

"Jack, if you want this argument to work you need to stop giving ammunition to the prosecuting team. A psychologist is going to evaluate you and assess whether or not you have affluenza. For this to work, he has to diagnose you with it," Mr. Jenkins responded sternly.

"So you're saying Ethan got off the hook by claiming this so-called 'affluenza?'" Jack shivered. He suddenly felt extremely cold.

"Yes. He was given no prison time and ten years of probation instead. The four victims' families were devastated at the time," Mr. Jenkins reflected. "In your case, the judge will probably count your current juvenile detention time as

---

65   Ibid.

time served, deport you back to China, and blacklist you from returning to the US."

"That sounds like a *great* deal to me," Jack exclaimed. He couldn't wait to be back with his best friend Tim and partying in high-end nightclubs with hot girls along the Shanghai Bund.

I'm so done with the US. I never liked it in the first place.

"Okay, so what do I need to do now, Mr. Jenkins?" Jack said eagerly.

"For starters, you can just be yourself. I suspect the psychologist will have no problem coming up with a diagnosis of affluenza."

Jack shot Mr. Jenkins a glare. "What is *that* supposed to mean? Isn't this some made up diagnosis just like all the other random mental health issues Americans like to come up with?"

Mr. Jenkins stiffened. "I'd recommend simply conversing with the psychologist and letting the doctor make his or her own diagnosis. I'm assuming your trophies and accolades were oftentimes driven by parental pressure and self-image, which should strengthen the diagnosis. The psychologist will make the right judgment."

"Time's up!" a prison guard barked from the corner of the room.

"Guess that's my cue to leave. Keep on holding up, kid."

Jack could have sworn he heard Mr. Jenkins sigh a breath of relief before he gathered up his leather briefcase, gave a quick nod, and disappeared out the door swiftly.

Jack was left all alone again.

"Time to go back to your cell, *chink*," the prison guard shouted.

Jack got up slowly with a scowl but ignored the guard. He was so used to all the racial slurs at the prison that he was completely numb to them. "Yup," he responded.

He dragged his feet toward the metal exit door. He had never yearned for his bespoke memory foam mattress so badly in his life. Instead, all he had here was a cellmate covered in face tattoos and filthy toilets with no privacy.

How am I going to survive?

CHAPTER 30

FELIX, PAUL, AND SIERRA

———

FELIX

Felix rubbed his nose. After Paul broke it two months ago, it had healed completely. But he still flinched at the memory. The fact that Sierra had profusely apologized to Felix for the experience, as if *she* was the one who threw a crazy temper tantrum, certainly didn't help either.

The edge of his lips twitched. *He's finally getting what he deserves. After this, he'll know what it's like to drop from the top of the world into absolute hell.*

Any day now, Paul was going to get arrested. Felix had waited patiently for this for almost a year. Paul had, unsurprisingly, received his USC acceptance letter earlier this morning.

Even with Paul's shitty AP scores he still got into USC. Felix smirked. *Must be due to his athlete and legacy status, I guess. Works great for my plan at least.*

Felix purposely waited for April 1, USC's college admissions notification date (and ironically also April Fool's), to send the police the video recording of Paul studying the stolen AP exams. He wanted them to arrest his older brother right when Paul thought he was utterly invincible.

Felix calculated and charted out every type of scenario in his brain, including the police department questioning the origins of the evidence. Luckily, Felix had attached his spy camera to Paul's backpack, where anyone, inside the house or at Winchester, could have planted it.

Felix walked over to his laptop to see if the download was complete. He had encrypted the video recording and made an untraceable throwaway email account. With the help of his VPN, the sender's location for the evidence would be from the middle-of-nowhere Russia. Seeing the loaded green bar, Felix smiled and cracked his knuckles.

Paul will never see what's coming.

PAUL

"Paul? Are you coming down?" his mom shouted from downstairs. "Sergeant Gomez is waiting!"

Paul detected a tinge of worry in her voice. He wanted to punch a hole in the wall. After his last conversation with Sergeant Gomez about the AP tests, he thought he was off the hook. But now she was in his living room.

I literally just got into USC yesterday. I should be partying it up right now, not talking to a cop.

"Coing, Mom!" he shouted. "Just, uh, getting dressed!" In reality, he was throwing things around in his room trying to figure out what to do next.

Will Mom and Dad have my back? They always do.

Paul got up, took a deep breath, straightened his back, and glanced at the mirror. He saw a smart, handsome, future Trojan college student with the signature Jones bright blue eyes staring right back at him. He flashed a sideways grin at himself in the mirror. There was no way the police could suspect him. How could they? He was the golden boy, Paul Jones.

***

"Good to see you again, Paul," Sergeant Gomez stated in a voice devoid of emotion as Paul emerged in the doorway of his father's massive study. Shelves of rare and unread first-edition books circulated the room as sunlight spilled in through floor-to-ceiling windows.

He greeted Sergeant Gomez with a masked peppy "great to see you again" before glancing at his dad seated in the large Herman Miller leather chair. Paul gulped. He could see his dad's fingers drumming impatiently against the mahogany desk as his mom motioned for him to take a seat in an engraved oak chair across from Sergeant Gomez.

He confidently strode over to take a seat and raised his eyebrows. *Wow, Mom must be really stressed. Is Sergeant Gomez holding a cup from her British Royal collection?*

The china was only reserved for the most important guests in the Joneses' house.

"What's up, Sergeant Gomez?" Paul hoped Sergeant Gomez didn't detect the hint of anxiety in his voice.

Sergeant Gomez's foreboding gaze latched onto his. "Paul, I'll get straight to the point. There has been a breakthrough in the case. It involves you."

"What? Me?" Paul asked innocently, hoping she didn't notice his eye twitching. He slicked back his hair with one hand, attempting to put on the most befuddled expression.

"Yes. You." Sergeant Gomez took a sip of coffee from the china cup.

"Paul, what is Sergeant Gomez talking about?" his dad boomed in a deep voice laced with dangerous anger.

Paul felt the hairs on the back of his neck shoot straight up. His dad was not the most patient person, and having a police officer inquiring about Paul was surely going to lead to painful consequences later. "I have no idea, Dad," he quickly replied in a small voice. "I seriously don't. Sergeant Gomez, I don't know what you're implying."

"There's evidence that shows the culprit studying the AP tests."

Paul's entire body went stiff. "And you think that's me?" *Is it possible? How could anyone have filmed me that night? Was it through the window?* A cascade of questions twisted in his brain, and each scenario seemed more implausible than the next.

"Yes. In fact, we're confident," Sergeant Gomez maintained, her gaze never leaving Paul's.

His mom looked frantically between him, the sergeant, and his dad. She turned to Sergeant Gomez. "Sergeant Gomez, please, you're being so cryptic. What video? Are you sure you saw this correctly? I know my son very well, and he would never do something like what you're talking about."

Yes, Mom. Thank you. I knew you'd have my back.

"Mrs. Jones, I know this may come as a shock to you, but without a doubt, your son was the one studying the AP exams in the video." She turned to Paul. "Paul, this is your last chance. If you willingly turn yourself in, the charges will be lighter."

This. Is. Not. Happening. Paul wanted to sprint out of the room. Why did the sergeant make it sound like he was about to get arrested? *Could I be criminally charged for this? What about USC?* He couldn't be involved in a police investigation now. They would rescind their offer without any hesitation. The sergeant was probably bluffing anyway.

"Sergeant Gomez, I have no idea what you're talking about," he declared defiantly.

"See. My son is telling the truth," his mom immediately added on.

"Well, then, you leave me no choice." Sergeant Gomez set down her cup and stood from her seat. "Paul Jones, I hereby place you under arrest for a school break-in and burglary. You have the right to remain silent and refuse to answer questions. Anything you say may be used against you in a court of law. You have the right to consult an attorney before speaking to the police and to have an attorney present during questioning now or in the future." She whipped out handcuffs.

Paul felt his stomach drop. *Shit. Shit. Shit!*

"Sergeant Gomez, there will be no such arrest in my house!" his dad slammed down a fist, knocking over his own coffee and splattering it all over the desk. "This arrest is illegal without any evidence!"

"Mr. Jones, like I said, we have evidence," Sergeant Gomez replied. She snapped her attention back to Paul. "Hands, please."

Paul felt like the air had been taken out of him. He couldn't move. He couldn't think of any words. Nothing. He numbly held out his hands and felt the metal clasps clink shut around his wrists. Sergeant Gomez began to push him out of the room.

"Sergeant Gomez, please! There must be some mistake!" his mom screamed behind him. In a split-second decision, Paul tried to make a run for it. Like lightning, Sergeant Gomez grabbed his shirt by the scruff of his neck and threw him to the ground. "Don't even think about it," she barked.

"Get your hands off of him! He just got accepted into college!" his mom continued shouting, attempting to pull Sergeant Gomez away from Paul. All one hundred pounds of her stood no chance against Sergeant Gomez's strong grip on his arms.

Paul looked up from the ground and saw Sierra and Felix peering into the study from the hallway. *Is Felix smiling?* He thought about his brother's lights the night of him receiving the AP tests. A realization dawned on him.

"It was you, Felix! It was you!" Paul began to tear against the handcuffs like a hyena.

"Stop blaming everyone but yourself!" Sergeant Gomez shouted, continuing to drag him away.

He heard his dad behind him already on the phone with a lawyer. *Maybe this will be okay. I'm going to be okay.*

He dropped his head and began to bawl. Paul Jones no longer felt like a golden child.

SIERRA

Sierra helplessly watched as Paul, releasing earth-shattering sobs, was dragged away.

Why is he in handcuffs? Only minutes earlier, she was video chatting with Stacy about her future K-1 visa stepmom from Thailand[66] when she heard her mom screaming. Against Stacy's protests to stay on the phone (they hadn't yet gossiped about the new rumor that Jack's jail cell was a room in the Ritz Carlton), Sierra hung up on her and raced

---

66 Stacy Williams's dad apparently went to Thailand on a "singles dad" trip when he met a girl twenty years his junior in a "cafe." It was love at first sight and he proposed to her three days later. Mr. Williams now plans to bring her back to the US on a K-1, a.k.a. fiancé, visa.

over to her dad's study to find Sergeant Gomez slamming Paul to the ground.

She knew Sergeant Gomez arrived earlier to speak with her parents about the stolen AP tests, but she never believed the culprit could be Paul. He was not smart enough for such an elaborate operation.

Felix stood beside her while Paul began to scream. Her eyes narrowed. *Why is Paul accusing Felix?*

She stared at her youngest brother. Sierra always felt bad for Felix. Ever since they were little, he had been a constant punching bag, both physically and mentally, for all of Paul's emotions. While she tried her best to stop those attacks, it was nearly impossible to monitor them at all times.

Felix's lips curled into a smile. Sierra's entire body paralyzed in response. *Could it be? Could it really have been Felix?*

Felix certainly was cunning enough to do it. She wasn't exactly sure what he did in his room all the time, but she knew, out of everyone in the family, Felix was smarter than all of them combined.

Paul and her parents' shouting began to muffle as the group moved outside toward the police cruiser.

Sierra decided to swoop in. "Felix, was it you?"

Felix jumped in surprise. "Oh, hey. Crazy what's going on, huh?"

"Answer my question," she demanded. "Was it you?"

"Was I what?" Felix mumbled.

"Did you steal the AP tests and then plant it on Paul?"

"Psh. Why would I do that?" Felix said with a wave of a hand.

"Felix, I'm not dumb." Her eyes narrowed. "I know you hate Paul, and I have to admit, I had my suspicions he had something to do with it when he received perfect scores after clearly not studying. But Paul isn't clever enough to actually steal anything. I just figured he knew who stole it and had threatened the answers out of the real thief."

For a split second, it looked like Felix's face broke into a flash of smugness, but it was quickly replaced again with a blank stare.

"Felix, just tell me the truth. I promise I won't be mad. In fact, if it really was you, I feel like you'd have all the right in the world to want to do something like this," Sierra implored.

"Can we go back to my room and chat?" Felix robotically marched into his room, not waiting for his sister's response.

As soon as Sierra entered her little brother's dark room with a distinct scent of cheesy crackers, Felix shut the door behind them.

Sierra waited for Felix to say something, but he just stared at her, mute.

"Felix... was it really you?" Sierra asked hesitantly. A long expanse of silence dragged between them.

Felix finally spoke up. "Sierra, you know I can never lie to you, right?" he said softly. "I just... he... he just needed to go." Sierra watched her little brother's expressionless mask break into dozens of tiny pieces of pain, anger, and resentment.

"Oh, Felix..." Sierra walked over to him, unsure whether to scold him or give him a hug. "What have you done? I don't think you realize how big this can get."

"I know exactly what is going to happen. Paul is going to get some misdemeanor charge and then expelled from Winchester. His USC dreams?" Felix snapped his fingers. "*Poof.*"

Sierra gaped in shock at her little brother, astonished at the coldness in his voice.

"But Felix, if Paul ever finds out you were the one who stole the AP tests, and it seems like he's already suspicious of you, he's *never* going to let you live this down," Sierra exclaimed. "He might actually *kill* you."

"He has already killed me in so many ways, Sierra," Felix replied, turning away from her. "I don't care anymore."

Sierra felt like her heart was about to crack open. *How did I never notice?* All the years of Paul's torture had turned Felix into a shell of himself. While Paul grew into a fiery monster at home, Felix had turned into a stone-cold kid.

"Felix, I'm so sorry that I haven't been there for you," Sierra whispered.

His eyes widened. "Sierra, what are you talking about? You're the only person I can genuinely call my family."

She felt her eyes begin to water. *Is it possible that doing the wrong thing could actually be the right thing?* She didn't want Paul to be falsely imprisoned, but staring into her little brother's eyes made her think maybe that's exactly where Paul belonged.

But if Paul's life is ruined, will it truly solve Felix's issues? Sierra certainly didn't think so.

"Felix," Sierra began. "I know you hate Paul and I know he's been nothing but horrible to you, but you can't go through with this. You have to tell the truth."

"You mean turn myself in?" Felix's face suddenly flared with anger. "After all of that—after months of plotting, of stealing the AP tests, of planting it onto Paul, you want me to turn *myself in*?"

"Yes," Sierra said, although she wasn't so sure herself. "I know this sounds crazy, but you can't have Paul go to jail for something he didn't do. He's awful, but still our brother."

"He'll only get up to a year if they actually charge him. Most likely, it will be some monetary fine. I already did my research about this. And he's *your* brother, not mine."

"Felix... think about how this will affect *you*. You're a bigger and better person than this. I know it. Can you handle the guilt?"

"Who are you to decide how I will feel?" Felix seethed. "You know what? I thought you were different from everyone else, but maybe you really are just like the rest of the family—doing anything it takes to protect the 'Jones' image, including sacrificing me in the process."

"No, Felix, that's one hundred percent not what I'm trying to say. I just—"

"Get out!" Felix screamed, cutting Sierra off. It was like a switch flipped in his head. He grabbed her arm and yanked her out of the room before slamming the door.

Sierra's entire face crumbled as she slumped down into a ball outside of Felix's room. *How did things become like this? We have everything, yet we have nothing.*

She had a sudden urge to be in Hunter's embrace. He always lent a shoulder for her to lean on whenever her family was blowing up, and it certainly was now more than ever. *But you broke up with him, remember?* a voice whispered in her head. At this point, Sierra didn't care. She whipped out her phone:

Sierra: What are you doing right now?

CHAPTER 31

HUNTER

—

April 1, the near-nationwide last day for colleges to notify students about their admissions decisions, had ended not with a bang, but with a whimper. Hunter had always imagined this day as one of celebration, but instead, it just felt... numb.

He soldiered through writing and submitting all of his other college applications following his Stanford rejection, but it felt like everything was done in a depressive haze. Without Sierra, without Stanford, everything felt meaningless.

Hunter looked at the Post-It notes with his messy handwriting stuck onto his wall. There were three piles—rejection, waitlist, and acceptances. Harvard? Rejection. Yale? Waitlist.[67] USC? Acceptance. The Post-It notes in the acceptance pile went on and on.

He knew he should be happy. He had acceptances from almost all of his target schools, but it still didn't dull the pain of not getting into any of the HYSP schools. Hunter let out a painful sigh and closed his eyes.

---

67 With a mere 1.7 percent of applicants getting off of Yale's waitlist last year, according to the forums on *College Confidential*, there was no way Hunter was getting in.

"What are you sighing about?" Hunter opened his eyes and turned to his sister by the doorway. Without asking, she marched straight into the room and laid down on his couch.

"I don't know, I just thought this moment would be different, you know?" Hunter replied dejectedly, turning away from his Post-It note wall.

Trisha scoffed. "Are you serious right now? Stop being a drama queen. Getting into schools like Berkeley, USC, and NYU are absolute *dreams* for most people."

Humiliation and shame pricked at Hunter's skin. "I *know*, okay?" he snapped. He marched over to his bed and laid down, staring at his blank, white ceiling. "I just can't stand the fact that Mom and Dad have barely acknowledged any of my acceptances. It's like they've completely given up on me."

"This is about the call last night, huh?"

Hunter winced. He hated to admit it, but he had become one of those kids who desperately wanted his parents to be happy together, even though he knew whatever relationship they had with one another was beyond repair.

His parents drilled that point home for him last night when they began arguing with one another over which college Hunter would attend.

"Hector, stop being an idiot. You know *I'm* the one paying most of his college tuition, not you. Your accountant's salary can barely cover the mortgage on this house," his mom had shouted into the speaker phone when his dad had suggested that Hunter attend Berkeley because tuition costs would be lower in-state.

"Maybe the mortgage of this house wouldn't be so high if you hadn't decided it was necessary to buy a gigantic mansion with eight rooms and a sauna no one ever uses," his dad had screamed back.

The night had ended with his mom screeching, "I can't wait until our divorce is finalized!"

Hunter blinked back tears. The worst part of not getting into some "name brand" college was his parents projecting all their frustrations out onto him *and* each other.

Hunter snapped himself out of his thoughts, realizing Trisha had come up to him and placed a hand on his shoulder.

"Hunter, you literally got into Paul Jones's dream school," she said softly.

"Again, I know," Hunter skulked with little enthusiasm. Not even the thought of Hunter potentially going to Paul's dream school instead of Paul himself could make him feel a twinge of joy.

"But you were hoping for Stanford, huh?" Trisha stared at a Stanford throw on Hunter's couch, one he would have already thrown away if it hadn't been a Christmas gift from Matt sophomore year.

"Yeah," Hunter huffed. "I know, I'm being ungrateful and horrible. I hate myself even more for not feeling happier when others would die for the acceptances that I've gotten."

"It's understandable to feel that way when we've been trained to think anything less than number one is not okay."

A buzzing sound turned Trisha's attention away to her phone.

"Sorry, I've got to get this," she said quickly. "It's Pam. She had some explosive conversation with her parents."

Hunter waved his hand, still staring at the ceiling. "Go. Just let me sulk in peace."

He didn't have to look to know that Trisha was eye-rolling at him right now. "You need to get out of your self-pitying head and get it together."

"You sound like Mom."

"Ugh!" Trisha flung her hands up in frustration. Her phone continued to buzz. She picked up. "Pam?" Hunter heard her walk away without another word.

I really should be happier. My life could be Paul's right now.

While he and Sierra stayed broken up, she had reached out to Hunter again yesterday after Paul was arrested for the stolen AP exam scandal.

Even though they had only been texting for one day, it almost felt like it was back to old times. Sierra even confided to Hunter about how Felix was the true mastermind behind stealing the AP tests and then planting them on Paul. *That sweet, awkward kid who could barely look me in the eye took down Paul Jones? Props to him.*

Hunter dug out his own phone from his pocket and saw he had two instant message notifications.

Matt: Yo. Game later?

Hunter quickly messaged back, "sure." While Matt's New Year's kiss was insanely awkward, and Hunter now made sure to not do anything remotely intimate with Matt, he was still his best friend. An accidental kiss was not going to change that, especially when Hunter knew neither one of them actually felt anything for one another. *Hopefully.*

He opened up his second message:

Sierra: Thx for the chat last night. The venting really helped...

He smiled.

Hunter: Yeah, anytime. I'm always here for you <3

While Hunter did not care that Paul's life was ruined, Sierra was extremely distraught. She didn't know what to do with the truth, and the Jones home had apparently turned into a nuclear war zone after Paul came back with a $1,000 fine, an expulsion from Winchester, and an instant revocation of his USC acceptance.

Serves him right.

Hunter had no sympathy for Paul, but for Sierra's sake, he hoped everything worked out okay. *I wonder if Sierra and I will ever be the same again?* Hunter drew in a long breath and opened up his photo album to scroll through old pictures of them together. He never stopped loving Sierra, and he knew she was the only one he ever wanted to be with for his entire life.

But I also majorly screwed it up. Hunter sighed. *At least I can be here for her during this rough patch, boyfriend or not.*

Later that night, as Hunter laid in bed about to close his eyes, he felt an immense sense of relief overcome him. The relief of knowing he was just going somewhere and bringing a conclusion to an entire lifetime of building up a rejection-proof resume meant that, for the first time in forever, Hunter could sleep without thinking about college admissions. He could now dream about how amazing college was going to be.

CHAPTER 32

RAY AND TRISHA

RAY

Ray cursed under his breath. *I'm a dumbass.*

He beat himself up for months now. He felt an energy shift in the dynamic between Trisha and him that day outside of the hospital. He had a perfect shot to kiss her.

But when she closed her eyes and waited for him to make a move, he became paralyzed with fear. It was as if his usual fearless and impulsive self abandoned him in that crucial moment.

What was I thinking?

He chewed the inside of his cheek. Trisha and he never talked about that moment again. Nowadays, she barely wanted to speak to him. He missed being with her and staring at the mirth in her eyes when she told dumb jokes, or when she scrunched up her face whenever she was about to call him out on his crap. It didn't take too many brain cells to figure out Ray had not only missed his shot but also ruined a friendship.

He scrubbed his face with his hands and groaned.

"What are you fussing about?" his mom said in Spanish from behind him. "Why do all the kids these days make it sound like the world is ending?"

Ray turned around. His mom had her back to him, preparing *masa harina* for the homemade corn tortillas they were having for dinner tomorrow. The cluttered kitchen had every type of cookware that one could think of. His mom, a serial cook and baker, had the entire block rotating through their kitchen around mealtimes in the hopes of getting a taste of Señora Martinez's classic Mexican dishes. Tonight was no different. Moving like a hurricane through the brightly colored and cozy kitchen, his mom was whipping up a storm.

"Nothing…" Ray mumbled in English, having almost forgotten that he had raw, marinating chicken in his hands.

His mom turned around and wiped her plump hands onto her apron. "*Hijo*, do you forget that I'm your mother? I always know when something is bothering you."

Ugh. Should I tell her? Ray felt torn. He didn't feel like his love life was her business, but then again… he was the ultimate mama's boy, a stark contrast to the chill, rebellious vibe that he liked to portray outside of the house.

"Do you remember Trisha?" Ray began hesitantly.

"Yes, the *chica* with the bright eyes and smooth skin." His mom reached over for a large kitchen knife and began dicing tomatoes like a professional sous chef. "Did you confess your love to her yet?"

Ray's face instantly flushed. "Mama, if you're going to be like this I'm not going to continue!"

"Sorry, continue," his mom replied with a wave of a hand. She set aside the diced tomatoes before taking out the molcajete to make the salsa.

Ray took a deep breath and continued again. "As you clearly have guessed, I really like her. We had a moment together a few months back, but I ended up kind of rejecting her."

"What do you mean, 'kind of?'" his mom asked. Ray felt like he could detect a hint of boredom in her voice, but he couldn't tell if he was imagining it. She heated up a cast iron pan and threw peppers, tomatoes, onion, and garlic into it.

"She thought I was going to kiss her, but instead I changed my mind last minute and asked to leave instead."

His mom raised her eyebrows. "Why would you do that?"

Ray frowned. "She's generous, beautiful, comes from a wealthy family, and I swear she's going to end up at Harvard one day. Meanwhile, I'm just some ordinary, unprosperous guy who is one of the only scholarship kids at the academy. In other words, we're too different for one another." Ray ignored his growling stomach as the aroma of the blackening vegetables swarmed the kitchen.

"So what? You're the smartest one in the school, and I don't just say that because I'm your mother." His mom returned to the *masa harina* mixture and began to aggressively beat it.

"I don't know if that's enough to keep Trisha happy. I feel like she's meant for some millionaire guy who wines and dines her and can converse with her family in Mandarin."

His mom turned toward him and put her hands on her hips. "Has Trisha ever said this to you?"

"Nope, but I just know."

His mom released a torrent of *tsks*. "*Ser valiente!*[68] From the sounds of it, she clearly feels the same way for you, but you chickened out instead. Who are you to decide who Trisha

---

68   Spanish for "be brave."

likes or dislikes? You've been watching way too many tele-novelas with me."

"But we're so different, Mama." Ray began to doubt himself even more. "She mentioned before how her parents struggled with the idea of dating outside of their own race too. Her older brother used to date this white girl in her class, and they had so many issues."

"Were they issues because the girl was white or issues because they were not a good fit for one another?"

Ray paused. He never considered this question before. He just assumed that Hunter and Sierra fell apart because their backgrounds didn't align. "I'm... I'm actually not too sure..."

"Then the *pareja*[69] have issues not because of race but because of their own personalities," his mother said in a matter-of-fact voice.

"I guess... I don't know... Is it even possible to go back? This happened months ago, and I haven't done anything to fix the situation." Ray initially wanted to apologize to Trisha right away, but the more time passed, and the more Trisha stayed away from him, the easier it was to go with the more convenient choice of not doing anything at all.

"Look, *chico*, you're just asking me for approval now on something you've clearly already made your mind up about." His mother shook her head, *tsk*ed again, and went back to the stove to fish out her vegetables and peel off the blackened skin. "If you like her, then say it. Don't beat around the bush. I don't care if she's black, yellow, white, or even blue. If you like her, I like her."

Ray furrowed his eyebrows. *Maybe I am overthinking this...* He stared out the window at the orange trees growing

---

69 Spanish for "couple."

in their backyard. He took a deep breath. *Screw the what ifs. I'm asking Trisha Wang out.*

"Mama," Ray grinned from ear to ear, "you're the best."

His mom shook her head like her son had just said the most obvious statement in the world. "Yes, yes, of course I am. I gave life to you. Just remember that maintaining a relationship is much harder than getting into one."

Ray nodded his head enthusiastically, his mom's last statement barely landing on him. He was already planning the next steps.

His mom snapped her fingers in his face without her eyes ever leaving another hot pan that she now filled with sizzling ground pork. "Stop standing there like a rock and go fetch me the dried beans from the pantry," his mom commanded.

Ray began to make a beeline for the closet, stuffed with all different types of spices, rice, beans, and chiles. "Yes, Mama."

***

The following day, Ray found himself on the swings in a park near Trisha's house. It took some intense coaxing for her to agree to meet up, especially one-on-one, but she finally gave in after he promised it would only take thirty minutes of her time.

As he swung up and down in the air, calming down his nerves, he didn't notice Trisha had walked up alongside the swing until she gave him a hard push that sent him flying even higher.

"Woah!" Ray shouted, clamoring to an immediate stop. He turned around and saw Trisha laughing mischievously on the side. *She's cute even when she's diabolical*, Ray thought to himself.

"Sorry," Trisha said, "I couldn't help myself."

"Uh huh, right," Ray responded with an exaggerated eye roll. "Anyway, thanks for coming."

"Yep," Trisha combed her fingers through her hair, avoiding direct eye contact with Ray. "What's up?"

"Nothing much... well, not nothing... I just..." Ray suddenly felt incredibly self-conscious. Only Trisha could turn him into a stammering, clammy kid. "Do you want to take a seat, actually?" Ray said pointing to the swing beside him.

"Um, sure... I haven't sat in one of these since I was in middle school. Maybe even elementary school?" Trisha sat down onto the swing anyway and then finally looked at Ray directly in the eye. "You're acting really... strange."

"Yeah... I guess it's because..." Ray felt his throat tighten as he dragged in a deep breath. "I wanted to talk to you about that afternoon at the hospital a couple months back. You know, when we were sitting by the fountain."

"Right... the fountain..." Trisha said awkwardly.

"Yeah... I just wanted to say..." Ray felt his voice hitch in his throat. "I, uh... I was going to tell you I really liked you at the fountain that day, Trisha, and I still really like you."

TRISHA

Trisha wanted to implode. Ray, *Ray Martinez*, just said he *liked* her. Yet, her swirl of butterflies was quickly eclipsed by pure confusion.

After that day at the fountain, she had been absolutely heartbroken. She always thought they might be something more, but he was so infuriatingly cryptic she always had doubts about his true feelings. When he finally leaned in toward her at the fountain, she believed she was finally going to get her answers. Instead, it felt like she was slapped in the face.

Trisha decided he did not share the same feelings as her and, in fact, might have just been playing her all along. Since then, in order to mend her broken heart, she pulled away from him and spoke to him less and less.

But I guess I was wrong. Trisha narrowed her eyes. *Then why did he pull away from me like I was nothing to him?*

"Trisha, why are you so silent?" Ray smothered her with his eyes. "Say something, anything."

She focused her attention back on him. "I'm just confused. I thought we might have been something more that day, but you just completely blew me off by pulling away when you clearly were leaning in to kiss me. Like, what am I supposed to do with these mixed messages?"

Ray reached over and wrapped his hand around hers, pulling her swing closer to him.

Trisha's heart involuntarily thrummed.

"I get that." Ray gazed apologetically into her eyes. "And you have every right to be confused. It's not that I didn't want to kiss you that day. I just... I had a lot of doubts about how we would be together, romantically. I didn't think our backgrounds were a good fit for one another."

While the feeling of Ray's warm hand over hers definitely made Trisha's head spin, it wasn't enough to stop her confusion, sadness, and heartbreak from the past few months to rise to the surface. She snatched her hand away from Ray's.

"But who are you to decide that for the both of us?" Her eyes blazed and she stood up from the swing to tower over Ray. "So what? Ray Martinez decides we won't work out, so he makes no move, and out of thin air decides it's okay now?"

Adrenaline coursed through her veins. *This is bull-shit. I don't need someone who is has doubts.* She turned to walk away.

"No, no," Ray quickly grabbed Trisha's wrist. "That's not what I meant. That came out wrong. I just wanted to be absolutely sure about us before making a decision. I was scared I wasn't good enough for you."

Trisha startled at Ray's last sentence. "Not good enough?" Trisha flipped around to face him again. "How could you ever possibly think that? You're literally the smartest and funniest guy I've ever met. I love being around you. If anything, *I'm* the one who isn't good enough for *you*."

Ray let go of Trisha's wrist and looked down at the sand in shame and embarrassment.

"It's because you mean so much to me, Trish. And while we're amazing friends, I also want to spoil you as a boyfriend." Ray grimaced. "Let's be real. Just look at my car and then look at yours. I don't know if I can give you all the gifts and dates you want." Ray dug his shoe back and forth into the sand beneath it. "There won't be Michelin-star meals, fancy gifts, or even those surfing lessons Hunter used to take Sierra on."

What Ray was trying to say finally dawned on Trisha. *Why are boys so clueless?*

"Are you being serious?" Trisha was so incredulous that she almost laughed. She sat back down onto the swing and leaned toward Ray. "Did it ever seem like I even cared about nice gifts or dates? My happiest time with you was when we went to a *grocery store*, for goodness' sakes."

"I... I guess... I didn't think about that..." Ray's eyes looked up from the ground and met Trisha's. "I didn't mean to hurt you."

"Why today? Why this minute? Why are you now telling me this?" Trisha pressed. She felt like she was gaining more questions than answers.

"To be honest... I talked to my mom and realized I was being an idiot..."

She burst out laughing.

"Hey!" Ray shouted, his face bright red. "Leave me alone. She gives good advice! It's a stereotype that girls are always the ones overthinking."

"Clearly, considering the list of excuses you made about us not working out without even asking for my opinion first. I'm just glad your mom brought you back to your brain." Trisha gasped for breath from laughing so hard. He began laughing with her, breaking the intense mood that clouded over them.

As their laughter finally wore down, Ray started talking again. "I *do* think with my brain. I just needed time. I like you too much to screw it up."

Trisha fell silent for a moment, staring deep into his emerald green eyes that never ceased to make her heart skip a beat—the same twinkling eyes that stared at her on day one in Mr. Johnson's Calculus class. "I like you too," Trisha confessed. "I really like you." Trisha didn't hold back this time or wait for Ray to make a move. She leaned toward him and brushed her lips against Ray's. His lips curved against hers in a smile before leaning in deeper.

Trisha felt so blissfully alive.

CHAPTER 33

FELIX

———

One thousand and two. One thousand and three. One thousand and four. Felix paced back and forth in his room, counting each step as it fell lightly across the hardwood floor.

"Three months? That's outrageous. The AP tests weren't even worth any monetary value," his dad stormed. "Paul is already expelled from school. Isn't that punishment enough?"

He flinched at the loud volume and turned it down. Felix had planted a spy camera in the family living room long ago, and the room's conversation was now playing directly into his wireless headphones. Thanks to Mr. Jenkins, a lawyer and family friend, Paul quickly returned home after his parents paid the measly bail amount. Now, his parents and Mr. Jenkins sat downstairs discussing the plan to negotiate a fine and probation time instead of jail time.

"What college will ever accept him now?" his mom whimpered in the background.

"Unfortunately, the school's decision to punish him is not mutually exclusive from the charges he's currently facing by the prosecutor," Mr. Jenkin's calm and steady voice responded.

As an eighteen-year-old, Paul faced up to three months in county jail. There was no denying that Paul had studied the AP tests, and while Sergeant Gomez still struggled to link him directly to the burglary of Winchester, she still charged Paul with a misdemeanor.

Felix turned the volume on his headphones back up and continued pacing. *One thousand one hundred and three. One thousand one hundred and four...*

Mr. Jenkin's continued, "While Dean Rand has elected not to press charges, the district attorney's office has taken a special interest in the case given the fact that her nephew, who also attends Winchester, had to retake his AP exams again due to the theft."

"My poor baby!" Mrs. Jones began to wail. Felix quickly threw off his headphones. *Should have kept it at the original volume.* His mom had been in a constant state of hysterics since Paul's arrest. It certainly didn't help that Paul had barely stepped foot out of his room, or eaten, since the scandal.

Felix rubbed his ears, attempting to soothe the pain.

Darn, I lost count. He cursed under his breath. *Now I have to restart.* His OCD had taken a new turn once Paul returned home. He was barely keeping it under control these days and found himself counting every single action. He walked over to his computer. *One. Two. Three.* He flipped it on. Based on the webpages Paul was visiting on his laptop (Felix had created a dashboard on the side to continue monitoring what his brother was up to), Winchester's social media flurry was tearing Paul's reputation apart.

Desperate messages from Paul to his old friends went unanswered, and "#DeletePaulJones" was now the number-one trending tag in the SGV. Paul Jones was officially a social pariah.

Felix felt a twinge of guilt. He hated to admit it, but Paul was getting punished way more than he expected. Not only that—Sierra wouldn't even look Felix in the eye anymore. For someone who always felt like a stranger to his family, he had never felt as invisible as he did now.

Felix got up again and began to pace even faster than before. *Four. Five. Six. Seven. Eight. Nine.* His long-time night owl habits had lately transformed to insomnia. Felix found it harder and harder to think every day because something inside kept gnawing at his conscience.

What is wrong with me? Felix rubbed his bloodshot eyes with his hands. He knew the answer, but he didn't like it one bit. *Am I really going to just throw years of planning down the drain? Sierra admitted it too. If anyone deserved to be in this mess it should be Paul.*

Felix stopped pacing and looked over at Buttercup, who was completely passed out on his hoodie. He walked over and began to stroke him, his mind still racing. Buttercup slowly opened his eyes and then tried to bite him. Felix barely dodged in time. *What the...?* He stared at Buttercup and swore he saw judgement in his eyes.

Will you ever be able to live this down? a tiny voice said in his head. *You clearly thought you'd be happy if Paul's life was destroyed, but you're not.*

Felix pulled his hair in frustration. Buttercup got up, clearly perturbed by Felix, and turned to face away from him.

Wow, even my cat hates me now.

Felix groaned in exasperation. *I can't live like this any-more.* He walked over to Sierra's room. *Twenty-three. Twenty-four. Twenty-five.* He quietly knocked on the door. There was some shuffling behind before she opened it up a crack.

"Oh, Felix, hey…" she said in surprise.

"Hey, um…" Felix faltered. "I… I need your help."

Concern immediately flooded her eyes. "What's wrong?" She opened her door wider. "Want to come in?"

"No," he quickly responded, turning away from her. "I need you to come out." He gestured with his hand. "I'm going to tell Mom and Dad."

Sierra's eyes widened. "What?" She stepped out into the hallway. "About… the tests?"

"I guess," he responded, still unsure about his decision. "I've thought about it, and you're right; I don't want to deal with the guilt anymore. Plus, it will be fun seeing them agonize a bit when they realize both their sons are fuck-ups."

Sierra struggled to process Felix's words. She finally spoke up, "Okay, not sure if I agree with how you arrived at the decision, but I'm still happy that you're telling the truth."

She walked toward Felix and put a hand on his shoulder. "What can I do to help?"

Felix gave a half-hearted smile. "You're just emotional support."

***

A few minutes later, Felix and Sierra walked downstairs. *Thirty-eight. Thirty-nine. Forty. Forty-one.* As they got closer to the living room, they heard his mom begin to wail again. Mr. Jenkins had just told her Paul's charge would go on his permanent record as an adult.

"Mom, Dad?" Felix asked hesitantly. Instead of looking at any one person in the room, he elected to stare at the statue of the ghastly marble bust of Ares, the Greek god of war, in the center of the living room. He felt the room fall silent as the three adult heads turned toward his sister and him.

"Kids, can't you see we're busy right now? Go back to your room," his dad demanded impatiently.

His dad turned toward Mr. Jenkins. "As I was saying—"

"Dad, this is important," Felix interjected, turning his burning eyes onto his dad. "I have something to say."

The room fell silent for a second time.

"Well, spit it out son. I swear, if—" his dad snapped.

"Dad, can you stop being a dick?" Sierra interjected.

Felix's breath hitched. It felt like all the oxygen left the room at once. *I can't believe she just—*

Without even realizing what was happening, Felix saw his dad bolt from the couch. A loud clap reverberated around the room. He looked over in shock as Sierra held her cheek in one hand, glaring at their dad.

His mom gasped, and Felix balled his hands into a tight fist. "Don't you *ever* lay a hand on her *ever* again!"

His dad turned his menacing eyes onto Felix. "And why not, especially when my daughter is being a disrespectful brat?"

"Because, *Dad*, I was the one who did everything, and I can just as likely plot and turn your lives upside down all over again if I wanted to," Felix lashed out.

His parents stared at him, unsure of what they heard.

"Sweetie, that's so kind of you to want to protect your brother," his mom said in a condescending voice. "But you're just a little boy. No one is going to believe that. Leave helping Paul to the adults."

Felix's blood began to boil. He glanced at Sierra, whose cheek was now blossoming into a bright red color. Never in his life did he want to murder his own parents than right now.

"Maybe you should act like an adult and *listen* to me for once in your life, Mom," Felix hissed. He took two steps toward them. *Fifty-one. Fifty-two.* "*I'm* the one that did everything. *I'm* the one who filmed Paul studying the AP exams. *I'm* the one who hired someone to break in. *I'm* the one who planned *everything*. And you know why? Because I *hate* Paul. I *hate* this family. And I especially *hate* both of you for never caring about anyone but your precious whittle Paul, boo, boo."

The room fell silent for a third time. It stretched long and wide—so much so that Felix began to pace. *Fifty-three. Fifty-four. Fifty-five. Fifty-six.*

"Kelsey, John, I can see this is a family conversation," Mr. Jenkins finally said. Everyone in the room looked at him in surprise, clearly forgetting there was a guest present. "I'm going to excuse myself now. If what Felix is saying is true, we'll have a lot to discuss."

With that, Mr. Jenkins grabbed his coat, fixed his large round spectacles, and walked out of the front door without another word.

Felix felt any thread of respect for Mr. Jenkins leave him. *Some lawyer you are to bounce right after seeing your client hit his kid.*

"Sierra, explain to us. What is this all about?" his mom asked his sister, barely registering Mr. Jenkins' swift departure.

"Mom, stop looking at me and look at Felix. *He's* the one who you should listen to," Sierra shrieked. Her eyes brimmed with tears of rage.

His dad turned toward him with a cruel, twisted expression. "Well, explain then."

Felix stopped pacing and stared at his dad, hating how his icy blue eyes were the same as his own. "There's nothing to explain. You all suck. You both ignore my existence to the point where I wish I was never even born sometimes. In your eyes, I'm only a vessel for you to continue some deranged dream of being part of high-class society. You see so much perfection in Paul that, even though I planted it on him, he was stupid and cocky enough to go and study the AP tests. Meanwhile, Sierra has become a Barbie for you to play around with and let your male clients ogle over."

Felix couldn't believe what he was saying, but he didn't know how to stop the firehose of rage and contempt that bottled up over the years. "Congratulations, Mom and Dad, you've raised two criminals. One with such an inflated ego that he thinks terrorizing others means they should be grateful for his attention, and a second who hates life so much that he's willing to throw everything away just so he could wipe a smile off of his brother's face."

Felix began to slow clap. "Parents of the year."

His dad's jaw fell open, stunned speechless. His mom looked like she was on the verge of bursting into tears again.

However, Felix had hit a point where he no longer cared about his parents' feelings or fearing his dad's abusive hand. He stopped caring long ago.

"I'll be in my room," he snarled. "Find me when you can actually have a respectful conversation, since, let's be real—if you want the charges against Paul dropped, you would need me to fully confess to Winchester and the police. If you want that to happen, I refuse to be treated like some sacrificial pawn for your beloved golden boy."

With that, Felix turned around, pulling Sierra with him on his way out. He felt his parents' eyes on them the entire time. After making sure Sierra was okay after the whole ordeal and apologizing for what had happened to her (she had proudly declared that was the best thing she had ever done and would take a dozen slaps to curse even worse things at their dad again), Felix returned to his own room. As he closed his door behind him the tiny voice in his came back and said, *Finally.* For the first time in a long time, Felix felt happy.

I just stuck it to my trash parents. Felix furrowed his eyebrows. *What number was I on again?*

CHAPTER 34

TRISHA AND PAMELA

TRISHA

"I love you."

Trisha turned her head to look at Ray, who had declared his love for perhaps the tenth time that day.

Trisha rolled her eyes. "I love you too—just don't count on me saying it every single waking moment."

Ray leaned in and caught a piece of hair that had fallen against her cheek and tucked it behind her ear. He smiled a devilish grin and pulled Trisha to his chest, wrapping his arms around her.

"Sorry, I just feel like I need to keep on reminding you that... especially after our rocky start," Ray whispered into her ear.

Trisha pulled away and lightly punched his arm. "That's right. I hope you feel guilty about it forever."

Ray laughed and gave her an intimate peck on the forehead. Trisha felt her heart beat faster. Even now, weeks into dating, every moment with Ray still took her breath away. She snuggled against him, letting the comforting, minty scent of Ray envelop her.

Shortly after they got together, Ray and Trisha (or more like Ray) didn't waste any time to declare their love for one another. She hadn't expected him to be so forward about it at the time, but Ray had surprised her. Once he had made up his mind about being together, he went all in.

Now, the two of them couldn't get enough of each other. Sure, after Ray's idiotic decision-making process when confessing his feelings, Trisha still felt a sense of bitterness enter the edges of her bliss now and then. But because he overcompensated for his mistake ever since (like now), she didn't mind.

And the make out sessions, Trisha thought to herself with a happy sigh. The one thing missing now was... sex... but that was a conversation for another day. Today wasn't about Trisha and Ray—today was about Pamela.

They sat outside of the Shah mansion in Trisha's car to say goodbye before Pamela headed off to an in-patient rehab center the next morning. Following the confession of her drug addiction to her parents, Pamela confided to Trisha that her relationship with her parents had ironically improved. For the first time in her life, Pamela had a heart-to-heart with them.

Trisha turned her head toward Ray. "You ready?"

"Are you ready?" Ray said, taking off his seatbelt.

She considered the question for a moment, sifting through her conflicted feelings. "Not ready to see Pamela leave for the entire summer, but ready to see her get better."

Trisha had spent summers away from Pamela before, but never without texting her daily. With electronics prohibited in the rehab center, Trisha would have to deal with a summer devoid of sassy remarks, crude jokes, and tear-inducing laughter from her best friend.

Trisha looked up at the Shah's picturesque home with purple flowers dancing across the doorstep. She suddenly thought back to a time when they were in middle school and had picked all of the flowers in the garden to make floral crowns. Mrs. Shah was so aghast at her bare front garden that she almost fainted.

Trisha's lips curved into a nostalgic smile. *I'm really going to miss her.* She stepped out of Ray's truck and began to walk toward the massive front door with his hand in hers.

PAMELA

Why in the world is therapy so expensive?

Pamela's head was drowning in numbers. After her charged and lengthy conversation with her maybe-not-so-unloving-after-all parents, Pamela was finally getting the help she so desperately needed.

Her parents, while still struggling to believe in the American system of therapy, tried their best to find a reasonable in-patient program. A part of them still didn't understand why Pamela couldn't "just stop taking drugs." However, despite their skepticism, they agreed it was time to try a new system that didn't involve brushing problems under the rug. After way too many phone calls with various centers and an insurance agent, her parents narrowed down the list of SoCal treatment centers to a beautiful, sprawling center in Dana Point.

While Pamela knew it was costing her parents a small fortune to send her there, they certainly didn't mention it. Instead, they continued to remind her that her arranged marriage was only temporarily delayed and the complete dissolution of it would entail Pamela "performing well" in rehab. She smirked. Even in rehab, her parents could not help but try to goad her into overachieving.

Some things I guess never change, but this is certainly better than nothing.

Regardless, Pamela discovered a newfound appreciation for her parents. *Thousands of dollars each day.* That was the cost of in-patient rehab. Insurance luckily was covering some of it, but Pamela knew her parents were not so rich where spending tens of thousands in one summer just to get her the best help available didn't make any financial dent.

Pamela had never been so eternally grateful to have money until now. She couldn't understand how those without money and resources could get access to the mental health resources they needed. Actually, Pamela already knew the answer to that. *They don't,* she thought with a frown.

Ding dong.

Must be Trisha and Ray. Pamela quickly dropped the crop top she was shoving into her luggage and ran for the door. She knew she had been an awful friend to Trisha the past couple of months, and her heart swelled whenever she thought about how her friend never gave up on her, even when Pamela tried to push her away.

I'm going to miss her, she thought sadly.

"Trish!" Pamela cried while wrapping Trisha into a big hug as soon as she flung open the door. She made eye contact with Ray. "Hey, Ray," she greeted with a wink. Pamela was not surprised when the pair became an official couple. *It was about time.*

"Hi, how is packing going?" Trisha asked, trying to gasp for air within Pamela's tight hug.

"It's *awful.* Who knew packing clothes for one month would require so much thought and effort?" Pamela groaned and let go of Trisha, who looked like she was turning blue.

"I hate the fact that you're leaving for so long." Trisha frowned. "Will you even be able to choose who you room with?"

"Oh, stop it," Pamela waved her hand like it was nothing. "We've spent plenty of summers apart before, Trish. Our families are always going back to Beijing or Karachi to meet relatives. Plus, you've got your *boyfriend* now," Pamela emphasized her last sentence in a sing-song voice. "As for roomies, I'll get by. It will be like summer camp."

"I know, but I want to be there for you, you know?" Trisha offered. "Oh, and I almost forgot. We picked up your favorite pastries from Porto's."

"Porto's!" Pamela exclaimed. Ray handed her a plastic bag holding a big bakery box filled with Cuban potato balls, cheese rolls, and guava-filled pastries.

"Oh my gosh, you know me too well. This must have taken forever to wait for!" Pamela gave Trisha a hug again. "I'm totally getting fat this summer." Pamela pinched her flat stomach dramatically. "With restricted phone access, I'm going to be chomping down on whatever I want knowing there aren't a million people staring at my tummy."

Trisha rolled her eyes. "Why do I highly doubt that's going to happen? Although I really can't imagine you without your phone around twenty-four-seven, even though it's been confiscated for a while now."

Pamela's eyes went from thoughtful to focused as they resettled onto Trisha's. "You know what's weird? I started out devastated without my phone, but after a while, I kind of enjoy it. I didn't realize how much time it sucked up. I'm also not in a permanent state of frenzy now, knowing I don't have to plot my next post or figure out some way to gain more followers." Pamela paused. "The best part is actually not having to read the posts ripping me apart all the time, especially by Reddy's ex. They bothered me more than I realized, to the point that I just numbed out completely and started to believe the comments were true."

Pamela felt Trisha put her hand around hers as she looked past Trisha's shoulder to the sprawling, manicured lawn outside. "A part of me still thinks it's true, but I'm hoping maybe this summer will be the time where I can find myself again, away from what the world thinks of me."

Trisha gave Pamela's hand a gentle squeeze. "For what it's worth, you'll always be, and have always been, my beautiful, brave, and ridiculously hilarious best friend."

Pamela gave Trisha an appreciative glance and let herself get lost in thought for a moment. She always knew high school would be hard and full of change, but the direction it was taking was not what she expected. Even now, Pamela didn't 100 percent regret taking Adderall that fateful night freshman year. It did get her through so many essays, exams, and emotionally empty nights, after all. She wasn't sure if she ever would regret entering this void—at least a small part never would.

This is something to figure out this summer, I guess.

Pamela let her attention refocus into the present. She spoke up again with some sass: "It's a good thing I'm shipping myself off to an in-patient center surrounded by psychiatrists and whatever other crazy docs they have going on there to help me. Come on, stop lingering by the door and come in. Speaking of social media, I want you two to help me make one last video before I leave."

"I wouldn't have it any other way," Trisha grinned from ear to ear.

CHAPTER 35

JACK, PAUL, AND FELIX

JACK

Jack's entire body hurt. It had been months since his arrest, and he felt like every day was going to be his last.

After prosecutors agreed not to escalate his case to the adult criminal justice system, Jack was placed in Central Juvenile Hall. It was the most dangerous and chaotic place he had ever encountered. The other inmates were absolutely barbaric. The windows were either cracked or completely shattered by other juveniles repeatedly banging or shoving up against them, walls and floor tiles had cracks that either meant there were major structural issues or weight had repeatedly flung against them, and there was even graffiti on the walls. *How do these lunatics even get their hands on a sharpie?* Jack thought to himself miserably.

He even overheard one of the guards chatting the other day, saying how he was afraid to come to work because the inmates had become so violent. For Jack, this also meant violence against him. As someone who was a clear outsider from the get-go (Jack made the mistake of bragging on about how wealthy he was), he was the target of the many gangs that had formed within the facility. Overnight, Jack had become a punching bag for the smallest infractions, and the guards didn't even seem to care.

Earlier today, Jack was walking out of the food hall after a disgusting dinner of boiled string beans, mashed potatoes, and questionable-looking meatloaf and didn't bother holding the door on his way out for the guy behind him.

"Hey, China man, do you not have any manners?" Jack turned around to face a piercing covered, scowling inmate with the name "Warren" scrawled onto his jumpsuit.

"Oh, shoot. Sorry. I'm really sorry," Jack apologized profusely. The past two months had wiped away the overconfidence and aloofness he once projected. Now all he wanted to do was hide in a corner and not have anyone notice him.

"That's not going to cut it, squinty eyes." Jack was immediately slammed against the wall with his arm twisted behind his back. He felt his shoulder pop before yelping out in pain. A group of boys near them began cheering, "Yeah, you teach him, Warren!"

Jack crumpled to the ground while Warren stepped over him. There had been a guard posted only a few meters away from him the whole time, and the guard did nothing. Jack ended up dragging himself off to receive medical attention, which had become a weekly occurrence.

Now, Jack laid in his cell in the fetal position, with his head against his curled-up knees. He missed home. He missed China. Heck, he even missed his mom.

He closed his eyes. His mom, whom his dad was also ignoring now (minus a limitless credit card he continued to pay off), instantly burst into tears the last time she saw him. The fresh bruises on Jack's once blemish-free face were too much for her. She and Mr. Jenkins tried to arrange more protection for Jack, but his wealth couldn't help him. Jack was alone inside the detention hall.

With his trial date still one month away, Jack had no idea how he was going to make it out alive. He wasn't even sure he wanted to.

I have no future anymore, Jack thought miserably. He stuck a fist into his mouth and tried to stifle his gut-wrenching sobs.

PAUL

Paul enthusiastically stabbed his pencil through a piece of paper, creating a hole straight in the middle. It was another Wednesday afternoon consisting of sitting in a room flooded with the scent of sage and way too many pillows. Paul toyed with thoughts of slowly burning every single large leaf of the toddler-sized plant in the corner of the room. *One of these days...*

He jerked his head toward a figure on an armchair beside the plant. He gave Dr. Jackson, the court-mandated therapist staring at him with a poker face, an overly wide grin.

I wish I could just stab that expressionless face with this pencil.

After his life was torpedoed by his sociopathic little brother, Paul became absolutely numb to the world. His friends from school dropped him so quickly that he questioned whether they were friends to begin with.

I was the one who made them all popular in the first place, Paul thought to himself miserably. Even the underclassmen were talking trash about him. He almost stormed into Sierra's room when he overheard Stacy gossiping about him. He decided to drop it once he considered how Loudmouth Stacy would just gossip to everyone about how sensitive he was.

One day, when everyone least expects it... I will destroy them all. Paul flared his nostrils and tried to ignore the fact that Felix was sitting right beside him. Both of them had been given a clean slate from the legal system in exchange for attending therapy sessions with Dr. Jackson on a twice-a-week basis.

Paul was less than pleased. Even though he'd been given a clean slate from the judicial system, that didn't change the fact that Winchester expelled him and now USC black-listed him.

He wanted to murder Felix for destroying his life. Well, okay, maybe not murder, but he really wanted to beat the shit out of him. However, his sporadic rage had now transformed into something much deadlier—a grudge. He would never forget what Felix did to him, and he would never let it go.

I'll just play the charade until the day comes for revenge. A small part of Paul knew he was just repeating the cycle of hate, but he didn't care.

"I know we've spoken about this question already one-on-one, but I want to ask you this in front of Paul. Do you regret stealing the AP exams?" Dr. Jackson asked Felix.

Paul rolled his eyes. He already knew the answer to this one.

Felix stopped playing with his own pencil and looked Dr. Jackson in the eye. A strong "no" ricocheted around the room.

According to Dr. Jackson, Paul was bipolar, which helped explain why he had so much uncontrollable rage and mood swings at times. Felix, on the other hand, was diagnosed (or re-diagnosed?) with social anxiety, OCD, and PTSD that stemmed from all the bullying he experienced over the years at the hands of Paul.

Paul hated the bullshit medical diagnoses. It made Felix out as a victim and Paul as some crazy monster.

It's not my fault he's so fragile.

Still, Paul decided he needed to at least *pretend* he was trying to become a "better" person in order for Felix to let his guard down and get his parents off his back. Everyone would accept the good-hearted, reinvented Paul Jones again, even if it meant having to play nice with the useless creature sitting beside him.

"Paul, how do you feel about Felix's response?" Dr. Jackson asked. He simultaneously scribbled little notes into some grungy old leather notebook on his lap.

Paul took a deep breath. *Here goes nothing.* He plastered the best impression of a sympathetic look on his face and turned to Dr. Jackson with remorseful eyes.

"I get it. I understand why Felix set me up. I forced him into that position." He shyly peered at Felix. "Hey, little bro, I'm... I'm sorry for all the pain I've caused." Paul stammered out the last sentence, hoping that it would make it sound like he was in agonizing pain when he thought about his past actions.

Man, they need to give me an Oscar for this performance.

Felix looked at Paul skeptically. He didn't say anything in response.

The least that this piece of shit can do is respond to my apology. Even him, Paul Jones, just apologized. He felt a flare of anger spark inside of him. He fought the urge to take Felix by the scruff of his neck and throw him against the wall.

Dr. Jackson nodded in approval at Paul's response.

"And what do you think, Sierra?" Dr. Jackson asked, turning toward the corner of the room.

Paul almost forgot that she was with them for the "special sibling" session today. She had opted for the corner of the couch in the corner of the room, basically blending in with the furniture. He felt a tiny droplet of guilt when he thought of Sierra. His beautiful sister shouldn't have been caught up into Felix's antics. He even heard that his dad hit her at some point. He had never raised a hand against Sierra before. Still, Paul's opinion of her dropped steeply, knowing she knew about Felix's crimes for weeks and stayed mute about it.

Dr. Jackson continued. "You've stayed mostly quiet during these sibling sessions. What do you think about this whole AP exam situation between your brothers?"

"I... I don't know. I do think Felix has been punished fairly for his actions already. Winchester revoked his acceptance for next fall. As for Paul..." Sierra drifted off.

She cleared her throat. "As for Paul... honestly, he deserved it. Paul has beaten, shoved, hurt, and destroyed Felix's self-confidence. I know he's my brother, but he's honestly awful."

"It's not like you two are perfect either!" Paul snarled. Hearing his sister take Felix's side ignited a second flame inside.

"Paul, deep breaths," Dr. Jackson said calmly. "Why are you upset right now?"

"Isn't it obvious?" Paul snapped. "They're saying I deserved to have my entire life ruined."

Sierra scoffed, gaining more confidence. "Look, Paul. You cannot keep moping around, wallowing in self-pity, and blaming everyone except yourself for your so-called 'tragedies' in life. Your life is not over. Let's be real, did you really even want to go to USC? Or was it just something you felt obligated to do because Mom and Dad went there and it looked good?"

"Of course I wanted to go. USC has some of the hottest girls, after all," he flashed a filthy grin.

"Asshole," Sierra muttered.

Paul shrugged, feeling satisfied that he got under Sierra's skin. He threw himself back into the creaking chair and crossed his arms. He needed to start holding in his anger better or else his goody two shoes facade was going to go tumbling down real soon.

Dr. Jackson cleared his throat, drawing the three siblings' attention to him. "Clearly, there is still a lot of healing and mending to do, and this is normal. Everything takes time, especially with your family history. However, I do have a challenge for everyone before we meet individually next time—I want you all to come with a two-sided collage. One side will be pictures and words of who you think you are, and the other side will be pictures of who you believe others think you are."

Easy... Perfect. Jock. Trojan. Paul felt a stab of sadness at the thought of a Trojan, remembering his offer rescinding letter. He, Sierra, and Felix mumbled a thanks as they left the doctor's office to find their parents in the waiting room surrounded by bamboo plants and Zen music.

FELIX

Felix walked out of Dr. Jackson's herbal-smelling room, trailing behind Paul and Sierra. He shot Dr. Jackson a grateful glance and a wave goodbye before shutting the door.

He had to admit he started looking forward to his family therapy sessions. It was oddly nice to shit on Paul directly without any consequences. Paul was faker than ever, but because he had to show that he was "recovering" from anger management issues, Felix had the luxury of hearing apologies and kind words he never received growing up.

Felix knew everything Paul said was just empty words though.

He thinks he can fool everyone, again, but I know that this is all just an act. It's now Paul Jones 2.0. Felix smirked. He really should make his brother's sociopathic tendencies into a book or movie.

The three of them walked into the living room, where his mom waited anxiously in a chair wringing her hands and his dad typed furiously into his work phone.

His mom's face lit up upon seeing Paul step out. "How was it, honey?" she asked, making a beeline for Paul.

Before his mom could take a few steps forward, his dad's hand shot out and grabbed his mom roughly by the wrist. "You're doing that favoritism thing again," he muttered.

Felix felt his stomach do a flip. His parents had begun therapy sessions with Dr. Jackson as well, and it seemed like his dad was following the doctor's advice, but he followed them like military commands. If they didn't obey something Dr. Jackson suggested, there would be consequences. The worst part was, Dr. Jackson had no idea, and Felix certainly wasn't dumb enough to reveal that his dad was occasionally abusive, like when he hit Sierra. He hated his family, but he hated the idea of child services more.

"How was therapy, kids?" his dad roughly addressed all three of them. Felix, Paul, and Sierra turned to look at each other, not sure what to say.

"We're doing arts and crafts next week," Paul responded with a shrug.

"Arts and crafts? We're paying Dr. Jackson two hundred dollars per hour for three sessions a week to do *arts and crafts?*" His dad looked like he was about to storm into Dr. Jackson's office.

"Honey," Mrs. Jones said disapprovingly. Their tone of voices seemed to have swapped with one another. "*You* were the one who said to trust the process. So, trust it."

His dad scowled at his mom, but let it drop. He had enough common sense to avoid making a scene within earshot of the doctor.

Sierra and Felix exchanged glances. Sierra reached over and squeezed her brother's arm.

"Let's get out of here," she said softly.

***

Felix watched Paul slice his very rare steak with a rabid expression. Paul stared happily as the blood oozed out of the center before bringing the piece to his mouth. Paul was playing nice now, but Felix knew he would never change. He was simply waiting for the moment to cut into Felix the same way he did into his steak.

"I've decided to get my GED and go to community college this fall," Paul announced to the whole family sitting around the table. The glaring white light of the chandelier made his brother's lips look bloody red.

"Really?" his dad said stiffly. "That's great news, son." In the past, even the remote idea of Paul going to community college would have launched his dad into a raging firestorm. However, that was no longer the case. *Or maybe it's still the case, but Dr. Jackson convinced Dad not to get mad about it.* Felix was always curious what was going on behind the scenes of his parents' individual therapy sessions.

"Paul, dear, that's great!" his mom exclaimed, lifting up her glass of wine as if in a toast. "You can be around all the time then!"

And Paul will still be at home with me. Felix felt a part of him internally scream.

Maybe I shouldn't have confessed at all. Being a good person is not worth living with a sociopath.

CHAPTER 36

SIERRA AND HUNTER

SIERRA

This is nice. Sierra surveyed the clusters of Winchester students sprinkled across the quad, gossiping (probably about the downfall of Jack and Paul), planning for summer, and simply enjoying the LA sunshine like she and Hunter currently were. *I wish every day could be as peaceful.*

"What are you thinking about?"

Sierra turned her head toward Hunter, her heart skipping a beat as his eyes caught hold of hers. Sporting a new haircut, shorts, and a t-shirt that emphasized his firm chest, Sierra couldn't help but think *hot* when she looked at Hunter today. She broke the stare and turned away before her blush could take over her entire body.

For the first time since they broke up, they were sitting together again underneath the big oak tree in front of Winchester's library.

"Just about summer vacation," Sierra replied as nonchalantly as she could. She knew Hunter secretly hoped she was thinking whether they could ever be together again. Truthfully, Sierra had never stopped loving him. How could she, when he had been the only one in her life who ever truly connected with her? His laugh, his musty, earthy scent, and the way his touch felt like electricity on her skin—how could she ever forget that? Yet Sierra knew she couldn't go running back to him, not now.

Hunter leaned closer in until she could feel the warm breath on her cheek. Her breath caught in her throat. "What are—?" He lifted his hand toward her head and pulled away.

"There was a leaf in your hair," he chuckled with a dimpled grin. Sierra glanced at his hand and, sure enough, there was a small leaf in between his fingers.

I need to get out of here before he breaks down all my defenses.

While every pore in her yearned to be back in Hunter's embrace, she knew she needed to figure out who she was on her own before dating again. The whole fallout of her entire family had forced her to confront what she had been doing with her life. She had always been happy to be an ironic twist as a wallflower—the center of attention, but as the reflection of what everyone else wanted her to be. But the collapse of Felix's pain, Paul's rage, and her parents distorted reality all spiraled toward her, forcing her to realize that as long as she lived this way, she'd become either an empty robot or an exhausted doormat, if she wasn't one already.

Sierra felt familiar fingers wrap themselves over her hand on the grass. Her eyes widened in surprise.

"Hunter, I—"

"I've missed us," he interjected, although in some way his response also completed the sentence for a good chunk of her heart.

Sierra sighed long and sadly. "I have too, Hunter, but you know I need more time." She pulled her hand out from underneath his. "All my life I've been letting myself become smaller and emptier for the sake of someone else—my parents, Paul, and then even you once college applications rolled around." Sierra closed her eyes. "I can't let people step on me anymore. I need to learn to love myself first before putting all that time and effort into someone else again."

And I don't know if that someone else should be you. Sierra didn't say the last thought out loud in fear that it would hurt Hunter further.

"I know." Hunter looked down at the grass. "It makes sense. I've been a douche to you. I took advantage of you in so many ways and didn't appreciate you the way I should have. I'll always be sorry for that."

"Hey, stop it," Sierra demanded softly. "Stop beating yourself up. You'll only make me feel worse if you behave this way."

"Sorry," Hunter smiled tightly. "I just don't know how to forgive myself."

HUNTER

Hunter stared gloomily across the quad, resisting the intense urge to pull Sierra toward him and kiss her like he always did. *More like, always used to.* It was the last week of school and Hunter was about to take his senior class trip to the Grand Canyon in a few days. He should be happy—he was graduating as class valedictorian and heading off to USC in the fall on a full-ride merit scholarship that the school offered him last minute. Yet, knowing that his relationship with Sierra would never be the same anymore, he felt like there was a gigantic void that would never fill.

His hands clenched a fistful of grass.

I just wish it didn't ever get to the point of being dysfunctional. Hunter thought to himself. In his mind, he had already become a changed man after the events of the past several months. He no longer was some prestige-hungry person who only saw college as the end goal. It took losing Sierra to realize there was so much more to life than getting the fanciest degree possible. Unfortunately, that realization came too late.

Will we ever have a chance again? Hunter was determined to keep trying and waiting, even when he went off to college. He snuck a peek at Sierra, who had laid down next to him and was now watching the clouds gently float by. Hunter swallowed. She looked stunning today with her white shorts and sky-blue tank top.

Hunter's iPhone buzzed. He pulled it out of his pocket and looked at the caller ID. His heart stopped.

"Who's that?" Sierra asked, seeing the alarm on Hunter's face.

"Some number from New Haven, Connecticut," Hunter quickly replied. "New Haven... I think it's—" He picked up the phone.

"Hello?"

"Hi, is this Hunter Wang? This is Nancy calling from the Yale Admissions Office." Hunter's jaw fell open.

He cleared his throat. *Pull yourself together.* "Hi, yes, uh, this is Hunter." *What in the world is going on?* He felt like he was about to have a heart attack.

"I'm calling to let you know you've been identified as a potential candidate off of our waitlist. Are you still interested in joining us in New Haven this coming fall?"

Hunter was floored. Never in his lifetime did he think he'd actually get off of Yale's waitlist. Yes, there was a small part of him hoping so this entire time, but he had always been realistic about the minuscule chances. *Is this real? Am I hallucinating?*

"Hello? Hunter? Are you still there?" Hunter realized he had yet to respond.

"Yes, Nancy, yes! You have no idea how much this means to me." Hunter sprung up from the grass and threw his fist in the air. He couldn't wait to share the news with his family.

"Excellent. You will receive an email shortly from our admissions office with details. We look forward to having you with us this fall, Hunter."

"Thank you! Can't wait!" Hunter hung up the phone and looked over at Sierra, who had bewilderment etched across her face.

He broke into a smile so large his face hurt. "Sierra. That was just *Yale*. I'm going to Yale!" Hunter grabbed her hands, pulled her up, and began to spin her around.

"Oh my gosh, that's amazing, Hunter! I'm so proud of you!" Sierra began to jump up and down too. "Congratulations!" she threw her arms around him. He broke into a laugh as he squeezed her in his arms.

Something warm and wet dropped onto his arm. He looked down. *Is that a tear?* He pulled away from the embrace.

"Sierra, are you crying?" Hunter asked, confused. "I didn't expect you to be so happy that you'd cry."

"I... I just..." Sierra stammered while wiping away her tears, "It's just that... I don't know... I know we're broken up and all now, but you're still my best friend." She turned away trying to shield Hunter from the steady stream of tears. "Don't get me wrong. I'm super happy for you, but you can't blame me for being a little bit sad seeing you move across the country."

"Oh, Sierra," Hunter pulled her back toward him. "We'll make it work. There are so many virtual options. Imagine how our parents used to do it with just letters and pagers!"

Hunter couldn't help but feel a flicker of joy at seeing Sierra's tears as well.

It means that she still has some sort of feelings for me.

"Yeah... yeah, I guess you're right," Sierra said with a sniff. "I'm so happy for you, Hunter. Seriously, you deserve it after all of that hard work."

But was it worth losing you in the process to get here? a tiny voice in him wanted to ask. Hunter didn't know the answer to that question.

"Gah, I'm so excited, Sierra," Hunter said as he brushed away some lingering tears on her face.

Sierra gave him a tearful grin. "Everything happens for a reason."

"Agreed." Hunter grinned back. Without thinking, he leaned in and pressed his mouth against Sierra's soft, warm lips. Her body stiffened for a moment and then relaxed into it.

Hunter's heart burst with love and hope for the sweet, smart, and beautiful girl in his arms. *Maybe there's a second chance for me after all.*

EPILOGUE

———

MATT

What the heck? Matt stuffed his hands into his pockets.

Hunter had told him to meet up after class to grab some AYCE sushi, but Matt stopped in his tracks across the quad when he saw Hunter fist pump into the air and pull Sierra in for a kiss.

He cursed under his breath. While Matt liked Sierra, he couldn't help but feel selfishly happy when they broke up. With everything that was going on at home, having a single Hunter versus in-a-relationship Hunter meant his best friend and crush had more time to spend supporting him.

Especially when Dad still won't accept that I'm gay. He kicked a rock in front of him.

As soon as Hunter got the slightest whiff of having a chance with Sierra again, it was like his friend had gone underneath a rock. Matt initially suspected it might have been because Hunter felt weirded out about their kiss months ago, but he soon realized it was just because Sierra had entered Hunter's orbit once again. He was back to being the third-wheel sidekick who would occasionally tag along on their "hangouts" that were definitely not dates.

Some friend. Matt thought bitterly. It certainly didn't help that Hunter still occupied so much of Matt's heart. He knew his feelings would never be reciprocated, but it didn't help to lessen the pain and jealousy.

Out of the corner of his eye, Matt saw another angry figure standing a few feet away from him looking wretchedly at Sierra and Hunter make out.

Eyebrows raised, Matt felt his heart soften a little bit for the person in the shadows. *At least I'm not in this boat alone.*

He shook his head and walked away from the scene.

LAURA

Laura was furious. She looked across the quad as Hunter reached over and kissed Sierra.

Didn't she say she didn't want to get back together again? That hypocritical bitch.

Ever since she was little, Laura knew Hunter was meant to be with her—not with that Blake Lively-looking doll with no personality. That fateful day back at Hunter's house when Stanford rejected him, Laura knew Sierra had entered the room. She had seen Sierra's car pull up through the window. That's when Laura decided she would put Hunter and her in a compromising position. She thought it worked.

It clearly didn't.

Now, Sierra and Hunter were nearly inseparable, even though they weren't "official" again. Hunter even had the nerve to kick their friendship off to the curb to keep Sierra happy. Just last week, he texted Laura that they needed to take a break from one-on-one hangouts in case there could be another chance to date Sierra again. He was so smitten with that dumb doe-eyed girl it was disgusting.

Well, hope you're happy now, Sierra, because you won't be for much longer. No matter how long it would take, no matter how painful it would be, Laura was going to make Hunter hers and hers alone. Sierra was going down.

AUTHOR'S NOTE

———

This is a book about race, money, education, and young love—a book about families, immigration, adversity, and tragedy. However, first and foremost, this is an ode to the San Gabriel Valley, affectionately known as the SGV, in Southern California. SGV is home to 524,000 Asian Americans—a third of LA County's Asian American population—and what I consider the foundation of my identity as an Asian American.[70]

Early Life

Like many families in my area, my immigrant Chinese American family raised me and my older sister with a relentless hope of us graduating from a top-tier college—the pinnacle of success in my community. Their intense college desires motivated me to apply for and enroll in a college preparatory boarding school. Walking onto campus on day one, I distinctly remember Price Dining Hall, a large structure surrounded by palm trees that could serve four hundred

---

70 Frank Shyong, "Asian Americans Surpass Whites in San Gabriel Valley, Marking a Demographic Milestone," *Los Angeles Times,* February 22, 2018.

students at once. I was astounded to discover that meals consisted of a buffet of selections, including multiple entrees, a soup station, and a salad bar.[71] Coming from a public-school system where my lunches were $2.50 and consisted of soggy tater tots and rib sandwiches made from questionable meat sources, the boarding school dining hall felt like a food haven. To this day, with a mixture of fondness and humor, I remember my boarding school's beloved peanut butter and jelly sandwich station. It was available at all times of the day as a snack. For me, coming from a family that never wasted food and treasured every last bit of peanut butter in a jar, what had once been a staple meal in my life had somehow been devalued into a snack in this new world.

Slathering peanut butter onto a slice of toast with such glee and biting into its gooey sweetness, my thirteen-year-old self suddenly felt uprooted from everything I considered normal. Gone were the days of walking to school, daily home-cooked Chinese dinners, and dropping by my best friend's house to make Rice Krispie treats. Instead, my life had become a mix of signing in and out of binders in order to leave campus, grocery shopping with teachers, and having my closest friends living right next door to me. Every day, week, and year was different in my new school, and I don't think I ever found a new normal again.

SGV

I grew up in the suburbs of East Los Angeles in a region called San Gabriel Valley, the "capital of Asia America" as sociologists refer to it, or—as those from the area like to abbreviate

---

71 Apparently, the dining hall has only grown in its selection since my time there due to a plethora of complaints about poor tasting food and selection.

it—the SGV.[72] It's what outsiders think of as a quintessential melting pot, and you can easily access some of the best ethnic cuisine in the world by living in the region amongst tri-ethnic Latino, Caucasian, and Asian neighborhoods.

However, SGV natives will tell you that rather than a melting pot, it is really a huge salad bowl—a cultural concept that suggests residents are mixed together based on distinctive cultures rather than a homogenous "melting pot."[73] In the Greater LA region, as many as 224 languages are spoken, and the mix of cultures, languages, ethnicities and socio-economic statuses are largely in separate enclaves.[74] Growing up, I knew that Diamond Bar is where you'd go for Korean food, Rowland Heights for Chinese food, and West Covina for Mexican food. The best ethnic food spots were obvious to me and my peers because of the geographic representation in each city. Like many US communities, the SGV was divided by race, not by religious, political, or socio-economic ties.

While the Asian American population has been swelling in the region, unique forms of white flight and Latino migration have also taken place due to tears in the fabrics of SGV society that had, up until a few decades ago, been associated with tri-ethnic suburbs.[75] Between 2000 and 2010, the Asian American population grew by 22 percent, while the white population declined more than any other ethnic group, by

72   Jennifer Medina, "New Suburban Dream Born of Asia and Southern California," *The New York Times*, April 28, 2013.

73   Bruce Thornton, "Melting Pots and Salad Bowls," *Hoover Digest* 2012, no. 4 (October 2012).

74   County of Los Angeles, "Residents," accessed September 22, 2020.

75   Merlin Chowkwanyun and Jordan Segall, "The Rise of the Majority-Asian Suburb," *Bloomberg,* August 24, 2012.

17 percent.[76] These days, majority-Asian suburbs have become cultural bubbles where first generation immigrants, second generation immigrants, and multi-generational Asian families face challenges to adapt in a country that often sees them as the "invisible minority," impacting all areas of life.[77] While this rapid Asianization has led to positive externalities, such as the region being known for some of the best and most authentic Asian food in the US, it has also led to disturbing stories of educational opportunities being increasingly divided by race and economic privilege.

When I began attending boarding school, I left my everyday life of being Asian American and surrounded by Asian Americans to a new bubble tucked away in the hills of Claremont, California, ironically still considered part of, or adjacent to, the SGV, yet in its own little world. In my new bubble, I no longer knew how to fit in. Everyone and every group were so different from one another. My understanding of what was "cool" was shattered, and my ideas about wealth became completely skewed. By the time I hit high school, my own family had achieved what many would consider the "American Dream." While my parents had moved to the United States with next to nothing, our household income had grown well into the upper middle-class range. I understood that my family had achieved financial success, yet in my boarding school, mine felt like an average household figure with hundreds of millions, if not billions, in household earnings being a not-so-rare demographic.

---

76 Frank Shyong, "Asian Americans Surpass Whites in San Gabriel Valley, Marking a Demographic Milestone," *Los Angeles Times,* February 22, 2018.

77 Keun-Joo Christine Pae, "To Make the Invisible Visible: Interrogating Race and Racism," *The Future of Race,* January 23, 2013, 17.

It didn't reflect the SGV that I knew, but in reality my high school was already reflecting what the SGV was becoming. Only a few miles outside of my boarding school bubble, the SGV's historical reputation for agriculture, country clubs, and flashes of *La La Land* in Pasadena began to slowly fade away. Immense levels of foreign wealth poured into the region, which I saw up close through the lifestyles of my classmates. Unfortunately, with the gentrification and the erection of an "Asian Beverly Hills," many families across all cultures continued to struggle with poverty, educational attainment, and language barriers, but with more invisibility than ever before.

The Model Minority Stereotype

This book was originally meant to be a work of nonfiction. I wanted to interview leaders across a diverse range of industries to highlight their struggles and accomplishments as Asian Americans. Having been raised to almost imitate the model minority stereotype—the myth that all Asian Americans are a law-abiding, hardworking, overachieving, silent, and also (in the wake of the COVID-19 pandemic) a virus-spreading minority group—I aimed to write a book that could shatter the model minority myth after being unable to break out of the mold myself. But as I began a series of interviews with Asian Americans across industries from entertainment to politics, ethnicities from Vietnamese American to Chinese American, and generations from first to third, I began to see a unique trend in everyone's experiences. Notably, many of the conversations mentioned the amount of empowerment, or lack thereof, during childhood when it came to embracing their Asian American identity. On one side of the spectrum, those who happened to grow up in predominantly Asian American communities highlighted the privilege of never feeling like an outsider or experiencing racism until moving out of those communities. On the other side of the spectrum, those who grew up as the only Asian American in their entire community felt particularly isolated; some even admitted to hating their identity and rejecting anything related to their parents' or grandparents' cultures.

As my interview list grew longer, I realized the immense privilege I had growing up in a strong Asian American community like the SGV. As a child, I got to witness firsthand the many different shades of being an Asian American as the daughter of first-generation Chinese immigrants. My home was traditionally Chinese in many ways. My parents' marriage was arranged, and my sister and I were brought up by my grandparents in a multi-generational and extended household. Besides my sister, parents, and maternal grandparents, my maternal uncles and cousin also lived with us. In our nine-person household, we ate home-cooked Chinese food for every meal, and my grandparents—who had lived through the Great Chinese Famine that had taken the lives of tens of millions in the late 1950s and early '60s—collected everything from old newspapers to plastic utensils in order to reuse them. We did not have much in my toddler years, but we were scrappy.[78]

In addition, my sister and I were raised in a stereotypical "academics are everything" fashion that seemed to extend to the entire valley. Regardless of time or cost, my sister and I were enrolled in piano, art, and dance classes on top

78 Louisa Lim, "A Grim Chronicle Of China's Great Famine," NPR, November 10, 2012.

of all sorts of academic activities from a young age. We did not participate in sports teams—we'd get too "tan" playing sports outside, and that was a big no-no in a culture that equates fair skin with the elite. When Amy Chua's book, *The Battle Hymn of the Tiger Mother*, came out while I was in high school, I remember suddenly understanding that my experience was by no means confined to my family or my region. It was perhaps a cultural one, or a cultural stereotype many families were reinforcing.[79] Perhaps what I loved about the book was that no matter how outrageous Chua got, I felt that the region of mothers in the SGV were superior to her. The reason? I had witnessed and experienced firsthand situations that made her notorious parenting practices seem lovely.

While Amy Chua's book gave a glimpse of what Asian parenting could be like for some, Asian Americans are by no means a homogenous group of high achievers. While there are many Asian Americans achieving socioeconomic success, especially with rising wealth among new immigrants all across Asia, there are still just as many Asian Americans at the lower end of the socioeconomic spectrum. Furthermore, the millennial and Gen Z generations, a group that is swelling with heterogeneity, are redefining what it means to be Asian American. Rather than being just "Asian American," there's now the Asian American defined by geographic areas like the "SoCal Asian American" and the "Flushing Asian American," as well as stereotypes defined by Asian Americans like the

---

79   In the book "Tiger Mother," Amy Chua utilizes strict and sometimes cruel parenting tactics to drive her children toward her definition of success while dismantling Western child rearing philosophies as "worrying too much about a child's self-esteem"; Amy Chua, *Battle Hymn of the Tiger Mother* (London: Bloomsbury, 2012), 118.

"Asian Baby Girl" and the "Yappie." Rather than being the salad bowl I grew up in, I've begun to realize the SGV has now transformed into a salad bar of cultures from different states, countries, and socioeconomic backgrounds.

A Look Ahead

I hope this young adult book will provide not only a fun, dramatic read for teenagers and those who have grown up in ethnic enclaves but also for those who are interested in exploring a dynamic subset of the Asian American community. I also aimed to stay as true to the real world as possible in my book. The excessive price tags of luxury items, the concerns about not creating the perfect college "resume," and the reflections on generational divides in Asian American identities are all loosely inspired by real people and stories. Scenes such as trips to 99 Ranch Market, getting boba tea, and even the AP test booklet heist are also based on my personal experiences growing up in the San Gabriel Valley. It is necessary to point out, though, that the stories I've weaved only highlight a small sliver of the diversity and struggles in the area. I don't believe my book even comes close to representing the unique fabric of the San Gabriel Valley as a whole, nor do I believe it should be treated as a critique or cultural analysis of the area. However, I do hope my book will inspire others to reflect on their own identities in an increasingly globalized and diversified world. I certainly did.

It's in this backdrop that I launch readers into the story of *Not THAT Rich*, where teenagers from various ethnic, socioeconomic, and political backgrounds attend a private school in the Valley and are tossed into the grueling process that is today's high-pressure college admissions process. While they try to navigate their own identities as burgeoning young adults, they also face the struggles of understanding what it means to understand where they fall within the fabric of the rapidly changing SGV region.

CHARACTER LIST

The Zhous

- Jack Zhou—A new junior transfer to Winchester who is the illegitimate son of billionaire Wang Zhou.
- Zi Wei Xu/Auntie Xu—Jack's mom and the mistress of Wang Zhou.
- Wang Zhou—Billionaire tycoon who made his wealth in the garment industry. He lives in Shanghai with his wife and oldest son, Sam Zhou.

The Wangs

- Hunter Wang—Senior at Winchester. Dating Sierra. Older brother to Trisha Wang. Dreams of attending Stanford.
- Trisha Wang—Sophomore at Winchester. Best friends with Pamela Shah.
- Phoebe Wang—Mother of Hunter and Trisha Wang. Real estate agent who has come into a lot of wealth in the past decade due to the immigrant Chinese wealth pouring into the San Gabriel Valley.
- Hector Wang—Accountant and father of Hunter and Trisha Wang.

- Uncle Mike—Younger brother of Phoebe. Uncle to Trisha and Hunter.

The Joneses
- Paul Jones—Oldest child of the Jones family and senior at Winchester. Dreams of attending USC.
- Sierra Jones—Middle child of the Jones family. Sophomore at Winchester. Dating Hunter.
- Felix Jones—Youngest child of the Jones family. Eighth grader who is applying to Winchester this year.
- Kelsey Jones—Mother of the Jones kids. Head of the Winchester Parents Committee.
- John Jones—Father of the Jones kids. Famous plastic surgeon in the area.

Additional Winchester Students
- Ray Martinez—New junior transfer to Winchester.
- Pamela Shah—Trisha's best friend and from a second-generation Pakistani American family. Has three younger siblings—Anika, Rohan, and Nirav. Parents have their own tech firm.
- Matt Miller—Hunter's best friend and quarter Korean, quarter Chinese, and half German. Mom is Susan Lee.
- Laura Tan—Freshman at Winchester and childhood friends with Matt Miller and the Wang siblings.

Additional Moms of SGV
- Susan Miller/Auntie Miller—Half Chinese/Korean Wife to Chris Miller and mother of Matt Miller. Phoebe's confidant. Married to one of the most sought-after producers in Hollywood.

- Caroline Tan/Auntie Tan—Single mother of Laura Tan. Has a successful toy manufacturing empire.

Additional Characters
- Dean Rand—Dean of School at Winchester.
- Fiona and Chris Lu—Twins who graduated from Winchester and are now freshmen at Stanford and Harvard, respectively. Uncle Lu and Auntie Lu are their parents.
- Stacy Williams—Sierra's best friend. Father is a faculty member at Winchester.
- Coach Bron—Water polo coach at Winchester.
- Mr. Johnson—AP Calc teacher and triathlon and cross-country coach at Winchester.
- Sergeant Gomez—Lead sergeant on the stolen AP tests case.
- Mrs. Browser—Winchester counselor with a twenty-year career in college counseling.

ACKNOWLEDGMENTS

———

A year before this book was published, I fully intended for *Not THAT Rich* to live and die on my laptop. I never imagined the amount of love, support, and enthusiasm I would receive when I finally made the decision on a late Friday night to take this book beyond the confines of my old laptop. Fulfilling this dream would not have been possible without it.

Thank you first and foremost to my family for supporting me through every step of the way and believing in me even when I didn't quite believe in myself.

Thank you to my gracious sister and friends turned editors—Ann, Vanessa, Rebecca, and Daniyal—who went above and beyond to make sure my book would be a good one. Special thank you to Shane for reading multiple versions of my manuscript, despite the fact that he, unfathomably and ironically, hates reading.

And thank you to everyone who gave me their time for a personal interview; pre-ordered the e-book, paperback, and multiple copies to make publishing possible; helped spread the word about *Not THAT Rich* to gather amazing momentum; and helped me publish a book I am proud of. I am sincerely grateful for all of your help:

Lynn Chao, John Zhao, Amy Zhao, Olivia Zhao, Charles Zhao, Dahlia Chiu, Iris Chiu, Lily Chiu, Tracy Hou, Ryan Wang, Betty Wang, Linda Lin, Elizabeth Kor, Shernia Wang, Jiali Xiong, Valerian Jiang, Lily Shi, Dana Zeng, Mary Dong, Shuo Fang, Sidney Leung, Martha Xiang, Tianhao Cai, Lisa Fang Zhou, Annie and Bonnie Yan, Fan Wen, Fabio Acero, Shawn Xiao Wang, Frank Wang, Conghui Wu, Richard Leong, Ana Diaz, Hiranthip Intaranukulkij, Nuttpasint Chet-udomlap, Trisha Shastri, Ann Lei, Rebecca Liu, Vanessa Hung, Shane Drangel, Maulik Pancholy, Melissa Medina, Bessie Chan, Andrew Gu, Jeffrey Pak Shing Ho, Megan Ananian, Ben Ma, Clyde Hunt III, Elaine Li, Katie Takahashi, Kevin Pandji, Ruby Chi, Jessica Y Li, Pamela Hung, Jea Yun Sim, June Wu, Mae Louise Lee, Dev Shah, Genevieve Chan, Maya Kushmail, Ayana Usui, Pengyun Ma, Nandini Srinivasan, Gerry Songgerry, Lussandra Rosenfeld, Ken Rosenfeld, Mei Zhang, Christina Lee, Josh Tsung, Elizabeth Coh, Jennifer Mojun Jin, Tiffany Sakurada, Yajuan Chen, Tracy Li, Mei Li, Betty Wang, James Tan, Shae Wang, Rebecca Lee, Sarah Mackenzie, Eric Koester, Ivy Yeung, Lucy Tan, Sophia Zhang, Melissa Medina, Amy Resnik, Dana Dootson, Vanessa Hung, Mariah Qian, Gary Huang, Tracy Jaffe, Jiayu Chen, Tony Lin, Daniyal Kiani, Huijun Wang, Daniel Ahn, Mason Balbera, Sally Choi, Kelly Zhang, Melissa Mazzeo, Yehsen Lin, Marlynn Ma, Shahsin Pai, Heidi Peng, Vincent Chang, Sean Nam, Zoe Chen, Jamie Lok, Marissa Pang, Suzanne Hirasuna, Naomie Gendron, Shuchi Goyal, Ryan Au, Simone Lamont, Michelle Hur, Daniel Kent, Xin Qiao, Sara Laffin, Genevieve Chan, Jun Wang, Sharon Yam, Luke Xing, Jeffrey Lin, Addie Liang, Edmund Liang, Wendy Cheung, Jennifer Tang

Lastly, thank you to the dream team at New Degree Press, especially Eric Koester, Brian Bies, Amanda Brown, Elissa Graeser, Amanda Moskowitz, Venus Bradley, Kayla LaFevre, Gjorgi Pejkovski, Mateusz Cichosz, Noemi Bazon, and everyone else who touched my book to make a dream a reality. I can't even begin to imagine what this book would have been like without having you all every step of the way. My gratitude truly extends beyond words.

APPENDIX

———

Chapter 29: Jack

Park, Madison. "Ethan Couch of 'affluenza' case released from jail." *CNN*, April 2, 2018. https://www.cnn.com/2018/04/02/us/ethan-couch-affluenza-jail-release/index.html.

Author's Note

Chowkwanyun, Merlin, and Jordan Segall. "The Rise of the Majority-Asian Suburb." *Bloomberg,* August 24, 2012. https://www.citylab.com/equity/2012/08/rise-majority-asian-suburb/3044/.

Chua, Amy. *Battle Hymn of the Tiger Mother.* London: Bloomsbury, 2012.

County of Los Angeles. "Residents." Accessed September 22, 2020. https://lacounty.gov/residents/.

Lim, Louisa. "A Grim Chronicle of China's Great Famine." *NPR*, November 10, 2012. https://www.npr.org/2012/11/10/164732497/a-grim-chronicle-of-chinas-great-famine.

Medina, Jennifer. "New Suburban Dream Born of Asia and Southern California." *The New York Times*, April 28, 2013. https://nyti.ms/16902tS.

Pae, Keun-Joo Christine. "To Make the Invisible Visible: Interrogating Race and Racism." *The Future of Race*, January 23,
2013. https://reflections.yale.edu/sites/default/files/reflections_
spring_2013_01.pdf.

Shyong, Frank. "Asian Americans Surpass Whites in San Gabriel
Valley, Marking a Demographic Milestone." *Los Angeles Times*,
February 22, 2018. https://www.latimes.com/local/lanow/
la-me-asians-sgv-data-20180221-story.html.

Thornton, Bruce. "Melting Pots and Salad Bowls." Hoover Digest
2012, no. 4 (2012). https://www.hoover.org/research/melting-
pots-and-salad-bowls.

CPSIA information can be obtained
at www.ICGtesting.com
Printed in the USA
LVHW052035100221
678950LV00014B/2034

9 781636 765143